POSTMODERNISM,

FEMINISM, AND

CULTURAL POLITICS

SUNY Series, Teacher Empowerment and School Reform
Henry A. Giroux and Peter L. McLaren

HENRY A. GIROUX, *EDITOR*

POSTMODERNISM,

FEMINISM, AND

CULTURAL POLITICS

REDRAWING EDUCATIONAL
BOUNDARIES

STATE UNIVERSITY OF NEW YORK PRESS

Published by
State University of New York Press, Albany

© 1991 State University of New York

For information, address State University of New York
Press, State University Plaza, Albany, N.Y., 12246

Library of Congress Cataloging in Publication Data

Postmodernism, feminism, and cultural politics : redrawing educational
    boundaries / Henry A. Giroux, editor.
        p.   cm. — (SUNY series, teacher empowerment and school
    reform)
        Includes bibliographical references (p.   ) and index.
        ISBN 0-7914-0576-1 (alk. paper). — ISBN 0-7914-0577-X (pbk. :
    alk. paper)
        1. Education — Social aspects — United States. 2. Educational
    sociology — United States. 3. Postmodernism — United States.
    4. Education — United States — Philosophy. I. Giroux, Henry A.
    II. Series: Teacher empowerment and school reform.
    LC191.4.P67   1991
    370.19'0973 — dc20   90-36679
                                                                          CIP

10   9   8   7   6   5   4   3   2

"Natasha has just come to the window so that the air
may enter more freely into my room. I can see the bright
green strip of grass beneath the wall, and the clear blue
sky above the wall, and sunlight everywhere. Life is
beautiful. Let future generations cleanse it of all evil,
oppression, and violence and enjoy it to the full."
                    Leon Trotsky, *Trotsky's Diary in Exile* –1935

This book is dedicated to four editors, Sophy Craze, Candy
Mitchell, Ralph Page, and Priscilla C. Ross, who express
in their work and friendship the highest standards of integrity,
scholarship, and courage.

For Bell Hooks who exhibits in her work and life what it
means to make the political more pedagogical and the
pedagogical more political.

Contents

Acknowledgments

This book would not have been possible without the help of a number of friends. I am particularly grateful to Donaldo Macedo, Jeanne-Brady Giroux, Roger Simon, Ralph Page, Peter McLaren, Stephen Haymes, and Stanley Aronowitz for reading various drafts of the first and last chapters included in this volume. I am particularly grateful to Candy Mitchell who supported me right from the beginning of this project. I am especially grateful to my graduate students Martin O'Neill and Honor Fagan who read endless drafts of my work and played a major role in getting me to rethink and rewrite various sections. One could not expect more from my editor, Priscilla Ross, at SUNY Press. Her intelligent advice and warm support were crucial in getting this volume started and completed. Thanks to my wife, Jeanne-Brady, and my three boys, Jack, Chris and Brett, for reminding me that productive work cannot be done outside a context that provides meaning, warmth, and love. Goodbye to Rosa, my friend for the last decade. While I am solely responsible for my own work, this volume represents a collective effort on the part of a group of authors who have been a pleasure to work with. Without their collective effort this book could not have been put together.

I would like to thank the *Boston University Journal of Education* for permission to publish the following articles:

Douglas Kellner, "Reading Images Critically: Toward a Postmodern Pedagogy."

Peter McLaren, "Schooling and the Postmodern Body: Critical Pedagogy and the Politics of Enfleshment."

Linda Brodkey and Michelle Fine, "Presence of Mind in the Absence of Body."

Leslie Gotfrit, "Women Dancing Back: Disruption and the Politics of Pleasure."

Philip D. R. Corrigan, "The Making of the Boy: Mediations on What Grammar School did With, To, and For My Body."

A highly modified version of "Modernism, Postmodernism, and Feminism-Rethinking the Boundaries of Educational Discourse: An Introduction" has been published in *College Literature*, Vol. 17, No.'s 2 & 3 (1990).

Henry A. Giroux

Introduction

Modernism, Postmodernism, and Feminism: Rethinking the Boundaries of Educational Discourse

Modern citizenship was formulated in a way that played a crucial role in the emergence of modern democracy, but it has become an obstacle to making it wider and more pluralistic. Many of the new rights that are being claimed by women or ethnic minorities are no longer rights that can be universalized. They are the expression of specific needs and should be granted to particular communities. Only a pluralistic conception of citizenship can accommodate the specificity and multiplicity of democratic demands and provide a pole of identification for a wide range of democratic forces. The political community has to be viewed, then, as a diverse collection of communities, as a forum for creating unity without denying specificity. (Mouffe 1989, 7)

Chantal Mouffe's comments suggest we have entered a new age, one that is marked by a crisis of power, patriarchy, authority, identity, and ethics. This new age has been described, for better or worse, by many theorists in a variety of disciplines as the age of postmodernism.[1] It is a period torn between the ravages and benefits of modernism; it is an age in which the notions of science, technology, and reason are associated not only with social progress but also with the organization of Auschwitz and the scientific creativity that made Hiroshima possible (Poster 1989). It is a time in which the humanist subject seems to no longer be in control of his or her fate. It is an age in which the grand narratives of emancipation, whether from the political Right or Left, appear to share an affinity for terror and oppression. It is also a historical moment in which culture is no longer seen as a reserve of white men whose contributions to the arts, literature, and science constitute the domain of high culture. We live at a time in which a strong challenge is being waged against a modernist discourse in which knowledge is legitimized almost exclusively from a European model of culture and civilization. In part, the struggle for democracy can be seen in the context of a broader struggle against certain features of modernism that represent the worst legacies of the Enlightenment tradition. And it is against these features that a variety of oppositional movements have emerged in an attempt to rewrite the relationship between modernism and democracy. Two of the most important challenges to modernism have come from divergent theoretical discourses associated with postmodernism and feminism.

Postmodernism and feminism have challenged modernism on a variety of theoretical and political fronts, and I will take these up shortly, but there is another side to modernism that has expressed itself more recently in the ongoing struggles in Eastern Europe. Modernism is not merely about patriarchy parading as universal reason, the increasing intensification of human domination over nature in the name of historical development, or the imperiousness of grand narratives that stress control and mastery (Lyotard 1984). Nor is modernism simply synonomous with forms of modernization characterized by the ideologies and practices of the dominating relations of capitalist production. It exceeds this fundamental but limiting rationality by offering the ideological excesses of democratic possibility. By this I mean, as Ernesto Laclau and Chantal Mouffe (1985) have pointed out, modernism becomes a decisive point of reference for advancing certain and crucial elements of the democratic revolution. Beyond its claims to certainty, foundationalism, and epistemological essentialism, modernism provides theoretical elements for analyzing both the limits of its own historical tradition and for developing a political standpoint in which the breadth and specificity of democratic struggles can be expanded through the modernist ideals of freedom, justice, and equality. As Mark Hannam points out, modernism does have a legacy of progressive ambitions which have contributed to substantive social change, and these ambitions need to be remembered in order to be reinserted into any developing discourses on democracy. For Hannam (1990) these include: "economic redistribution towards equality, the emancipation of women, the eradication of superstition and despotism, wider educational opportunities, the improvement of the sciences and the arts, and so forth. Democratization was one of these ambitions and frequently was perceived to be a suitable means towards the realization of other, distinct ambitions" (113). What is important to note is that the more progressive legacies of modernism have been unleashed not in the West, where they have been undermined by modernism's undemocratic tendencies, but in Eastern Europe where the full force of political modernism has erupted to redraw the political and cultural map of the region. What this suggests is neither the death of modernism, nor the facile dismissal of the new oppositional discourses that have arisen within postmodernism and feminism, but a rethinking of how the most critical aspects of these discourses can be brought to bear to deepen the democratic possibilities within the modernist project itself. For what is at stake here is not simply the emergence of a new language in order to rethink the modernist tradition, but also the reconstruction of the political, cultural, and social preconditions for developing a radical conception of citizenship and pedagogy.

That we live in an age in which a new political subject is being constructed can be seen most vividly in the events that have recently taken place in Eastern Europe. Within a matter of months, the Berlin wall has fallen; the Stalinist communist parties of the Eastern bloc are, for all intent and purposes, in disarray; the Soviet Union is radically modifying an identity forged in the legacy of Leninism and Bolshevism; the master narratives of Marxism are being refigured within the shifting identities, and cultural practices, and imaginary possibilities unleashed in the nascent discourse of a radical democracy. In Eastern Europe, the theoretical and political preconditions for a postmodern citizen are being constructed, even if only at the present they exist as a faint glimmer. This is a political subject that rejects the authoritarianism of master narratives, that refuses traditions that allow only for a reverence of what already is, that denies those instrumental and universalized forms of rationality which eliminate the historical and the contingent, that opposes science as a universal foundation for truth and knowledge, and that discredits the Western notion of subjectivity as a stable, coherent self. What these shifting perspectives and emergent social relations have done is to radicalize the possibilities of freedom, and to affirm the capacity of human beings to shape their own destinies as part of a larger struggle for democracy.

In the Western industrial countries, the revolutions in Eastern Europe for freedom, equality, and justice appear in the dominant media as the valiant struggle of the Other against enslavement through communism. But in the United States these are events that take place on the margins of civilization, related but not central to the political and cultural identity of the West except as mimesis. In the mass media, the struggles for equality and freedom in Eastern Europe have been analyzed through the lens of a modernist discourse that reproduces highly problematic notions of the Enlightenment tradition. For example, many Western theorists view the redrawing of the political and social borders of Eastern Europe in reductionist modernist terms as the "end of history," a metaphor for the already unquestionable triumph of capitalist liberal democracy. In this scenario, the ideological characteristics that define the center of civilization through the discourse of the Western democracies has now been extended to the culturally and politically "deprived" margins of civilization. This is a curious position, because it fails to recognize that what the revolutions in Eastern Europe may be pointing to is not the "end of history" but to the exhaustion of those hierarchical and undemocratic features of modernism that produce state oppression, managerial domination, and social alienation in various countries in both the East and the West. It is curious because the "end of history" ideology, when applied to the Western democracies, is quite revealing; that is, it points to a political smugness which presupposes that democracy in the West has reached its culmination. Of course, beneath this smugness lies the indifference of Western-style democracy toward substantive political life; in effect, what has become increasingly visible in this argument is the failure of democracy itself. Hannam captures this point, "Formal democracy has failed because it has generated indifference towards many of the substantive goals of political activity. Western democracy believes itself to be at its own endpoint; it has given up the ambition of social change, of which it was once a central, but never an exclusive part" (Hannam 1990, 113).

While Western ruling groups and their apologists may choose to see only the triumph of liberal ideology beneath the changes in Eastern Europe, there is more being called into question than they suspect. In fact, the revolutions in Eastern Europe call into question not only the master narrative of Marxism, but all master narratives that make a totalizing claim to emancipation and freedom. In this case, the events taking place in Eastern Europe and in other places like South Africa represent part of a broader struggle of oppressed peoples against all totalizing forms of legitimation and cultural practice that deny human freedom and collective justice. What the West may be witnessing in Eastern Europe is the emergence of a new discourse, one that does not pit socialism against capitalism, but democracy against all forms of totalitarianism. In opposition to a limited modernist version of democracy, the struggles in Eastern Europe implicitly suggest the conditions for creating a radical democracy, one in which people control the social and economic forces that determine their existence. In this case, the struggle for democracy exceeds its modernist framework by extending the benefits of freedom and justice beyond the strictly formal mechanisms of democracy. What appears at work in these revolutions is a discourse that has the potential to deepen the radical implications of modernism through considerations of a rather profound set of questions: What set of conditions are necessary to create social relations for human liberation within historically specific formations? How might individual and social identities be reconstructed in the service of human imagination and democratic citizenship? How can the assertion of history and politics serve to deconstruct all essentialisms and totalizing rationalities? How can political and social identities be constructed within a politics of difference that is capable of struggling over and deepening the project of radical democracy while constantly asserting its historical and contingent character? Put another way, what can be done to strengthen and extend the oppositional tendencies of modernism?

I want to argue that modernism, postmodernism, and feminism represent three of the most important discourses for developing a cultural politics and pedagogical practice capable of extending and theoretically advancing a radical politics of democracy. While acknowledging that all three of these discourses are internally contradictory, ideologically diverse, and theoretically inadequate, I believe that when posited in terms of the interconnections between *both* their differences and the common ground they share for being mutually correcting, they offer critical educators a rich theoretical and political opportunity for rethinking the relationship between schooling and democracy. Each of these positions have much to learn from the theoretical strengths and weaknesses of the other two discourses. Not only does a dialogical encounter among these discourses offer them the opportunity to re-examine the partiality of their respective views, such an encounter also points to new possibilities for sharing and integrating their best insights as part of broader radical democratic project. Together these diverse discourses offer the possibility for illuminating how critical educators might work with other cultural workers in various movements to develop and advance a broader discourse of political and collective struggle. At stake here is an attempt to provide a political and theoretical discourse which can move beyond a postmodern aesthetic and a feminist separatism in order to develop a project in which a politics of difference can emerge within a shared discourse of democratic public life. Similarly, at issue is also the important question of how the discourses of modernism, postmodernism, and feminism might be pursued as part of a broader political effort to rethink the boundaries and most basic assumptions of a critical pedagogy consistent with a radical cultural politics.

I want to develop these issues through the following approach: First, I will analyze in schematic terms some of the central assumptions which characterize various modernist traditions, including Jurgen Habermas's spirited defense of social and political modernism. Second, I will analyze some of the central issues that postmodernism has made problematic in its encounter with modernism. Third, I will highlight the most progressive aspects of what can be loosely labeled as postmodern feminist theory to be used in the service of advancing both its own critical tendencies and the most radical aspects of modernism and postmodernism. Finally, I will indicate how these three discourses might contribute to developing some important principles in the construction of a critical pedagogy for democratic struggle. It is to these issues that I will now turn.

MAPPING THE POLITICS OF MODERNISM

To invoke the term modernism is to immediately place oneself in the precarious position of suggesting a definition that is itself open to enormous debate and little agreement (Groz 1986;

Appignanensi and Bennington 1986). Not only is there a disagreement regarding the periodization of the term, there is enormous controversy regarding to what it actually refers.[2] To some it has become synonomous with terroristic claims of reason, science, and totality (Lyotard 1984). To others it embodies, for better or worse, various movements in the arts (Newman 1985). While to some of its more ardent defenders, it represents the progressive rationality of communicative competence and support for the autonomous individual subject (Habermas 1981, 1983, 1987). It is not possible within the context of this chapter to provide a detailed history of the various historical and ideological discourses of modernism even though such an analysis is essential to provide a sense of the complexity of both the category and the debates that have emerged around modernism.[3] Instead, I want to focus on some of the central assumptions of modernism. The value of this approach is that it serves not only to highlight some of the more important arguments that have been made in the defense of modernism but also provides a theoretical and political backdrop for understanding some of the central features of various postmodernist and feminist discourses. This is particularly important with respect to postmodernism, which presupposes some idea of the modern and also of various feminist discourses, which have increasingly been forged largely in opposition to some of the major assumptions of modernism, particularly as these relate to notions such as rationality, truth, subjectivity, and progress.

The theoretical, ideological, and political complexity of modernism can be grasped by analyzing its diverse vocabularies with respect to three traditions: the social, aesthetic, and political. The notion of social modernity corresponds with the tradition of the new, the process of economic and social organization carried out under the growing relations of capitalist production. Social modernity approximates what Matei Calinescu (1987) calls the bourgeois idea of modernity, which is characterized by:

> The doctrine of progress, the confidence in the beneficial possibilities of science and technology, the concern with time (a measurable time, a time that can be bought and sold and therefore has, like any other commodity, a calculable equivalent in money), the cult of reason, and the ideal of freedom defined within the framework of an abstract humanism, but also the orientation toward pragmatism and the cult of action and success. (41)

Within this notion of modernism, the unfolding of history is linked to the "continual progress of the sciences and of techniques, the rational division of industrial work, [which] introduces into social life a dimension of permanent change, of destruction of customs and traditional culture" (Baudrillard 1987, 65). At issue here is a definition of modernity which points to the progressive differentiation and rationalization of the social world through the process of economic growth and administrative rationalization. Another characteristic of social modernism is the epistemological project of elevating reason to an ontological status. Modernism in this view becomes synonomous with civilization itself, and reason is universalized in cognitive and instrumental terms as the basis for a model of industrial, cultural, and social progress. At stake in this notion of modernity is a view of individual and collective identity in which historical memory is devised as a linear process, the human subject becomes the ultimate source of meaning and action, and a notion of geographical and cultural territorality is constructed in a hierarchy of domination and subordination marked by a center and margin legitimated through the civilizing knowledge/power of a privileged Eurocentric culture (Aronowitz 1987, 1988).

The category of aesthetic modernity has a dual characterization that is best exemplified in its traditions of resistance and formal aestheticism (Newman 1986). But it is in the tradition of opposition, with its all consuming disgust with bourgeois values and its attempt through various literary and avant-garde movements to define art as a representation of criticism, rebellion, and resistance that aesthetic modernism first gained a sense of notoriety. Fueling this aesthetic modernism of the nineteenth and early twentieth centuries was an alienation and negative passion whose novelty was perhaps best captured in Bakunin's anarchist maxim, "To destroy is to create" (cited in Calinescu 1987, 117). The cultural and political lineaments of this branch of aesthetic modernism is best expressed in those avant-garde movements which ranged from the surrealists and futurists, to the conceptualist artists of the 1970s. Within this movement, with its diverse politics and expressions, there is an underlying commonality and attempt to collapse the distinction between art and politics and to blur the boundaries between life and aesthetics. But in spite of its oppositional tendencies, aesthetic modernism has not fared well in the latter part of the twentieth century. Its critical stance, its aesthetic dependency on the presence of bourgeois norms, and its apocalyptic tone became increasingly recognized as artistically fashionable by the very class it attacked (Barthes 1972).

The central elements that bring these two traditions of modernism together constitute a powerful force for shaping not only the academic disciplines and the discourse of educational theory and practice, but also for providing a number of points where various ideological positions share a common ground. This is especially true in modernism's claim for the superiority of high culture over and against popular culture, its affirmation of a centered if not unified subject, its faith in the power of the highly rational, conscious mind, and its belief in the unequivocal ability of human beings to shape the future in the interest of a better world. There is a long tradition of support for modernism and some of its best representatives are as diverse as Marx, Baudelaire, and Dostoevsky. This notion of the self based on the universalization of reason and the totalizing discourses of emancipation have provided a cultural and political script for celebrating Western culture as synonomous with civilization itself and progress as a terrain that only needed to be mastered as part of the inexorable march of science and history. Marshall Berman (1982, 1988) exemplifies the dizzying heights of ecstasy made possible by the script of modernism in his own rendition of the modernist sensibility.

> Modernists, as I portray them, are simultaneously at home in this world and at odds with it. They celebrate and identify with the triumphs of modern science, art, technology, communications, economics, politics—in short, with all the activities, techniques, and sensibilities that enable mankind to do what the Bible said God could do—to "make all things new." At the same time, however, they oppose modernization's betrayal of its own human promise and potential. Modernists demand more profound and radical renewals: modern men and women must become the subjects as well as the objects of modernization; they must learn to change the world that is changing them and to make it their own. The modernist knows this is possible: the fact that the world has changed so much is proof that it can change still more. The modernist can, in Hegel's phrase, "look the negative in the face and live with it." The fact that "all that is solid melts into air" is a source not of despair, but of strength and affirmation. If everything must go, then let it go: modern people have the power to create a better world than the world they have lost. (Berman 1988, 11)

Of course, for many critics of modernism, the coupling of social and aesthetic modernism reveals itself quite differently. Modernist art is criticized for becoming nothing more than a commercial market for the museums and the corporate boardrooms and a depoliticized discourse institutionalized within the universities. In addition, many critics have argued that under the banner of modernism reason and aesthetics often come together in a technology of self and culture that combines a notion of beauty, which is white, male, and European with a notion of mastery that legitimates modern industrial technologies and the exploitation of vast pools of labor from the "margins" of Second and Third World economies. Robert Merrill (1988) gives this argument a special twist in claiming that the modernist ego with its pretentions to infallibility and unending progress has actually come to doubt its own promises. For example, he argues that many proponents of modernism increasingly recognize that what has been developed by the West in the name of mastery actually indicates the failure of modernism to produce a technology of self and power that can deliver on the promises of providing freedom through science, technology, and control. He writes:

> [A loss of faith in the promises of modernism]...is no less true for corporate and governmental culture in the United States which displays a...desperate quest for aestheticization of the self as modernist construct—white, male, Christian, industrialist—through monumentally styled office buildings, the Brooks Brothers suit (for male and female), designer food, business practices which amount only to the exercise of symbolic power, and most of all, the Mercedes-Benz which as the unification in design of the good (here functional) and the beautiful and in production of industrial coordination and exploitation of human labor is pre-eminently the sign that one has finally achieved liberation and mastery, "made it to the top" (even if its stylistic lines thematize what can only be called a fascist aesthetics). (Merrill 1988, ix)

It is against the claims of social and aesthetic modernism that the diverse discourses of postmodernism and feminism have delivered some of their strongest theoretical and political criticism, and these will be taken up shortly. But there is a third tradition of modernism that has been engaged by feminism but generally ignored by postmodernism. This is the tradition of political modernism. Political modernism, unlike its related aesthetic and social traditions, does not focus on epistemological and cultural issues as much as it develops a project of possibility out of a number of Enlightenment ideals (Laclau 1988; Mouffe 1988). It should be noted that political modernism constructs a project that rests on a distinction between political liberalism and economic liberalism. In the latter, freedom is conflated with the dynamics of the capitalist market place, whereas in the former, freedom is associated with the principles and rights embodied in the democratic revolution that has progressed in the West over the last three centuries. The ideals that have emerged out of this revolution include "the notion that human beings ought to use their reason to decide on courses of action, control their futures, enter into reciprocal agreements, and be responsible for what they do and who they are" (Warren 1988, ix–x). In general terms, the political project of modernism is rooted in the capacity of individuals to be moved by human suffering so as to remove its causes, to give meaning to the principals of equality, liberty, and justice, and to increase those social forms that enable human beings to develop those capacities needed to overcome ideologies and material forms that legitimate and are embedded in relations of domination.

The tradition of political modernism has largely been taken up and defended in opposition to and against the discourse of postmodernism. Consequently, when postmodernism is defined in relation to the discourse of democracy it is either pitted against the Enlightenment project and seen as reactionary in its political tendencies (Berman 1982; Habermas 1983, 1987), is grafted onto a notion of economic liberalism that converts it into an apology for rich Western democracies (Rorty 1985), or it is portrayed in opposition to the emancipatory project of Marxism (Eagleton 1985/86; Anderson 1984) and Feminism (Hartsock 1987; Christian 1987). In what follows, I want to examine some of the challenges that Jurgen Habermas (1983, 1987) presents to various versions of postmodernism and feminism through his defense of modernity as an unfinished emancipatory project (1983).

Habermas and the Challenge of Modernism

One of the most vigorous defenders of the legacy of modernism has been Jurgen Habermas (1981, 1983, 1987). Habermas's work is important because in forging his defense of modernism as part of a critique of the postmodernist and poststructuralist discourses that have emerged in France since 1968, he has opened up a debate between these seemingly opposing positions. Moreover, Habermas has attempted to revise and reconstruct the earlier work of his Frankfurt School colleagues, Theodor Adorno and Max Horkheimer, by revising their pessimistic view of rationality and democratic struggle.

Habermas identifies postmodernity less as a question of style and culture than as one of politics. The postmodern rejection of grand narratives, its denial of epistemological foundations, and its charge that reason and truth are always implicated in relations of power are viewed by Habermas as both a retreat and a threat to modernity. For Habermas, postmodernism has a paradoxical relation with modernism. On the one hand, it embodies the worst dimensions of an aesthetic modernism. That is, it extends those aspects of the avant-garde which "live [in] the experience of rebelling against all that is normative" (Habermas 1983, 5). In this sense, postmodernism echoes surrealism's attempt to undermine the cultural autonomy of art by removing the boundaries that separate it from everyday life. On the other hand, postmodernism represents a negation of the project of social modernity by rejecting its language of universal reason, rights, and autonomy as a foundation for modern social life. For Habermas, postmodernism's argument that realism, consensus, and totality are synonomous with terror represents a form of political and ethical exhaustion that unjustifiably renounces the unfinished task of the rule of reason (Habermas 1979). In Habermas's terms, the postmodernist thinkers are conservatives whose philosophical roots are to be found in various irrationalist and counter-Enlightenment theories that resemble a peculiar political kinship with fascism. According to Habermas, postmodernism undermines the still unfolding project of modernity, with its promise of democracy through the rule of reason, communicative competence, and cultural differentiation. Postmodernism is guilty of the dual crime, in this case, of rejecting the most basic tenets of the modernist ethos and failing to recognize its most emancipatory contributions to contemporary life. In the first instance, postmodernism recklessly overemphasizes the play of difference, contingency, and language against all appeals to universalized and transcendental claims. For the postmodernist, theory without the guarantee of truth redefines the relationship between discourse and power and in doing so destabilizes the modernist faith in consensus and reason. For Habermas, the latter represents a revolt against a substantive view of reason and subjectivity and negates the productive features of modernism.

For Habermas, modernity offers the promise of integrating the differentiating spheres of science, morality, and art back into society, not through an appeal to power, but through the rule of reason, the application of a universal pragmatics of language, and the development of forms of learning based on dictates of communicative competence. While Habermas accepts the excesses of technological rationality and substantive reason, he believes that it is only through reason that logic of scientific-technological rationality and domination can be subordinated to the imperatives of modernist justice and morality (Kellner 1988). Habermas (1982) admires Western culture and argues that "bourgeois ideals" contain elements of reason that should be at the center of a democratic society. He writes:

> I mean the internal theoretical dynamic which constantly propels the sciences—and the self-reflection of the sciences as well—beyond the creation of merely technologically exploitable knowledge; furthermore, I mean the universalist foundations of law and morality which have also been embodied (in no matter how distorted and imperfect a form) in the institutions of constitutional states, in the forms of democratic decision-making, and in individualistic patterns of identity formation; finally, I mean the productivity and the liberating force of an aesthetic experience with a subjectivity set free from the imperatives of purposive activity and from the conventions of everyday perception. (Habermas 1982, 18)

Central to Habermas's defense of modernity is his important distinction between instrumental and communicative rationality. Instrumental rationality represents those systems or practices embodied in the state, money, and various forms of power which work through "steering mechanisms" to stabilize society. Communicative rationality refers to the world of common experience and discursive intersubjective interaction, a world characterized by various forms of socialization mediated through language and oriented toward social integration and consensus. Habermas accepts various criticisms of instrumental rationality, but he largely agrees that capitalism, in spite of its problems, represents more acceptable forms of social differentiation, rationalization, and modernization than have characterized past stages of social and instrumental development. On the other hand, he is adamant about the virtues of communicative rationality, with its emphasis on the rules of mutual understanding, clarity, consensus, and the force of argument. Habermas views any serious attack on this form of rationality as in itself being irrational. In effect, Habermas's notion of communicative rationality provides the basis not only for his ideal speech situation but also for his broader view of social reconstruction. Rationality, in this case, with its distinctions between an outer world of systemic steering practices and a privileged inner world of communicative process represents in part a division between a world saturated with material power expressed in the evolution of ever growing and complex sub-systems of rational modernization and one shaped by universal reason and communicative action. At the core of this distinction is a notion of democracy in which struggle and conflict are not based on a politics of difference and power, but on a conceptual and linguistic search for defining the content of what is rational (Ryan 1989). Habermas's defense of modernity is not rooted in a rigorous questioning of the relationship between discourses, institutional structures and the interests they produce and legitimate within specific social conditions. Instead, he focuses on linguistic competence and the principle of consensus with its guiding problematic defined by the need to uproot the obstacles to "distorted communication." This points not only to a particular view of power, politics, and modernity, it also legitimates, as Stanley Aronowitz points out, a specific notion of reason and learning.

> He [Habermas] admonishes us to recognize [modernity's] unfinished tasks: the rule of reason. Rather than rules of governance based on power or discursive hegemonies, we are exhorted to create a new imaginary, one that would recognize societies able to resolve social conflicts, at least provisionally, so as to permit a kind of collective reflexivity. Characteristically, Habermas finds that the barriers to learning are not found in the exigencies of class interest, but in distorted communication. The mediation of communication by interest constitutes here an obstacle to reflexive knowledge. "Progressive" societies are those capable of learning—that is, acquiring knowledge that overcomes the limits of strategic or instrumental action. (Aronowitz 1987/88, 103)

Habermas's work has been both opposed and taken up by a number of critical and radical groups. He has been highly criticized by feminists such as Nancy Fraser (1985) and embraced by radicals who believe that his search for universal values represents a necessary ingredient in the struggle for human emancipation (Epstein 1990). In many respects, his writing provides a theoretical marker for examining how the debate over foundationalism and democracy, on the one hand, and a politics of difference and contingency, on the other, has manifested itself as a debate on the Left between those who line up for or against different versions of modernism or postmodernism.

A more constructive approach to both the specifics of Habermas's work as well as to the larger issue of modernism is that neither should be accepted or rejected as if the only choice was one of complete denial or conversion. In Habermas's case, for example, he is both right and wrong in his analyses of modernism and postmodernism. He is right in attempting to salvage the productive and emancipatory aspects of modernism and for attempting to develop a unifying principle which provides a referent point for engaging and advancing a democratic society. He is also right in claiming that postmodernism is as much about the issue of politics and culture as it is about aesthetics and style (Huyssen 1986). In this sense, Habermas provides a theoretical service by trying to keep alive as part of a modernist discourse the categories of critique, agency, and democracy. For better or worse, Habermas injects into the modernist versus postmodernist debate the primacy of politics and the role that rationality might play in the service of human freedom and the imperatives of democratic ideology and struggle. As Thomas McCarthy points out, Habermas

> believes that the defects of the Enlightenment can only be made good by further enlightenment. The totalized critique of reason undercuts the capacity of reason to be critical. It refuses to acknowledge that modernization bears developments as well as distortions of reason. Among the former, he mentions the "unthawing" and "reflective refraction" of cultural traditions, the universalization of norms and generalization of values, and the growing individuation of personal identities—all prerequisites for that effectively democratic organization of society through which alone reason can, in the end, become practical. (McCarthy 1987, xvii)

It is around these concerns that postmodern theorists have challenged some of the basic assumptions of modernism. For Habermas, these challenges weaken rather than mobilize the democratic tendencies of modernism. But as I hope to demonstrate in the remainder of this introduction, Habermas is wrong in simply dismissing all forms of postmodernism as anti-modernist and neo-conservative. Moreover, given his own notion of consensus and social action, coupled with his defense of Western tradition, his view of modernity is too complicitous with a notion of reason that is used to legitimate the superiority of a culture that is primarily white, male, and Eurocentric. Habermas speaks from a position that is not only susceptible to the charge of being patriarchal but is also open to the charge that his work does not adequately engage the relationship between discourse and power and the messy material relations of class, race, and gender. Postmodern and feminist critiques of his work cannot be dismissed simply because they might be labeled as anti-modern or anti-rationalist. In what follows, I want to take up some of the challenges that postmodernism has developed in opposition to some of the central assumptions of modernism.

POSTMODERN NEGATIONS

> If postmodernism means putting the Word in its place...if it means the opening up to critical discourse the line of enquiry which were formerly prohibited, of evidence which as previously inadmissible so that new and different questions can be asked and new and other voices can begin asking them; if it means the opening up of institutional and discursive spaces within which more fluid and plural social and sexual identities may develop; if it means the erosion of triangular formations of power and knowledge with the expert at the apex and the "masses" at the base, if, in a word, it enhances our collective (and democratic) sense of possibility, then I for one am a postmodernist. (Hebdige 1989, 226).

Hebdige's guarded comments regarding his own relationship to postmodernism are suggestive of some of the problems that have to be faced in using the term. As the term is increasingly employed both in and out of the academy to designate a variety of discourses, its political and semantic currency repeatedly becomes an object of conflicting forces and divergent tendencies. Postmodernism has not only become a site of conflicting ideological struggles—denounced by different factions on both the Left and the Right, supported by an equal number of diverse progressive groups, and appropriated by interests that would renounce any claim to politics—its varied forms also produce both radical and reactionary elements. Postmodernism's diffuse influence and contradictory character is evident within may cultural fields—painting, architecture, photography, video, dance, literature, education, music, mass communications—and in the varied contexts of its production and exhibition. Such a term does not lend itself to the usual topology of categories that serve to inscribe it ideologically and politically within traditional binary oppositions. In this case, the politics of postmodernism cannot be neatly labeled under the traditional categories of Left and Right.

In spite of the fact that many groups are making a claim for its use this should not suggest that the term has no value except as a buzzword for the latest intellectual fashions. On the contrary, its widespread appeal and conflict-ridden terrain indicate that something important is being fought over, that new forms of social discourse are being constructed at a time when the intellectual, political, and cultural boundaries of the age are being refigured amidst significant historical shifts, changing power structures, and emergent alternative forms of political struggle. Of course, whether these new postmodernist discourses adequately articulate rather than reflect these changes is the important question.

I believe that the discourse of postmodernism is worth struggling over, and not merely as a semantic category that needs to be subjected to ever more precise definitional rigor. As a discourse of plurality, difference and multinarratives, postmodernism resists being inscribed in any single articulating principle in order to explain either the mechanics of domination or the dynamic of emancipation. At issue here is the need to mine its contradictory and oppositional insights so that they might be appropriated in the service of a radical project of democratic struggle. The value of postmodernism lies in its role as a shifting signifier that both reflects and contributes to the unstable cultural and structural relationships that increasingly characterize the advanced industrial countries of the West. The important point here is not whether postmodernism can be defined within the parameters of particular politics, but how its best insights might be appropriated with a progressive and emancipatory democratic politics. I want to argue that while postmodernism does not suggest a particular ordering principle for defining a particular political project, it does have a rudimentary coherence with respect to the set of "problems and basic issues that have been created by the various discourses of postmodernism, issues that were not particularly problematic before but certainly are now" (Hutcheon 1988, 5). Postmodernism raises questions and problems so as to redraw and re-present the boundaries of discourse and cultural criticism. The issues that postmodernism has brought into view can be seen, in part, through its various refusals of all "natural laws" and transcendental claims that by definition attempt to "escape" from any type of historical and normative grounding. In fact, if there is any underlying harmony to various discourses of postmodernism it is in their rejection of absolute essences. Arguing along similar lines, Ernesto Laclau (1988b) claims that postmodernity as a discourse of social and cultural criticism begins with a form of epistemological, ethical, and political awareness based on three fundamental negations.

> The beginning of postmodernity can...be conceived as the achievement of multiple awareness: epistemological awareness, insofar as scientific progress appears as a succession of paradigms whose transformation and replacement is not grounded in any algorithmic certainty; ethical awareness, insofar as the defense and assertion of values is grounded on argumentative movements (conservational movements, according to Rorty), which do not lead back to any absolute foundation; political awareness, insofar as historical achievements appear as the product of hegemonic and contingent—and as such, always reversible—articulations and not as the result of immanent laws of history. (Laclau 1988b, 21)

Laclau's list does not exhaust the range of negations that postmodernism has taken up as part of the increasing resistance to all totalizing explanatory systems and the growing call for a language that offers the possibility to address the changing ideological and structural conditions of our time. In what follows, I shall address some of the important thematic considerations that cut across, what I define as a series of postmodern negations. I shall address these negations in terms of the challenge they present to what can be problematized as either oppressive or productive features of modernism.

Postmodernism and the Negation of
Totality, Reason, and Foundationalism

A central feature of postmodernism has been its critique of totality, reason, and universality. This critique has been most powerfully developed in the work of Jean-Francois Lyotard (1984). In developing his attack on Enlightenment notions of totality, Lyotard argues that the very notion of the postmodern is inseparable from an incredulity toward metanarratives. In Lyotard's view, "The narrative view is losing its functors, its great hero, its great dangers, its great voyages, its great goal. It is being dispersed in clouds of narrative language elements—narrative, but also denotative, prescriptive, descriptive, and so on. (Lyotard 1984, xxiv). For Lyotard, grand narratives do not problematize their own legitimacy, they deny the historical and social construction of their own first principles, and in doing so wage war on difference, contingency, and particularity. Against Habermas and others, Lyotard argues that appeals to reason and consensus, when inserted within grand narratives that unify history, emancipation and knowledge, deny their own implications in the production of knowledge and power. More emphatically, Lyotard claims that within such narratives are elements of mastery and control in which "we can hear the mutterings of the desire for a return of terror, for the realization of the fantasy to seize reality (Lyotard 1984, 82). Against metanarratives which totalize historical experience by reducing its diversity to a one-dimensional, all-encompassing logic, Lyotard posits a discourse of multiple horizons, the play of language games, and the terrain of micropolitics. Against the formal logic of identity and the transhistorical subject, he invokes a dialectics of indeterminancy, varied discourses of legitimation, and a politics based the "permanence of difference." Lyotard's attack on metanarratives represents both a trenchant form of social criticism and a philosophical challenge to all forms of foundationalism that deny the historical, normative, and the contingent. Nancy Fraser and Linda Nicholson (1988) articulate this connection well.

For Lyotard, postmodernism designates a general condition of contemporary Western civilization. The postmodern condition is one in which "grand narratives of legitimation" are no longer credible. By "grand narratives" he means, in the first instance, overarching philosophies of history like the Enlightenment story of the gradual but steady progress of reason and freedom, Hegel's dialectic of Spirit coming to

know itself, and, most important, Marx's drama of the
forward march of human productive capacities via class conflict culminating in proletarian revolution.... For what most
interests [Lyotard] about the Enlightenment, Hegelian, and
Marxist stories is what they share with other nonnarrative
forms of philosophy. Like a historical epistemologies and
moral theories, they aim to show that specific first-order discursive practices are well formed and capable of yielding true
and just results. True and just here mean something more
than results reached by adhering scrupulously to the constitutive rules of some given scientific and political games.
They mean, rather, results that correspond to Truth and
Justice as they really are in themselves independent of contingent, historical social practices. Thus, in Lyotard's view, a
metanarrative...purports to be a privileged discourse capable
of situating, characterizing, and evaluating all other discourses, but not itself infected by the historicity and contingency that render first-order discourses potentially distorted
and in need of legitimation. (86-87)

What Fraser and Nicholson point out by implication is that
postmodernism does more than "wage war on totality," it also
calls into question the use of reason in the service of power, the
role of intellectuals who speak through authority invested in a
science of truth and history, and forms of leadership that demand
unification and consensus within centrally administered chains of
command. Postmodernism rejects a notion of reason that is disinterested, transcendent, and universal. Rather than separating
reason from the terrain of history, place, and desire, postmodernism argues that reason and science can only be understood as
part of a broader historical, political, and social struggle over the
relationship between language and power. Within this context, the
distinction between passion and reason, objectivity and interpretation no longer exist as separate entities, but represent, instead, the
effects of particular discourses and forms of social power. This is
not merely an epistemological issue, but one that is deeply political and normative. Gary Peller (1987) makes this clear by arguing
that what is at stake in this form of criticism is nothing less than
the dominant and liberal commitment to Enlightenment culture.
He writes:

Indeed the whole way that we conceive of liberal progress

(overcoming prejudice in the name of truth, seeing through the distortions of ideology to get at reality, surmounting ignorance and superstition with the acquisition of knowledge) is called into question. [Postmodernism] suggests that what has been presented in our social-political and our intellectual traditions as knowledge, truth, objectivity, and reason are actually merely the effects of a particular form of social power, the victory of a particular way of representing the world that then presents itself as beyond mere interpretation, as truth itself. (30)

By asserting the primacy of the historical and contingent in the construction of reason, authority, truth, ethics, and identity, postmodernism provides a politics of representation and a basis for social struggle. Ernesto Laclau argues that the postmodern attack on foundationalism is an eminently political act since it expands the possibility for argumentation and dialogue. Moreover, by acknowledging questions of power and value in the construction of knowledge and subjectivities, postmodernism helps to make visible important ideological and structural forces, such as race, gender, and class. For theorists such as Ernesto Laclau (1988a) the collapse of foundationalism does not suggest a banal relativism or the onset of a dangerous nihilism. On the contrary, he argues that the lack of ultimate meaning radicalizes the possibilities for human agency and a democratic politics. He writes:

Abandoning the myth of foundations does not lead to nihilism, just as uncertainty as to how an enemy will attack does not lead to passivity. It leads, rather, to a proliferation of discursive interventions and arguments that are necessary, because there is no extradiscursive reality that discourse might simply reflect. Inasmuch as argument and discourse constitute the social, their open-ended character becomes the source of a greater activism and a more radical libertarianism. Humankind, having always bowed to external forces—God, Nature, the necessary laws of History—can now, at the threshold of postmodernity, consider itself for the first time the creator and constructor of its own history. (Laclau 1988a, 79–80)

The postmodern attack on totality and foundationalism is not without its drawbacks. While it rightly focuses on the importance of local narratives, and rejects the notion that truth precedes the notion of representation, it also runs the risk of blurring the distinction between master narratives that are monocausal and formative narratives which provide the basis for historically and relationally placing different groups or local narratives within some common project. To draw out this point further, it is difficult to imagine any politics of difference as a form of radical social theory if it doesn't offer a formative narrative capable of analyzing difference within rather than against unity. I will develop these criticisms in more detail in another section.

Postmodernism as the Negation of Border Cultures

Postmodernism offers a challenge to the cultural politics of modernism at a number of different levels. That is, it not only provides a discourse for retheorizing culture as fundamental to the construction of political subjects and collective struggle, it also theorizes culture as a politics of representation and power. Emily Hicks (1988) has presented the postmodern challenge to modernist culture as one framed within the contexts of shifting identities, the remapping of borders, and nonsynchronous memory. In her terms, modernist culture negates the possibility of identities created within the experience of multiple narratives and "border" crossings; instead, modernism frames culture within rigid boundaries that both privilege and exclude around the categories of race, class, gender, and ethnicity. Within the discourse of modernism, culture, in large part, becomes an organizing principle for constructing borders that reproduce relations of domination, subordination, and inequality. In this case, borders do not offer the possibility to experience and position ourselves within a productive exchange of narratives. Instead, modernism constructs borders framed in the language of universals and oppositions. Within the cultural politics of modernism, European culture becomes identified with the center of civilization, high culture is defined in essentialist terms against the popular culture of the everyday, and history as the reclaiming of critical memory is displaced by the proliferation of images. In effect, postmodernism constitutes a general attempt to transgress the borders sealed by modernism, to proclaim the arbitrariness of all boundaries, and to call attention to sphere of culture as a shifting social and historical construction.

I want to approach the postmodern challenge to a modernist cultural politics by focusing briefly on a number of issues. First, postmodernism has broadened the discussion regarding the relationship between culture and power by illuminating the changing conditions of knowledge embedded in the age of electronically mediated information systems, cybernetic technologies, and computer engineering (Lyotard 1984). In doing so, it has pointed to the development of new forms of knowledge that significantly shape traditional analyses relevant to the intersection of culture, power, and politics. Second, postmodernism raises a new set of questions regarding how culture is inscribed in the production of center/margin hierarchies and the reproduction of post-colonial forms of subjugation. At stake here is not only a reconsideration of the intersection of race, gender, and class but also a new way of reading history; that is, postmodernism provides forms of historical knowledge as a way of reclaiming power and identity for subordinate groups (Spivak 1987; Minh-ha 1989). Third, postmodernism breaks down the distinction between high and low culture and makes the everyday an object of serious study (Collins 1989).

In the first instance, postmodernism points to the increasingly powerful and complex role of the new electronic medium in constituting individual identities, cultural languages, and new social formations. In effect postmodernism has provided a new discourse that enables us to understand the changing nature of domination and resistance in late capitalist societies (Lash and Urry 1987). This is particularly true in its analyses of how the conditions for the production of knowledge have changed within the last two decades with respect to the electronic information technologies of production, the types of knowledge produced, and the impact they have had at both the level of everyday life and in larger global terms (Poster 1989). Postmodern discourses highlight radical changes in the ways in which culture is produced, circulated, read, and consumed; moreover, it seriously challenges those theoretical models which have inadequately analyzed culture as a productive and constituting force within an increasingly global network of scientific, technological, and information producing apparatuses.

In the second instance, postmodernism has provided an important theoretical service in mapping the relations of the center and periphery with respect to three related interventions into cultural politics. First, it has offered a powerful challenge to the hegemonic notion that Eurocentric culture is superior to other cultures and traditions by virtue of its canonical status as a universal measure of Western civilization. In exposing the particularity of the alleged universals that constitute Eurocentric culture, post-modernism has revealed that the "truth" of Western culture is by design a metanarrative which ruthlessly expunges the stories, traditions, and voices of those who by virtue of race, class, and gender constitute the "Other." Postmodernism's war on totality is defined, in this case, as a campaign against Western patriarchal culture and ethnocentricity (Mclaren and Hammer 1989). To the extent that Postmodernism has rejected the ethnocentricism of Western culture, it has also waged a battle against those forms of academic knowledge that serve to reproduce the dominant Western culture as a privileged canon and tradition immune from history, ideology, and social criticism (Aronowitz and Giroux 1990). Central to such a challenge is a second aspect of postmodernism's refiguring of the politics of the center and the margins. That is, postmoderism not only challenges the form and content of dominant models of knowledge, it also produces new forms of knowledge through its emphasis on breaking down disciplines and taking up objects of study that were unrepresentable in the dominant discourses of the Western canon.

Postmodern criticism provides an important theoretical and political service in assisting those deemed as "Other" to reclaim their own histories and voices. By problematizing the dominant notion of tradition, postmodernism has developed a power-sensitive discourse that helps subordinated and excluded groups to make sense out of their own social worlds and histories while simultaneously offering new opportunities to produce political and cultural vocabularies by which to define and shape their individual and collective identities (Lipsitz 1990). At stake here is both the rewriting of history within a politics of difference that substitutes totalizing narratives of oppression with local and multiple narratives which assert their identities and interests as part of a broader reconstruction of democratic public life. Craig Owens (1983) captures the project of possibility that is part of reclaiming voices that have been relegated to the marginal and therefore seem to be unrepresentable. While women emerge as the privileged force of the marginal in this account, his analysis is equally true for a number of subordinated groups.

> It is precisely at the legislative frontier between what can be represented and what cannot that the postmodernist operation is being staged—not in order to transcend representation, but in order to expose that system of power that autho-

rizes certain representations while blocking, prohibiting, or invalidating others. Among those prohibited from Western representation, whose representations are denied all legitimacy, are women. Excluded from representation by its very structure, they return within it as a figure for—a presentation of—the unrepresentable. (Owens 1983, 59)

Postmodernism's attempt to explore and articulate new spaces is not without its problems. Marginality as difference is not an unproblematic issue, and differences have to be weighted against the implications they have for constructing multiple relations between the self and the other. Moreover, resistance not only takes place on the margins but also at various points of entry within dominant institutions. Needless to say any notion of difference and marginality runs the risk of mystifying as well as enabling a radical cultural politics. But what is crucial is that postmodernism does offer the possibility for developing a cultural politics that focuses on the margins, for reclaiming, as Edward Said points out, "the right of formerly un- or mis-represented human groups to speak for and represent themselves in domains defined, political and intellectually, as normally excluding them, usurping their signifying and representing functions, overriding their historical reality" (Said, cited in Connor 1989, 233).

This leads to a third dimension of a postmodern cultural politics. As part of a broader politics of difference, postmodernism has also focused on the ways in which modernity functions as an imperialist masternarrative that links Western models of industrial progress with hegemonic forms of culture, identity, and consumption. Within this context, the project of modernity relegates all non-Western cultures to the periphery of civilization, outposts of insignificant histories, cultures, and narratives.

In the discourse of post-colonial modernism, the culture of the Other is no longer inscribed in imperialist relations of domination and subordination through the raw exercise of military or bureaucratic power. Power now inscribes itself in apparatuses of cultural production that easily transgress national and cultural borders. Data banks, radio transmissions, and international communications systems become part of the vanguard of a new global network of cultural and economic imperialism. Modernity now parades its universal message of progress through the experts and intellectuals it sends to Third World universities, through the systems of representations that it produces to saturate billboards all over Latin America, and/or and through advertising images it sends out from satellites to the television sets of inhabitants in Africa, India, and Asia.

Postmodernism makes visible both the changing technological nature of post-colonial imperialism and the new forms of emerging resistance that it encounters. On the one hand, it rejects the notion that the colonial relationship is an "uninterrupted psychodrama of repression and subjugation" (Roth 1988, 250). In this perspective, there is an attempt to understand how power is not only administered, but also taken up, resisted, and struggled over. The Other in this scenario does not suffer the fate of being generalized out of existence, but bears the weight of historical and cultural specificity. In part, this has resulted in a radical attempt to read the culture of the Other as a construction rather than a description, as a form of text that evokes rather than merely represents (Tyler 1987; Clifford and Marcus 1986; Clifford 1988). Within this scenario, the relationship between the subject and the object, invention and construction is never innocent and is always implicated in theorizing about the margins and the center. At issue here is an attempt to make problematic the voices of those who try to describe the margins, even when they do so in the interest of emancipation and social justice (Minh-ha 1989). This suggests yet another aspect of post-colonial discourse that postmodernism has begun to analyze as part of its own cultural politics.

In the postmodern age, the boundaries that once held back diversity, otherness, and difference, whether in domestic ghettos or through national borders policed by custom officials, have begun to break down. The Eurocentric center can no longer absorb or contain the culture of the other as something that is threatening and dangerous. As Renato Rosaldo (1989) points out, "the Third World has imploded into the metropolis. Even the conservative national politics of containment, designed to shield 'us' from 'them,' betray the impossibility of maintaining hermetically sealed cultures" (44). Culture in post-colonial discourse becomes something that Others have, it is the mark of ethnicity and difference. What has changed in this hegemonic formulation/strategy is that diversity is not ignored in the dominant cultural apparatus, but promoted in order to be narrowly and reductively defined through dominant stereotypes. Representation does not merely exclude, it also defines cultural difference by *actively* constructing the identity of the "Other" for dominant and subordinate groups. Postmodernism challenges post-colonial discourse by bringing the margins to the center in terms of their own voices and histories. Representation, in this sense, gives way to opposition and the struggle over questions of identity, place, and values (Spivak 1987; Minh-ha 1989). Difference in this context holds out the possibility of not only bringing the voices and politics of the "Other" to the centers of power, but also understanding how the center is implicated in the margins. It is an attempt to understand how the radicalizing of difference can produce new forms of displacement and more refined forms of racism and sexism. Understandably, the best work in this field is being done by writers from the "margins."

Finally, it is well known that postmodernism breaks with dominant forms of representation by rejecting the distinction between elite and popular culture and by arguing for alternative sites of artistic engagement and forms of experimentation (Hebdige 1988). As an anti-aesthetic, postmodernism rejects the modernist notion of privileged culture or art, it renounces "official" centers for "housing" and displaying art and culture along with their interests in origins, periodization, and authenticity (Foster 1983). Moreover, postmodernism's challenge to the boundaries of modernist art and culture has, in part, resulted in new forms of art, writing, film-making, and various types of aesthetic and social criticism. For example, films like *Whetherby* deny the structure of plot and seem to have no recognizable beginning or end, photographer Sherrie Levine uses a "discourse of copy" in her work in order to transgress the notions of origin and originality. Writer James Sculley (1988) blurs the lines between writing poetry and producing it within a variety of representational forms. The American band, Talking Heads, adopts an eclectic range of aural and visual signifiers to produce a pastiche of styles in which genres are mixed, identities shift, and the lines between reality and image are purposely blurred (Hebdige 1986). Most important, postmodernism conceives of the everyday and the popular as worthy of serious *and* playful consideration. In the first instance, popular culture is analyzed as an important sphere of contestation, struggle, and resistance. In doing so, postmodernism does not abandon the distinctions which structure varied cultural forms within and between different levels of social practice, instead, it deepens the possibility for understanding the social, historical, and political foundation for such distinctions as they are played out within the intersection of power, culture, and politics. In the second instance, postmodernism cultivates a tone of irony, parody, and playfulness as part of an aesthetic which desacralizes cultural aura and "greatness" while simultaneously demonstrating that "contingency penetrates all identity" and that "the primary and constitutive character of the discursive is...the condition of any practice" (Laclau 1988b, 17). Richard Kearney (1988) has noted that the postmodern notion of play, with its elements of undecidability and poetical imagining, challenges constricted and egocentric levels of selfhood and allows us to move toward a greater understanding of the Other.

> The ex-centric characteristics of the play paradigm may be construed as tokens of the poetical power of imagination to transcend the limits of egocentric, and indeed anthropocentric, consciousness—thereby exploring different possibilities of existence. Such "possibilities" may well be deemed impossible at the level of the established reality. (366–367)

Central to the postmodern rejection of elite culture as a privileged domain of cultural production and repository of "truth" and civilization is an attempt to understand modernist cultural practices in their hegemonic and contradictory manifestations. Similarly, postmodernism rejects the notion of popular culture as structured exclusively through a combination of commodity production and audience passivity, a site for both dumping commercial junk and the creation of consumer robots. Instead, postmodernism views popular culture as a terrain of accommodation and struggle, a terrain whose structuring principles should not be analyzed in the reductionistic language of aesthetic standards but rather through the discourse of power and politics (Giroux and Simon 1989). Of course, it must be stated that the postmodern elements of a cultural politics that I have provided need to be interrogated more closely for their excesses and absences, and I will take up this issue in another section, but in what follows I will analyze the third postmodern negation regarding language and subjectivity.

Postmodernism, Language, and the Negation of the Humanist Subject

Within the discourse of postmodernism, the new social agents become plural; that is, the discourse of the universal agent, such as the working class, is replaced by multiple agents forged in a variety of struggles and social movements. Here we have a politics which stresses differences between groups. But, as Sharon

Welch points out in her chapter in this book, subjects are also constituted within difference. This is an important distinction and offers an important challenge to the humanist notion of the subject as a free, unified, stable, and coherent self. In fact, one of the most important theoretical and political advances of postmodernism is its stress on the centrality of language and subjectivity as new fronts from which to rethink the issues of meaning, identity, and politics. This issue can best be approached by first analyzing the ways in which postmodernism has challenged the conventional view of language.

Postmodern discourse has re-theorized the nature of language as a system of signs structured in the infinite play of difference, and in doing so has undermined the dominant, positivist notion of language as either a genetic code structured in permanence or simply a linguistic, transparent medium for transmitting ideas and meaning. Theorists such as Jacques Derrida (1976), Michel Foucault (1977a, 1977b), Jacques Lacan (1968), and Laclau and Mouffe (1985), in particular, have played a major role in re-theorizing the relationship among discourse, power, and difference. For example, Derrida (1976) has brilliantly analyzed the issue of language through the principle of what he calls "differance." This view suggests that meaning is the product of a language constructed out of and subject to the endless play of differences between signifiers. What constitutes the meaning of a signifier is defined by the shifting, changing relations of difference that characterize the referential play of language. What Derrida, Laclau and Mouffe (1985), and a host of other critics have demonstrated is "the increasing difficulty of defining the limits of language, or, more accurately, of defining the specific identity of the linguistic object" (Laclau 1988a, 67). But more is at stake here than theoretically demonstrating that meaning can never be fixed once and for all.

The postmodern emphasis on the importance of discourse has also resulted in a major rethinking of the notion of subjectivity. In particular, various postmodern discourses have offered a major critique of the liberal humanist notion of subjectivity which is predicated on the notion of a unified, rational, self-determining consciousness. In this view, the individual subject is the source of self-knowledge and his or her view of the world is constituted through the exercise of a rational and autonomous mode of understanding and knowing. What postmodern discourse challenges is the liberal humanism's notion of the subject "as a kind of free, autonomous, universal sensibility, indifferent to any particular or moral contents" (Eagleton 1985/1986, 101). Teresa Ebert (1988) in her discussion of the construction of gender differences offers a succinct commentary on the humanist notion of identity:

> Postmodern feminist cultural theory breaks with the dominant humanist view...in which the subject is still considered to be an autonomous individual with a coherent, stable self constituted by a set of natural and pre-given elements such as biological sex. It theorizes the subject as produced through signifying practices which precede her and not as the originator of meaning. One acquires specific subject positions—that is, existence in meaning, in social relations—being constituted in ideologically structured discursive acts. Subjectivity is thus the effect of a set of ideologically organized signifying practices through which the individual is situated in the world and in terms of which the world and one's self are made intelligible. (22–23)

The importance of postmodernism's re-theorizing of subjectivity cannot be overemphasized. In this view, subjectivity is no longer assigned to the apolitical wasteland of essences and essentialism. Subjectivity is now read as multiple, layered, and non-unitary; rather than being constituted in a unified and integrated ego, the "self" is seen as being "constituted out of and by difference and remains contradictory" (Hall 1986, 56). No longer viewed as merely the repository of consciousness and creativity, the self is constructed as terrain of conflict and struggle, and subjectivity is seen as site of both liberation and subjugation. How subjectivity relates to issues of identity, intentionality, and desire is a deeply political issue that is inextricably related to social and cultural forces that extend far beyond the self-consciousness of the so-called humanist subject. Both the very nature of subjectivity and its capacities for self- and social-determination can no longer be situated within the guarantees of transcendent phenomena or metaphysical essences. Within this postmodern perspective, the basis for a cultural politics and the struggle for power has been opened up to include the issues of language and identity. In what follows, I want to take up how various feminist discourses reinscribe some of the central assumptions of modernism and postmodernism as part of a broader cultural practice and political project.

POSTMODERN FEMINISM AS POLITICAL
AND ETHICAL PRACTICE

Feminist theory has always engaged in a dialectical relationship with modernism. On the one hand, it has stressed modernist
concerns with equality, social justice, and freedom through an
ongoing engagement with substantive political issues, specifically
the rewriting of the historical and social construction of gender in
the interest of an emancipatory cultural politics. In other words,
feminism has been quite discriminating in its ability to sift
through the wreckage of modernism in order to liberate its victories, particularly the unrealized potentialities that reside in its categories of agency, justice, and politics. On the other hand, postmodern feminism has rejected those aspects of modernism in
which universal laws are exalted at the expense of specificity and
contingency. More specifically, postmodern feminism opposes a
linear view of history which legitimates patriarchal notions of subjectivity and society; moreover, it rejects the notion that science
and reason have a direct correspondence with objectivity and
truth. In effect, postmodern feminism rejects the binary opposition
between modernsim and postmodernism in favor of a broader theoretical attempt to situate both discourses critically within a feminist political project.

Feminist theory has both produced and profited from a critical appropriation of a number of assumptions central to both modernsim and postmodernism. The feminist engagement with modernsim has been taken up primarily as a discourse of self-criticism
and has served to radically expand a plurality of positions within
feminism itself. Women of color, lesbians, poor and working class
women have challenged the essentialism, separatism, and ethnocentricism that has been expressed in feminist theorizing and in
doing so have seriously undermined the Eurocentricism and totalizing discourse that has become a political straitjacket within the
movement. Nancy Fraser and Linda Nicholson (1988) offer a succinct analysis of some of the issues involved in this debate, particularly in relation to the appropriation by some feminists of "quasi
metanarratives."

They tacitly presuppose some commonly held but unwarranted and essentialist assumptions about the nature of
human beings and the conditions for social life. In addition,

they assume methods and/or concepts that are uninflected by temporality or historicity and that therefore function de facto as permanent, neutral matrices for inquiry. Such theories, then, share some of the essentialist and ahistorical features of metanarratives: they are insufficiently attentive to historical and cultural diversity; and they falsely universalize features of the theorist's own era, society, culture, class, sexual orientation, and/or ethnic or racial group....It has become clear that quasi metanarratives hamper, rather than promote, sisterhood, since they elide differences among women and among the forms of sexism to which different women are differentially subject. Likewise, it is increasingly apparent that such theories hinder alliances with other progressive movement, since they tend to occlude axes of domination other than gender. In sum, there is a growing interest among feminists in modes of theorizing that are attentive to differences and to cultural and historical specificity. (92, 99)

Fashioning a language that has been highly critical of modernism has not only served to make problematic what can be called totalizing feminisms, it has also called into question the notion that sexist oppression is at the root of all forms of domination (Malson, et al 1989b). Implicit in this position are two assumptions that have significantly shaped the arguments of mostly Western white women. The first argument simply inverts the orthodox Marxist position regarding class as the primary category of domination with all other modes of oppression being relegated to a second rate consideration. In this instance, patriarchy becomes the primary form of domination while race and class are reduced to its distorted reflection. The second assumption recycles another aspect of orthodox Marxism which assumes that the struggle over power is exclusively waged between opposing social classes. The feminist version of this argument simply substitutes gender for class and in doing so reproduces a form of "us" against "them" politics that is antithetical to developing community building within a broad and diversified public culture. Both of these arguments represent the ideological baggage of modernism. In both cases, domination is framed in binary oppositions which suggests that workers or women cannot be complicit in their own oppression and that domination assumes a form which is singular and uncomplicated. The feminist challenge to this ideological straitjacket of modernism is well expressed by Bell Hooks who avoids the politics of separatism by invoking an important distinction between the role that feminists might play in asserting their own particular struggle against patriarchy as well as the role they can play as part of a broader struggle for liberation.

> Feminist effort to end patriarchal domination should be of primary concern precisely because it insists on the eradication of exploitation and oppression in the family context and in all other intimate relationships....Feminism, as liberation struggle, must exist apart from and as a part of the larger struggle to eradicate domination in all of its forms. We must understand that patriarchal domination shares an ideological foundation with racism and other forms of group oppression, that there is no hope that it can be eradicated while these systems remain intact. This knowledge should consistently inform the direction of feminist theory and practice. Unfortunately, racism and class elitism among women has frequently led to the suppression and distortion of this connection so that it is now necessary for feminist thinkers to critique and revise much feminist theory and the direction of the feminist movement. This effort at revision is perhaps most evident in the current widespread acknowledgement that sexism, racism, and class exploitation constitute interlocking systems of domination—that sex, race, and class, and not sex alone, determine the nature of any female's identity, status, and circumstance, the degree to which she will or will not be dominated, the extent to which she will have the power to dominate. (Hooks 1989, 22)

I invoke the feminist critique of modernism to make visible some of the ideological territory it shares with certain versions of postmodernism and to suggest the wider implications that a postmodern feminism has in developing and broadening the terrain of political struggle and transformation. It is important to note that this encounter between feminism and postmodernism should not be seen as a gesture to displace a feminist politics with a politics and pedagogy of postmodernism. On the contrary, I think feminism provides postmodernism with a politics, and a great deal more. What is at stake here is using feminism, in the words of Meaghan Morris (1988) as "a context in which debates about postmodernism might further be considered, developed, transformed (or abandoned)" (16). Critical to such a project is the need to analyze the ways in which feminist theorists have used postmodernism to fashion a form of social criticism whose value lies in its critical approach to gender issues and in the theoretical insights it provides for developing broader democratic and pedagogical struggles.

The theoretical status and political viability of various postmodern discourses regarding the issues of totality, foundationalism, culture, subjectivity and language are a matter of intense debate among diverse feminist groups. I am less concerned with charting this debate or focusing on those positions which dismiss postmodernism as antithetical to feminism. Instead, I want to focus primarily on those feminist discourses which acknowledge being influenced by postmodernism but at the same time deepen and radicalize the assumptions most important in the interest of a theory and practice of transformative feminist, democratic struggles.[4]

Feminism's relationship with postmodernism has been fruitful but problematic (Kaplan 1988). Postmodernism shares a number of assumptions with various feminist theories and practices. For example, both discourses view reason as plural and partial, define subjectivity as multilayered and contradictory, and posit contingency and difference against various forms of essentialism.

At the same time, postmodern feminism has criticized and extended a number of assumptions central to postmodernism. First, it has asserted the primacy of social criticism and in doing so has redefined the significance of the postmodern challenge to founding discourses and universal principles in terms that prioritize political struggles over epistemological engagements. Donna Haraway (1989) puts it well in her comment, "the issue is ethics and politics perhaps more than epistemology" (579). Second, postmodern feminism has refused to accept the postmodern view of totality as a wholesale rejection of all forms of totality or metanarratives. Third, it has rejected the postmodern emphasis on erasing human agency by decentering the subject; in related fashion it has resisted defining language as the only source of meaning and in doing so has linked power not merely to discourse but also to material practices and struggles. Fourth, it has asserted the importance of difference a part of a broader struggle for ideological and institutional change rather than emphasizing the postmodern approach to difference as either an aesthetic (pastiche) or as an expression of liberal pluralism (the proliferation of difference without recourse to the language of power). Since I cannot analyze all these issues in great detail in this chapter, I will take up some of the more important tendencies implied in these positions.

Postmodern Feminism and the Primacy of the Political

> Working collectively to confront difference, to expand our awareness of sex, race, and class as interlocking systems of domination, of the ways we reinforce and perpetuate these structures, is the context in which we learn the true meaning of solidarity. It is this work that must be the foundation of feminist movement. Without it, we cannot effectively resist patriarchal domination; without it, we remain estranged and alienated from one another. Fear of painful confrontation often leads women and men active in feminist movement to avoid rigorous critical encounter, yet if we cannot engage dialectically in a committed, rigorous, humanizing manner, we cannot hope to change the world....While the struggle to eradicate sexism and sexist oppression is and should be the primary thrust of feminist movement, to prepare ourselves politically for this effort we must first learn how to be in solidarity, how to struggle with one another. (Hooks 1989, 25)

Bell Hooks speaks eloquently to the issue of constructing a feminism that is self-consciously political. In solidarity with a number of feminists, she provides a much needed corrective to the postmodern tendency to eclipse the political and ethical in favor of issues that center on epistemological and aesthetic concerns. Not only does she assert that intellectual and cultural work must be driven by political questions and issues, she also performs the theoretically important task of affirming a feminist politics which attempts to understand and contest the various ways in which patriarchy is inscribed at every level of daily life. But what is different and postmodern about Hooks's commentary is that she not only argues for a postmodern feminist practice that is oppositional in its appeal "to end sexism and sexist oppression" (Hooks 1989, 23) but she also calls into question those feminisms that reduce domination to a single cause, focus exclusively on sexual difference, and ignore women's differences as they intersect across other vectors of power, particularly with regards to race and class. What is at stake in this version of postmodern feminist politics is an attempt to reaffirm the centrality of gender struggles while simultaneously broadening the issues associated with such struggles. Similarly, there is an attempt to connect gender politics to broader politics of solidarity. Let me be more specific about some of these issues.

Central to the feminist movement since the 1970s in the United States has been the important notion of arguing that the personal is political. This suggests a complex relationship between the construction of subjectivity through the use of language and material social practices. Within this context, subjectivity was analyzed as a historical and social construction, engendered through the historically weighted configurations of power, language, and social formations. The problematization of gender relations in this case has been often described as the most important theoretical advance made by feminists (Showalter 1989). Postmodern feminism has extended the political significance of this issue in important ways.

First, it has strongly argued that feminist analyses cannot downplay the dialectical significance of gender relations. That is, such relations have to focus not only on the various ways in which women are inscribed in patriarchal representations and relations of power, but also on how gender relations can be used to problematize the sexual identities, differences, and commonalities of both men and women. To suggest that masculinity is an unproblematic category is to adopt an essentialist position which ultimately reinforces the power of patriarchal discourse (Showalter 1989).

Second, feminist theorists have redefined the relationship between the personal and political in ways that advance some important postmodern assumptions. In part, this has emerged out of an increasing feminist criticism which rejects the notion that sexuality is the only axis of domination or that the study of sexuality should be limited theoretically to an exclusive focus on how women's subjectivities are constructed. For example, theorists such as Teresa de Lauretis have argued that central to feminist social criticism is the need for feminists to maintain a "tension between [the personal and the political] precisely through the understanding of identity as multiple and even self-contradictory (de Lauretis 1986, 9). To ignore such as tension often leads to the trap of collapsing the political into the personal and limiting the sphere of politics to the language of pain, anger, and separatism. Bell Hooks elaborates on this point by arguing that when feminists reduce the relationship between the personal and the political merely to the naming of one's pain in relation to structures of domination they often undercut the possibilities for understanding the multifaceted nature of domination and for creating a politics of possibility. She writes:

That powerful slogan, "the personal is political," addresses the connection between the self and political reality. Yet it was often interpreted as meaning that to name one's personal pain in relation to structures of domination was not just a beginning stage in the process of coming to political consciousness, to awareness, but all that was necessary. In most cases, naming one's personal pain was not sufficiently linked to overall education for critical consciousness of collective political resistance. Focussing on the personal in a framework that did not compel acknowledgement of the complexity of structures of domination could easily lead to misnaming, to the creation of yet another sophisticated level of non- or distorted-awareness. This often happens in a feminist context when race and/or class are not seen as factors determining the social construction of one's gendered reality and most important, the extent to which one will suffer exploitation and domination. (1989, 32)

In this case, the construction of gender must be seen in the context of the wider relations in which it is structured. At issue here is the need to deepen the postmodern notion of difference by radicalizing the notion of gender through a refusal to isolate it as a social category while simultaneously engaging in a politics which aims at transforming the self, community, and society. Within this context, postmodern feminism offers the possibility of going beyond the language of domination, anger, and critique.

Third, postmodern feminism attempts to understand the broader workings of power by examining how it functions other than through specific technologies of control and mastery (de Lauretis 1987). At issue here is understanding how power is constituted productively. Teresa de Lauretis (1986) develops this insight by arguing that while postmodernism provides a theoretical service in recognizing that power is "productive of knowledges, meanings, and values, it seems obvious enough that we have to make distinctions between the positive effects and the oppressive effects of such production" (18). De Lauretis's point is important because it suggests that power can work in the interests of a politics of possibility, that it can be used to rewrite the narratives of subordinate groups not merely in reaction to the forces of domination but in response to the construction of alternative visions and futures. The exclusive emphasis on power as oppressive always runs the risk of developing as its political equivalent a version of radical cynicism and anti-utopianism. Postmodern feminism offers the possibility for redefining both a negative feminist politics (Kristeva 1988) and a more general postmodern inclination towards a despair that dresses itself up in irony, parody, and pastiche. Linda Alcoff put it well in arguing that, "As the Left should by now have learned, you cannot mobilize a movement that is only and always against: you must have a positive alternative, a vision of a better future that can motivate people to sacrifice their time and energy toward its realization" (Alcoff 1988, 418–419). Central to this call for a language of possibility are the ways in which a postmodern feminism has taken up the issue of power in more expansive and productive terms, one that is attentive to the ways in which power inscribes itself through the force of reason, and constructs itself at the levels of intimate and local associations (Diamond and Quinby 1988).

Postmodern Feminism and the Politics of Reason and Totality

Various feminist discourses have provided a theoretical context and politics for enriching postmodernism's analyses of reason and totality. Whereas postmodern theorists have stressed the historical, contingent, and cultural construction of reason, they have failed to show how reason has been constructed as part of a masculine discourse (Diamond and Quinby 1988). Postmodern feminists have provided a powerful challenge to this position, particularly in their analyses of the ways in which reason, language, and representation have produced knowledge/power relations, legitimated in the discourse of science and objectivity, to silence, marginalize, and misrepresent women (Jagger 1983; Keller 1985; Harding 1986; Birke 1986). Feminist theorists have also modified the postmodern discussion of reason in two other important ways. First, while recognizing that all claims to reason are partial, they have argued for the emancipatory possibilities that exist in reflective consciousness and critical reason as a basis for social criticism (Welch 1985; de Lauretis 1986). In these terms, reason is not merely about a politics of representation structured in domination or a relativist discourse that abstracts itself from the dynamics of power and struggle, it also offers the possibility for self-representation and social reconstruction. For example, Donna Haraway (1989) has qualified the postmodern turn towards relativism by theorizing reason within a discourse of partiality that "privileges contestation, deconstruction, passionate construction, webbed connections, and hope for transformation of systems of knowledge and ways of seeing" (585). Similarly, Bell Hooks (1989) and others have argued that feminists who deny the power of critical reason and abstract discourse often reproduce a cultural practice that operates in the interest of patriarchy. That is, it serves to silence women and others by positioning them in ways that cultivate a fear of theory which in turn often produce a form of powerlessness buttressed by a powerful anti-intellectualism. Second, feminists such as Jane Flax (1988) have modified postmodernism's approach to reason by arguing that reason is not the only locus of meaning:

> I cannot agree...that liberation, stable meaning, insight, self-understanding and justice depend above all on the "primacy of reason and intelligence." There are many ways in which such qualities may be attained—for example, political practices, economic, racial and gender equality; good childrearing; empathy; fantasy; feelings; imagination; and embodiment. On what grounds can we claim reason is privileged or primary for the self or justice? (202)

At issue here is not the rejection of reason but a modernist version of reason that is totalizing, essentialist, and politically repressive. Postmodern feminism has also challenged and modified the postmodern approach to totality or master narratives on similar terms. While accepting the postmodern critique of master narratives that employ a single standard and make a claim to embody a universal experience, postmodern feminism does not define all large or formative narratives as oppressive. At the same time, postmodern feminism recognizes the importance of grounding narratives in the contexts and specificities of peoples' lives, communities, and cultures, but supplements this distinctly postmodern emphasis on the contextual with an argument for meta-narratives which employ forms of social criticism that are dialectical, relational, and holistic. Metanarratives play an important theoretical role in placing the particular and the specific in broader historical and relational contexts. To reject all notions of totality is to run the risk of being trapped in particularistic theories that cannot explain how the various diverse relations that constitute larger social, political, and global systems interrelate or mutually determine and constrain one another. Postmodern feminism recognizes that we need a notion of large narratives that privileges forms of analyses in which it is possible to make visible those mediations, interrelations, and interdependencies that give shape and power to large political and social systems. Nancy Fraser and Linda Nicholson (1988) make very clear the importance of such narratives to social criticism.

> Effective criticism...requires an array of different methods and genres. It requires, at minimum, large narratives about changes in social organization and ideology, empirical and social-theoretical analyses of macrostructures and institutions, interactionist analyses of the micropolitics of everyday life, critical-hermeneutical and institutional analyses of cultural production, historically and culturally specific sociologies of gender....The list could go on. (91)

Postmodern Feminism and the Politics of
Difference and Agency

Feminists share a healthy skepticism toward the postmodern celebration of difference. Many feminist theorists welcome the postmodern emphasis on the proliferation of local narratives, the opening up of the world to cultural and ethnic differences, and the positing of difference as a challenge to hegemonic power relations parading as universals (Flax 1988; McRobbie 1986; Nicholson 1990; Kaplan 1988; Lather 1989). But at the same time, postmodern feminists have raised serious questions about how differences are to be understood so as to change rather than reproduce prevailing power relations. This is particularly important since difference in the postmodern sense often slips into a theoretically harmless and politically deracinated notion of pastiche. For many postmodern feminists, the issue of difference has to be interrogated around a number of concerns. These include questions regarding how a politics of difference can be constructed that will not simply reproduce forms of liberal individualism, or how a politics of difference can be "rewritten as a refusal of the terms of radical separation?" (Kaplan 1987, 194). Also at issue is the question regarding how a theory of difference can be developed that is not at odds with a politics of solidarity? Equally important is the issue of how a theory of the subject constructed in difference might sustain or negate a politics of human agency? Relatedly, there is the question of how a postmodern feminism can redefine the knowledge/power relationship in order to develop a theory of difference that is not static, one that is able to make distinctions between differences that matter and those that do not. All these questions have been addressed in a variety of feminist discourses not all of which support postmodernism. What has increasingly emerged out of this engagement is a discourse that radically complicates and amplifies the possibilities for reconstructing difference within a radical political project and set of transformative practices.

In the most general sense, the postmodern emphasis on difference serves to dissolve all pretentions to an undifferentiated concept of truth, man, woman, and subjectivity, while at the same time refusing to reduce difference to "opposition, exclusion, and hierarchic arrangement" (Malson, et al 1989a, 4). Postmodern feminism has gone a long way in framing the issue of difference in terms that give it an emancipatory grounding, that identify the "differences that make a difference" as an important political act. In what follows, I want to briefly take up how the issue of difference and agency has been developed within a postmodern feminist discourse.

Joan Wallach Scott (1988) has provided a major theoretical service in dismantling one of the crippling dichotomies in which the issue of difference has been situated. Rejecting the idea that difference and equality constitutes an opposition, she argues that the opposite of equality is not difference but inequality. In this sense, the issue of equality is not at odds with notion of difference, but depends on an acknowledgment of differences that promote inequality and those that do not. In this case, the category of difference is central as a political construct to the notion of equality itself. The implication this has for a feminist politics of difference according to Scott (1988) involves two important theoretical moves:

> In histories of feminism and in feminist political strategies there needs to be at once attention to the operations of difference and an insistence on differences, but not a simple sub-

stitution of multiple for binary difference, for it is not a happy pluralism we ought to invoke. The resolution of the "difference dilemma" comes neither from ignoring nor embracing difference as it is normatively constituted. Instead it seems to me that critical feminist position must always involve two moves: the first, systematic criticism of the operations of categorical difference, exposure of the kinds of exclusions and inclusions—the hierarchies—it constructs, and a refusal of their ultimate "truth." A refusal, however, not in the name of an equality that implies sameness or identity but rather (and this is the second move) of an equality that rests on differences—differences that confound, disrupt, and render ambiguous the meaning of any fixed binary opposition. To do anything else is to buy into the political argument that sameness is a requirement for equality, an untenable position for feminists (and historians) who know that power is constructed on, and so must be challenged from, the ground of difference. (176–177)

According to Scott, challenging power from the ground of difference by focusing on both exclusions and inclusions is to avoid slipping into a facile and simple elaboration or romanticization of difference. In more concrete terms, E. Ann Kaplan (1988) takes up this issue in arguing that the postmodern elimination of all distinctions between high and low culture is important but erases the important differences at work in the production and exhibition of specific cultural works. By not discriminating among differences of context, production, and consumption, postmodern discourses run the risk of suppressing the differences at work in the power relations that characterize these different spheres of cultural production. For example, to treat all cultural products as texts may situate them as historical and social constructions, but it is imperative that the institutional mechanisms and power relations in which different texts are produced be distinguished so that it becomes possible to understand how such texts, in part, make a difference in terms of reproducing particular meanings, social relations, and values.

A similar issue is at work regarding the postmodern notion of subjectivity. The postmodern notion that human subjectivities and bodies are constructed in the endless play of difference threatens to erase not only any possibility for human agency or choice, but also the theoretical means for understanding how the body becomes a site of power and struggle around specific differences that do matter with respect to the issues of race, class and gender. There is little sense in many postmodern accounts of the ways in which different historical, social, and gendered representations of meaning and desire are actually mediated and taken up subjectively by real, concrete individuals. Individuals are positioned within a variety of "subject positions" but there is no sense of how they actually make choices, promote effective resistance, or mediate between themselves and others. Feminist theorists have extended the most radical principles of modernism in modifying the postmodern view of the subject. Theorists such as Teresa de Lauretis (1984, 1986, 1987) insist that the construction of female experience is not constructed outside human intentions and choices, however limited. She argues that the agency of subjects is made possible through shifting and multiple forms of consciousness constructed through available discourses and practices, but always open to interrogation through the process of a self-analyzing practice. For de Lauretis and others like Linda Alcoff (1988) such a practice is theoretical and political. Alcoff's (1988) own attempt to construct a feminist identity-politics draws on de Lauretis' work and is insightful in its attempt to develop a theory of positionality.

> ...the identity of a woman is the product of her own interpretation and reconstruction of her history, as mediated through a cultural discursive context to which she has access. Therefore, the concept of positionality includes two points: First...the concept of woman is a relational term identifiable only with a (constantly moving) context; but second, that the position that women find themselves in can be actively utilized (rather than transcended) as a location for the construction of meaning, a place where a meaning can be discovered (the meaning of femaleness). The concept...of positionality shows how women use their positional perspective as a place from which values are interpreted and constructed rather than as a locus of an already determined set of values. (434)

Feminists have also raised a concern with the postmodern tendency to portray the body as so fragmented, mobile, and boundary-less that it invites a confusion over how the body is actually engendered and positioned within concrete configurations of power and forms of material oppression. The postmodern emphasis on the proliferation of ideas, discourses, and representations underplays both the different ways in which bodies are oppressed and how bodies are constructed differently through specific material relations. Feminists such as Sandra Lee Bartky (1988) have provided a postmodern reading of the politics of the body by extending Foucault's (1979, 1980) notion of how the growth of the modern state has been accompanied by an unprecedented attempt at disciplining the body. Where Bartky differs from Foucault is that she employs a discriminating notion of difference by showing how gender is implicated in the production of the body as a site of domination, struggle, and resistance. For example, Bartky points to the disciplinary measures of dieting, the tyranny of slenderness and fashion, the discourse of exercise, and other technologies of control. Bartky also goes beyond Foucault in arguing that the body must be seen as a site of resistance and linked to a broader theory of agency.

Postmodern feminism provides a grounded politics that employs the most progressive aspects of modernism and postmodernism. In the most general sense, it reaffirms the importance of difference as part of a broader political struggle for the reconstruction of public life. It rejects all forms of essentialism but recognizes the importance of certain formative narratives. Similarly, it provides a language of power that engages the issue of inequality and struggle. In recognizing the importance of institutional structures and language in the construction of subjectivities and political life, it promotes social criticism that acknowledges the interrelationship between human agents and social structures, rather than succumbing to a social theory without agents or one in which agents are simply the product of broad structural and ideological forces. Finally, postmodern feminism provides a radical social theory imbued with a language of critique and possibility. Implicit in its various discourses are new relations of parenting, work, schooling, play, citizenship, and joy. These are relations which link a politics of intimacy and solidarity, the concrete and the general; it is a politics which in its various forms is taken up by each of the essays in this book. All these essays provide, in different ways, a sense of the tension between the construction of new paradigms, and the creation of a pedagogy that makes concrete how they might be taken up by teachers and educators so as to create a postmodern pedagogical practice. In ending I want to briefly outline what some of the principles are that inform such a practice.

TOWARDS A POSTMODERN PEDAGOGY

As long as people are people, democracy in the full sense of the word will always be no more than an ideal. One may approach it as one would a horizon, in ways that may be better or worse, but it can never be fully attained. In this sense, you too, are merely approaching democracy. You have thousands of problems of all kinds, as other countries do. But you have one great advantage: You have been approaching democracy uninterruptedly for more than 200 years. (Vaclav Havel, cited in Oreskes 1990, 16)

How on earth can these prestigious persons in Washington ramble on in their sub-intellectual way about the "end of history"? As I look forward into the twenty-first century I sometimes agonize about the times in which my grandchildren and their children will live. It is not so much the rise in population as the rise in universal material expectations of the globe's huge population that will be straining its resources to the very limits. North-South antagonisms will certainly sharpen, and religious and national fundamentalisms will become more intransigent. The struggle to bring consumer greed within moderate control, to find a level of low growth and satisfaction that is not at the expense of the disadvantaged and poor, to defend the environment and to prevent ecological disasters, to share more equitably the world's resources and to insure their renewal—all this is agenda enough for continuation of "history." (Thompson 1990, 120)

A striking character of the totalitarian system is its peculiar coupling of human demoralization and mass depoliticizing. Consequently, battling this system requires a conscious appeal to morality and an inevitable involvement in politics. (Michnik 1990, 44)

All these quotes stress, implicitly or explicitly, the importance of politics and ethics to democracy. In the first quote, the newly elected president of Czechoslovakia, Vaclav Havel, addressing a joint session of Congress reminds the American people that democracy is an ideal that is filled with possibilities but always has to be seen as part of an ongoing struggle for freedom and human dignity. As a playwright and former political prisoner, Havel is a living embodiment of such a struggle. In the second quote, E. P. Thompson, the English peace activist and historian, reminds the American public that history has not ended but needs to be opened up in order to engage the many problems and possibilities that human beings will have to face in the twenty-first century. In the third quote, Adam Michnik, a founder of Poland's Workers' Defense Committee and an elected member of the Polish parliament, provides an ominous insight into one of the central features of totalitarianism, whether on the Right or the Left. He points to a society that fears democratic politics while simultaneously reproducing in people a sense of massive collective despair. None of these writers are from the United States and all of them are caught up in the struggle to recapture the Enlightenment model of freedom, agency, and democracy while simultaneously attempting to deal with the conditions of a postmodern world.

All of these statements serve to highlight the inability of the American public to grasp the full significance of the democratization of Eastern Europe in terms of what it reveals about the nature of our own democracy. In Eastern Europe and elsewhere there is a strong call for the primacy of the political and the ethical as a foundation for democratic public life whereas in the United States there is an ongoing refusal of the discourse of politics and ethics. Elected politicians from both sides of the established parties in the Congress complain that American politics is about "trivialization, atomization, and paralysis." Politicians as diverse as Lee Atwater, the Republican Party chairman, and Walter Mondale, former Vice President, agree that we have entered into a time in which much of the American public believes that "Bull permeates everything...[and that] we've got a kind of politics of irrelevance" (Oreskes, *The New York Times*, March 18, 1990, 16). At the same time, a number of polls indicate that while the youth of Poland, Czechoslovakia, and East Germany are extending the frontiers of democracy, American youth are both unconcerned and largely ill-prepared to struggle for and keep democracy alive in the twenty-first century.

Rather than being a model of democracy, the United States has become indifferent to the need to struggle for the conditions that make democracy a substantive rather than lifeless activity. At all levels of national and daily life, the breadth and depth of democratic relations are being rolled back. We have become a society that appears to demand less rather than more of democracy. In some quarters, democracy has actually become subversive. What does this suggest for developing some guiding principles in order to rethink the purpose and meaning of education and critical pedagogy within the present crises? Since I outline the particulars of a postmodern critical pedagogy in the last chapter of this book, I want to conclude with some suggestive principles for a critical pedagogy that emerge out of my discussion of the most important aspects of modernism, postmodernism, and postmodern feminism.

1. Education must be understood as producing not only knowledge but aslo political subjects. Rather than rejecting the language of politics, critical pedagogy must link public education to the imperatives of a critical democracy (Dewey 1916; Giroux 1988a). Critical pedagogy needs to be informed by a public philosophy dedicated to returning schools to their primary task: places of critical education in the service of creating a public sphere of citizens who are able to exercise power of their own lives and especially over the conditions of knowledge production and acquisition. This is a critical pedagogy defined, in part, by the attempt to create the lived experience of empowerment for the vast majority. In other words, the language of critical pedagogy needs to construct schools as democratic public spheres. In part, this means educators need to develop a critical pedagogy in which the knowledge, habits, and skills of critical rather than simply good citizenship are taught and practiced. This means providing students with the opportunity to develop the critical capacity to challenge and transform existing social and political forms, rather than simply adapt to them. It also means providing students with the skills they will need to locate themselves in history, find their own voices, and provide the convictions and compassion necessary for exercising civic courage, taking risks, and furthering the habits, customs, and social relations that are essential to democratic public forms. In effect, critical pedagogy needs to be grounded in a keen sense of the importance of constructing a political vision from which to develop an educational project as part of a wider discourse for revitalizing democratic public life. A critical pedagogy for democracy cannot be reduced, as some educators, politicians, and groups have argued, to forcing students to say the Pledge of Allegiance at the beginning of every school day or to speak and think only in the language of dominant English (Hirsch Jr. 1987). A critical pedagogy for democracy does not begin with test scores but with the questions: What kinds of citizens do we hope to produce

through public education in a postmodern culture? What kind of society do we want to create in the context of the present shifting cultural and ethnic borders? How can we reconcile the notions of difference and equality with the imperatives of freedom and justice?

2. Ethics must be seen as a central concern of critical pedagogy. This suggests that educators attempt to understand more fully how different discourses offer students diverse ethical referents for structuring their relationship to the wider society. But it also suggests that educators go beyond the postmodern notion of understanding how student experiences are shaped within different ethical discourses. Educators must also come to view ethics and politics as a relationship between the self and the other. Ethics, in this case, is not a matter of individual choice or relativism but a social discourse grounded in struggles that refuse to accept needless human suffering and exploitation. Thus, ethics is taken up as a struggle against inequality and as a discourse for expanding basic human rights. This points to a notion of ethics attentive to both the issue of abstract rights and those contexts which produce particular stories, struggles, and histories. In pedagogical terms, an ethical discourse needs to be taken up with regards to the relations of power, subject positions, and social practices it activates (Simon, forthcoming). This is neither an ethics of essentialism nor relativism. It is an ethical discourse grounded in historical struggles and attentive to the construction of social relations free of injustice. The quality of ethical discourse, in this case, is not simply grounded in difference but in the issue of how justice arises out of concrete historical circumstances (Shapiro 1990).

3. As Sharon Welch indicates in her chapter in this book, critical pedagogy needs to focus on the issue of difference in an ethically challenging and politically transformative way. There are at least two notions of difference at work here. First, difference can be incorporated into a critical pedagogy as part of an attempt to understand how student identities and subjectivities are constructed in multiple and contradictory ways. In this case, identity is explored through its own historicity and complex subject positions. The category of student experience should not be limited pedagogically to students exercising self reflection but opened up as a race, gender, and class specific construct to include the diverse ways in which their experiences and identities have been constituted in different historical and social formations. Second, critical pedagogy can focus on how differences between groups develop

and are sustained around both enabling and disabling sets of relations. In this instance, difference becomes a marker for understanding how social groups are constituted in ways that are integral to the functioning of any democratic society. Difference in this context does not focus only on charting spatial, racial, ethnic, or cultural differences but aslo analyzes historical differences that manifest themselves in public struggles.

As part of a language of critique, teachers can make problematic how different subjectivities are positioned within a historically specific range of ideologies and social practices that inscribe students in modes of behavior that subjugate, infantilize, and corrupt. Similarly, such a language can analyze how differences within and between social groups are constructed and sustained both within and outside the schools in webs of domination, subordination, hierarchy, and exploitation. As part of a language of possibility, teachers can explore the opportunity to construct knowledge/power relations in which multiple narratives and social practices are constructed around a politics and pedagogy of difference that offers students the opportunity to read the world differently, resist the abuse of power and privilege, and construct alternative democratic communities. Difference in this case cannot be seen as simply a politics of assertion, of simply affirming one's voice or sense of the common good, it must be developed within practices in which differences can be affirmed and transformed in their articulation with categories central to public life: democracy, citizenship, public spheres. In both political and pedagogical terms, the category of difference must be central to the notion of democratic community.

4. Critical pedagogy needs a language that allows for competing solidarities and political vocabularies that do not reduce the issues of power, justice, struggle, and inequality to a single script, a master narrative that suppresses the contingent, historical, and the everyday as a serious object of study (Cherryholmes 1988). This suggests that curriculum knowledge not be treated as a sacred text but developed as part of an ongoing engagement with a variety of narratives and traditions that can be re-read and re-formulated in politically different terms. At issue here is constructing a discourse of textual authority that is power-sensitive and developed as part of a wider analysis of the struggle over culture fought out at the levels of curricula knowledge, pedagogy, and the exercise of institutional power (Aronowitz and Giroux 1990). This is not merely an argument against a canon, but one that disavows

the very category. Knowledge has to be constantly re-examined in terms of its limits and rejected as a body of information that only has to be passed down to students. As Ernesto Laclau (1988a) has pointed out, setting limits to the answers given by what can be judged as a valued tradition (a matter of argument also) is an important political act. What Laclau is suggesting is the possibility for students to creatively appropriate the past as part of a living dialogue, an affirmation of the multiplicity of narratives, and the need to judge them not as timeless or as monolithic discourses, but as social and historical inventions that can be refigured in the interests of creating more democratic forms of public life. This points to the possibility for creating pedagogical practices characterized by the open exchange of ideas, the proliferation of dialogue, and the material conditions for the expression of individual and social freedom.

5. Critical pedagogy needs to create new forms of knowledge through its emphasis on breaking down disciplinary boundaries and creating new spaces where knowledge can be produced. In this sense, critical pedagogy must be reclaimed as a cultural politics and a form of counter-memory. This is not merely an epistemological issue, but one of power, ethics, and politics. Critical pedagogy as a cultural politics points to the necessity of inserting the struggle over the production and creation of knowledge as part of a broader attempt to create a public sphere of citizens who are able to exercise power over their lives and the social and political forms through which society is governed. As a form of counter-memory, critical pedagogy starts with everyday and the particular as a basis for learning, it reclaims the historical and the popular as part of an ongoing effort to legitimate the voices of those who have been silenced, and to inform the voices of those who have been located within narratives that are monolithic and totalizing. At stake here is a pedagogy that provides the knowledge, skills, and habits for students and others to read history in ways that enable them to reclaim their identities in the interests of constructing forms of life that are more democratic and more just. This is a struggle that deepens the pedagogical meaning of the political and the political meaning of the pedagogical. In the first instance, it raises important questions about how students and others are constructed as agents within particular histories, cultures, and social relations. Against the monolith of culture, it posits the conflicting terrain of cultures shaped within asymmetrical relations of power, grounded in diverse historical struggles. Similarly, culture has to be under-

stood as part of the discourse of power and inequality. As a pedagogical issue, the relationship between culture and power is evident in questions such as "Whose cultures are appropriated as our own? How is marginality normalized?" (Popkewitz 1988, 77). To insert the primacy of culture as a pedagogical and political issue is to make central how schools function in the shaping of particular identities, values, and histories by producing and legitimating specific cultural narratives and resources. In the second instance, asserting the pedagogical aspects of the political raises the issue of how difference and culture can be take up as pedagogical practices and not merely as political categories. For example, how does difference matter as a pedagogical category if educators and cultural workers have to make knowledge meaningful before it can become critical and transformative? Or what does it mean to engage the tension between being theoretically correct and pedagogically wrong? These are concerns and tensions that make the relationship between the political and the pedagogical both mutually informing and problematic.

6. The Enlightenment notion of reason needs to be reformulated within a critical pedagogy. First, educators need to be skeptical regarding any notion of reason the purports to reveal the truth by denying its own historical construction and ideological principles. Reason is not innocent and any viable notion of critical pedagogy cannot exercise forms of authority that emulate totalizing forms of reason that appear to be beyond criticism and dialogue. This suggests that we reject claims to objectivity in favor of partial epistemologies that recognize the historical and socially constructed nature of their own knowledge claims and methodologies. In this way, curriculum can be viewed as a cultural script that introduces students to particular forms of reason which structure specific stories and ways of life. Reason in this sense implicates and is implicated in the intersection of power, knowledge, and politics. Second, it is not enough to reject an essentialist or universalist defense of reason. Instead, the limits of reason must be extended to recognizing other ways in which people learn or take up particular subject positions. In this case, educators need to understand more fully how people learn through concrete social relations, through the ways in which the body is positioned (Grumet 1988), through the construction of habit and intuition, and through the production and investment of desire and affect, issues that are taken up in Peter Mclaren's contribution to this volume.

7. Critical pedagogy needs to regain a sense of alternatives by combining a language of critique and possibility. Postmodern feminism exemplifies this in both its critique of patriarchy and its search to construct new forms of identity and social relations. It is worth noting that teachers can take up this issue around a number of considerations. First, educators need to construct a language of critique that combines the issue of limits with the discourse of freedom and social responsibility. In other words, the question of freedom needs to be engaged dialectically not only as one of individual rights but also as part of the discourse of social responsibility. That is, whereas freedom remains an essential category in establishing the conditions for ethical and political rights, it must also be seen as a force to be checked if it is expressed in modes of individual and collective behavior that threatens the ecosystem or produces forms of violence and oppression against individuals and social groups. Second, critical pedagogy needs to explore in programmatic terms a language of possibility that is capable of thinking risky thoughts, that engages a project of hope, and points to the horizon of the "not yet." A language of possibility does not have to dissolve into a reified form of utopianism; instead, it can be developed as a precondition for nourishing convictions that summon up the courage to imagine a different and more just world and to struggle for it. A language of moral and political possibility is more than an outmoded vestige of humanist discourse. It is central to responding not only with compassion to human beings who suffer and agonize but also with a politics and a set of pedagogical practices that can refigure and change existing narratives of domination into images and concrete instances of a future which is worth fighting for.

There is a certain cynicism that characterizes the language of the Left at the present moment. Central to this position is the refusal of all utopian images, all appeals to "a language of possibility." Such refusals are often made on the grounds that "utopian discourse" is a strategy employed by the Right and therefore is ideologically tainted. Or, the very notion of possibility is dismissed as an impractical and therefore useless category. In my mind, this represents less a serious critique than a refusal to move beyond the language of exhaustion and despair. Essential to developing a response to this position is a discriminating notion of possibility, one which makes a distinction between a discourse characterized as either "dystopian" or utopian. In the former, the appeal to the future is grounded in a form of nostalgic romanticism, with its call for a return to a past, which more often than not serves to legitimate relations of domination and oppression. Similarly, in Constance Penley's terms a "dystopian" discourse often "limits itself to solutions that are either individualist or bound to a romanticized notion of guerrilla-like small-group resistance. The true atrophy of the utopian imagination is this: we can imagine the future but we *cannot* conceive the kind of collective political strategies necessary to change or ensure that future" (Penley 1989, 122). In contrast to the language of dystopia, a utopian discourse rejects apocalyptic emptiness and nostalgic imperialism and sees history as open and society worth struggling for in the image of an alternative future. This is the language of the "not yet", one in which the imagination is redeemed and nourished in the effort to construct new relationships fashioned out of strategies of collective resistance based on a critical recognition of both what society is and what it might become. Paraphrasing Walter Benjamin, this is a discourse of imagination and hope that pushes history against the grain. Nancy Fraser (1989) illuminates this sentiment by emphasizing the importance of a language of possibility for the project of social change: "It allows for the possibility of a radical democratic politics in which immanent critique and transfigurative desire mingle with one another "(107).

8. Critical pedagogy needs to develop a theory of teachers as transformative intellectuals who occupy specifiable political and social locations. Rather than defining teacher work through the narrow language of professionalism, a critical pedagogy needs to ascertain more carefully what the role of teachers might be as cultural workers engaged in the production of ideologies and social practices. This is not a call for teachers to become wedded to some abstract ideal that removes them from everyday life, or one that intends for them to become prophets of perfection and certainty; on the contrary, it is a call for teachers to undertake social criticism not as outsiders but as public intellectuals who address the most social and political issues of their neighborhood, nation, and the wider global world. As public and transformative intellectuals, teachers have an opportunity to make organic connections with the historical traditions that provide them and their students with a voice, history, and sense of belonging. It is a position marked by a moral courage and criticism that does not require educators to step back from society in the manner of the "objective" teacher, but to distance themselves from those power relations that subjugate, oppress, and diminish other human beings. Teachers need to

take up criticism from within, to develop pedagogical practices that not only heighten the possibilities for critical consciousness but aslo for transformative action (Walzer 1987). In this perspective, teachers would be involved in the invention of critical discourses and democratic social relations. Critical pedagogy would represent itself as the active construction rather than transmission of particular ways of life. More specifically, as transformative intellectuals, teachers can engage in the invention of languages so as to provide spaces for themselves and their students to rethink their experiences in terms that both name relations of oppression and offer ways in which to overcome them.

9. Central to the notion of critical pedagogy is a politics of voice that combines a postmodern notion of difference with a feminist emphasis on the primacy of the political. This suggest taking up the relationship between the personal and the political in a way that does not collapse the political into the personal but strengthens the relationship between the two so as to engage rather than withdraw from addressing those institutional forms and structures that contribute to racism, sexism, and class exploitation. This suggest some important pedagogical interventions. First the self must be seen as a primary site of politicization. That is, the issue of how the self is constructed in multiple and complex ways must be analyzed both as part of a language of affirmation and a broader understanding of how identities are inscribed in and between various social, cultural, and historical formations. To engage issues regarding the construction of the self is to address questions of history, culture, community, language, gender, race, and class. It is to raise questions regarding what pedagogical practices need to be employed that allow students to speak in dialogical contexts that affirm, interrogate, and extend their understandings of themselves and the global contexts in which they live. Such a position recognizes that students have several or multiple identities, but also asserts the importance of offering students a language that allows them to reconstruct their moral and political energies in the service of creating a more just and equitable social order, one that undermines relations of hierarchy and domination. Second, a politics of voice must offer pedagogical and political strategies that affirm the primacy of the social, intersubjective, and collective. To focus on voice is not meant to simply affirm the stories that students tell, it is not meant to simply glorify the possibility for narration. Such a position often degenerates into a form of narcissism, a carthartic experience that is reduced to naming anger without

the benefit of theorizing in order to both understand its underlying causes and what it means to work collectively transform the structures of domination responsible for oppressive social relations. Raising one's consciousness has increasingly become a pretext for legitimating hegemonic forms of separatism butressed by self-serving appeals to the primacy of experience. What is often expressed in such appeals is an anti-intellectualism that retreats from any viable form of political engagement, especially one willing to address and transform diverse forms of oppression. The call to simply affirm one's voice has increasingly been reduced to a pedagogical process that is as reactionary as it is inward looking. A more radical notion of voice should begin with what Bell Hooks (1989) calls a critical attention to theorizing experience as part of a broader politics of engagement. In referring specifically to feminist pedagogy, she argues that the discourse of confession and memory can be used to "shift the focus away from mere naming of one's experience....to talk about identity in relation to culture, history, politics" (110). For Hooks, the telling of tales of victimization, or the expression of one's voice is not enough; it is equally imperative that such experiences be the object of theoretical and critical analyses so that they can be connected rather than severed from a broader notions of solidarity, struggle, and politics.

CONCLUSION

This essay attempts to introduce readers to some of the central assumptions that govern the discourses of modernism, postmodernism, and postmodern feminism. But in doing so, it rejects pitting these movements against each other and tries instead to see how they converge as part of a broader political project linked to the reconstruction of democratic public life. Similarly, I have attempted here to situate the issue of pedagogical practice within a wider discourse of political engagement. Pedagogy, in this case, is not defined as simply something that goes on in schools. On the contrary, it is posited as central to any political practice that takes up question of how individuals learn, how knowledge is produced, and how subject positions are constructed. In this context, pedagogical practice refers to forms of cultural production that are inextricably historical and political. Pedagogy is, in part, a technology of power, language, and practice that produces and legitimates forms of moral and political regulation which construct and offer human beings particular views of themselves and the world. Such views are never innocent and are always implicated in the discourse and relations of ethics and power. To invoke the importance of pedagogy is to raise questions not simply about how students learn but also how educators (in the broad sense of the term) construct the ideological and political positions from which they speak. At issue here is a discourse that both situates human beings within history and makes visible the limits of their ideologies and values. Such a position acknowledges the partiality of all discourses so that the relationship between knowledge and power will always be open to dialogue and critical self-engagement. Pedagogy is about the intellectual, emotional, and ethical investments we make as part of our attempt to negotiate, accommodate, and transform the world in which we find ourselves. The purpose and vision which drives such a pedagogy must be based on a politics and view of authority which links teaching and learning to forms of self and social empowerment, that argues for forms of community life which extend the principles of liberty, equality, justice, and freedom to the widest possible set of institutional and lived relations.

Pedagogy as defined within the traditions of modernsim, postmodernism, and postmodern feminism offers educators an opportunity to develop a political project that embraces human interests that move beyond the particularistic politics of class, ethnicity, race, and gender. This is not a call to dismiss the postmodern emphasis on difference as much as it is an attempt to develop a radical democratic politics that stresses difference within unity. This means developing a public language that can transform a politics of assertion into one of democratic struggle. Central to such a politics and pedagogy is a notion of community developed around a shared conception of social justice, rights, and entitlement. This is especially necessary at a time in our history in which the value of such concerns have been subordinated to the priorities of the market and used to legitimate the interests of the rich at the expense of the poor, the unemployed, and the homeless. A radical pedagogy and transformative democratic politics must go hand in hand in constructing a vision in which liberalism's emphasis on individual freedom, postmodernism's concern with the particularistic, and feminism's concern with the politics of the everyday are coupled with democratic socialism's historic concern with solidarity and public life.

We live at at time in which the responsibilities of citizens exceed national borders. The old modernist notions of center and margin, home and exile, and familiar and strange are breaking apart. Geographic, cultural, and ethnic borders are giving way to shifting configurations of power, community, space and time. Citizenship can no longer ground itself in forms of Eurocentricism, patriarchy, and the language of colonialism. New spaces, relationships, identities, and social movements have to be created which allow teachers, students and others to move across borders, to engage difference and Otherness as part of a discourse of justice, social engagement and democratic struggle. Academics can no longer retreat into their careers, classrooms, or symposiums as if they were the only public spheres available for engaging the power of ideas and the relations of power. Foucault's (1977b) notion of the specific intellectual taking up struggles connected to particular issues and contexts must be combined with Gramsci's (1971) notion of the engaged intellectual who connects his or her work to broader social concerns that deeply affect how people live, work, and survive. But there is more at stake here than defining the role of the intellectual, or the relationship of teaching to democratic struggle. The struggle against racism, class structures, and sexism needs to move away from simply a language of critique, and redefine itself as part of a language of transformation and hope. This suggests that educators combine with others engaged in public struggles in order to invent languages and provide spaces both in and out of schools that offer new opportunities for social movements to come together in order to rethink and re-experience democracy as a struggle over values, practices, social relations, and subject positions which enlarge the terrain of human capacities and possibilities as a basis for a compassionate social order. At issue here is the need to create a politics which contributes to the multiplication of sites of democratic struggles, sites which affirm specific struggles while recognizing the necessity to embrace broader issues that enhance the life of the planet while extending the spirit of democracy to all societies (Mouffe, 1988, Bookchin, 1990).

All the essays in this book attempt to offer educators a language that allows them to create new ways of conceiving pedagogy and its relationship to social, cultural, and intellectual life. In various ways, this book challenges some of the major categories and practices that have dominated educational theory and practice in the United States and in other countries for the last two decades. Rejecting the apolitical nature of some postmodern discourses and the separatism characteristic of some versions of feminism, all these essays take a political stand rooted in a concern with politics of difference rooted in a radical democratic project. What these essays share is a refusal of the old political categories that hermetically labeled educational theories under the rubric of various master narratives. None of the theorists in this book attempt to legitimate themselves by appealing to the "religious" discourse of a specific ideological doctrine or grand narrative, whether it be a particular form of Marxism, feminism, or any other "ism". Instead all of these essays ground their politics in self-reflective attempts to deepen the possibilities for democratic struggle and social justice. This approach will not sit well with the new separatists who have given up a sense of humility and solidarity for a rabid politics of assertion and essentialism. What these essays do attempt to do is reveal the complexity and variance of human domination and the need for postmodern politics that ties education to the broader struggle for establishing public spaces that address the possibilities for overcoming through dialogue and collective struggle diverse forms of injustice and human suffering. At the same time, these essays represent a linguistic shift regarding how we think about foundationalism, difference, culture, and ethics. As a whole, these essays reflect in diverse ways a concern with developing a language that is critical of master narratives and technologies of power which reproduce forms of gender, racist, and class oppression both in and out of the schools.

All these essays share an attempt to develop a discourse which analyzes how power can be linked productively to knowledge; how knowledge and power might come together in the interests of creating public spheres informed by the principles of justice, freedom, and equality (Dewey 1916). In various ways, the essays in this book develop a language that both implicitly and explicitly raises questions as to how educators might contribute to an identity politics that is situated in democratic relations, and how analyses can be developed that enable students, teachers, and others to become self-reflective actors in the attempt to transform themselves and the conditions of their social existence. More specifically, this book demonstrates how postmodern and feminist theories can contribute to a critical pedagogy of race and ethnicity, how the body is schooled and engendered, how a politics of representation can be used to deconstruct specific subject positions, and how difference is central to a politics and pedagogy of ethics and solidarity. In short, this book provides both an introduction to the various aspects of modernism, postmodernism, and feminism while also offering its readers new ways of understanding how experience is constructed pedagogically and how to rethink the horizons and limits of educational theory and practice as a form of cultural politics.

DOUGLAS KELLNER

Chapter One

Reading Images Critically:
Toward a Postmodern Pedagogy

Modernity is interpreted as both the best and worst of things. It has been characterized in terms of progressive advances over premodern, or traditional, societies, and as a motor of innovation, creativity, change, and progress. Modernity has been identified with individuality, enlightenment, science and technology, the industrial and political revolutions, and thus with democracy and freedom (Berman 1982; Kolb 1986; Habermas 1987; Cahoone 1988). More negative postmodern critiques, however, associate modernity with repression, homogeneity, and a totalitarian domination which has epistemological, sexual, political, and cultural dimensions. Postmodern theorists, such as Jean Baudrillard, Jean-Francois Lyotard, Arthur Kroker, and David Cook, claim that we have left modernity behind for a new postmodern condition or scene. An extreme version of postmodern theory (Baudrillard; Kroker/Cook) claims that postmodernity constitutes a fundamental break or rupture in history which forms an entirely new

society, while Lyotard, Foucault, and others simply recommend
new ways of knowing, doing, and being which Lotard characterizes
as postmodern knowledge, or a "postmodern condition."[1] These
theorists recommend postmodern positions over modern ones and
thus positively valorize the discourse of the postmodern, while it
is presented in more negative terms and images in the pessimistic
writings of Baudrillard and some of his followers.

Fredric Jameson (1984), by contrast, represents postmodernism as both progressive and regressive, both positive and negative. With this and some other exceptions, most responses to the
postmodern debate have been one-sided with some enthusiasts
jumping on the bandwagon to trumpet the latest advances in
Theory, Culture, and Society, while others aggressively assault the
postmodern attacks on the modern (Habermas 1987), deny that
anything like a postmodern condition even exists (Britton 1988), or
they react with ambivalence and perhaps confusion. Some of my
own studies (Kellner 1987, 1988, 1989a, 1989b) have taken a primarily critical posture toward what I considered to be the pretensions and inflated bombast of much postmodern theory, while
exhibiting, no doubt, some degree of ambivalence. In this essay,
however, I will assume a different posture by stressing some of the
positive openings in postmodern thought and those postmodern
positions that might be productive for critical pedagogy. Yet I will
continue to deflate certain pretensions and criticize certain
excesses and dubious and reactionary aspects of so-called postmodern thought. I should stress in advance that I do not believe that
any coherent and shared postmodern theory exists, nor that we are
in something like a completely new postmodern condition or
scene. Rather, we should be aware of the diversity of postmodern
theory and positions and read postmodern theory as pointing to
new trends and social conditions that require a loosening up and
development of our old theories and that might be productive for
new theoretical syntheses. The latter will be the aim of this study,
which will sketch outlines of a critical pedagogy that makes use of
both modern and postmodern theory and positions.

POSTMODERN POSITIONS: SOME THEORETICAL
ADVANCES AND OPENINGS

One such postmodern position that I find salient to pedagogical concerns is the breakdown of the boundaries between "high" and "low" culture which Jameson (1983 and 1984) and others claim is at the very heart of the postmodern. Jameson argues that one of the defining features of postmodernism

> is the effacement in it of some key boundaries or separations, most notably the erosion of the older distinction between high culture and so-called mass or popular culture. This is perhaps the most distressing development of all from an academic standpoint, which has traditionally had a vested interest in preserving a realm of high or elite culture against the surrounding environment of philistinism, of schlock and kitsch, of TV series and *Reader's Digest* culture, and in transmitting difficult and complex skills of reading, listening and seeing to its initiates (Jameson, 1983: 112; compare Jameson, 1984: 54f.).

Other postmodern positions—associated with Jacques Derrida, Foucault, Gilles Deleuze and Felix Guattari, etc.—extend notions of reading, writing, and textuality to a variety of cultural texts, ranging from philosophical treatises to harlequin novels and films. Through critiques of the boundaries between high and low culture and the emphasis on extension of notions of textuality, writing, etc., Ulmer (1985) and others have developed a postmodern populism. They attack the elitism inscribed in the conservative model of education which canonizes great books, complex literary skills, and the artifacts of high culture. Although traditional high culture provides unique pleasures and enticements, its enshrinement and canonization also serves as an instrument of exclusion, marginization, and domination by oppressive sex, race, and class forces. Furthermore it operates with a highly limited concept of culture and excludes from the domain of serious cultural artifacts precisely those phenomena which most immediately engage most individuals in our society. Consequently one of the merits of certain postmodern positions is expanding the concept of culture while breaking down barriers between "high" and "low" culture, thus opening a vast terrain of cultural artifacts to scrutiny and critical discussion.

These positions are important, I believe, in developing a new critical pedagogy which attempts to expand literacy. Modern pedagogy is organized around books and gaining literacy in reading and writing, centering its notion of education and literacy on the acquisition of skills that are especially applicable to print culture.

Conservative educators bewail decline in this sort of print literacy and prescribe traditional educational curricula and methods as the solution, calling for a return to the great books, the established canons, and traditional methods for teaching literacy (see the discussion in Aronowtiz/Giroux 1985 and Giroux 1988). Other more liberal commentators (Hirsch 1987) prescribe a broader notion of cultural literacy; they urge teaching a wide spectrum of cultural knowledge and skills, applied to texts ranging from the great books to classified ads in order to make its recipient a more adequate knower and doer in the contemporary society. Although this liberal program has its merits in contrast to the conservative model, it also has its limitations. Giroux (1988), by contrast, argues for a notion of critical literacy connected to a discourse of emancipation, possibility, hope, and struggle.

Building on this program, I will make some proposals that concern developing *critical media literacy* and the development of competencies in reading images critically, concentrating on some examples from print advertisements. These examples pose in a provocative way the need to expand literacy and cognitive competencies in order to survive the onslaught of media images, messages, and spectacles which are inundating our culture. The goal will be to teach a critical media literacy which will empower individuals to become more autonomous agents, able to emancipate themselves from contemporary forms of domination and able to become more active citizens, eager and competent to engage in processes of social transformation.

READING IMAGES CRITICALLY

One insight central to postmodern theory is the emphasis on the increasingly central role of image in contemporary society. Baudrillard (1981, 185f.) describes the transition from a metallurgic society, defined as a society of production, to a semiurgic order characterized by the proliferation of signs, simulacra, and images. For Baudrillard, postmodern society is one defined by radical semiurgy, by the proliferation and dissemination of images and the entry into a new culture saturated with images. Indeed, from the moment we wake up to clock radios and/or turn on the television for the morning news to our last moments of consciousness at night with Johnny Carson, Bruce Springsteen, or Sylvester Stallone we find ourselves immersed in an ocean of images, in culture saturated with a flora and flauna of diverse species of images which contemporary cultural theory has only begun to sort out.

Building on this postmodern position without presenting it as such, Neil Postman (1985) argues that around the turn of the century, Western society left print—typographical—culture behind and entered a new "Age of Entertainment" centered on a culture of the image. Accompanying the new image culture, Postman argues, is a dramatic decline in literacy, a loss of the skills associated with rational argumentation, linear and analytical thought, and critical and public discourse. In particular, this change in literacy and consciousness has led to degeneration of public discourse and a loss of rationality in public life.[2] Postman attributes this "great transformation" primarily to television which indeed can be interpreted as the most prolific image machine in history, generating between fifteen and thirty images per minute and thus millions of images per day.

Other image machines generate a panoply of print, sound, environmental, and diverse aesthetic artifacts within which we wander, trying to make our way through this forest of symbols. And so we need to begin learning how to read these images, these fascinating and seductive cultural forms whose massive impact on our lives we have only begun to understand. Surely education should attend to the new image culture and should teach a critical pedagogy of reading images as part of media literacy. Such an effort would be part of a new radical pedagogy that attempts to get at the roots of our experience, knowledge, and behavior and that aims at liberation from domination and the creation of new, plural, enhanced, and more potent selves—ideals characteristic of both modern and some postmodern theory.

Reading images critically involves learning how to appreciate, decode, and interpret images concerning both *how* they are constructed and operate in our lives and *what* they communicate in concrete situations. Certain postmodern theory (Foucault, Derrida, Deleuze/Guattari, and Lyotard) helps make us aware of how our experience and selves are socially constructed, how they are overdetermined by a diverse range of images, discourses, codes, and the like. This strand of postmodern theory excels in deconstructing the obvious, taking the familiar and making it strange and unfamiliar and thus in making us attend to how our language, experience, and behavior are socially constructed and are thus constrained, overdetermined, and conventional, subject to change and transformation. Following an anti-hermeneutical thrust of structuralism, however, one strand of postmodern thought (Deleuze/Guattari) is overly restrictive concerning what it wants critical theory to do. This approach limits theoretically correct inquiry to either descriptive analysis of how phenomena work, or formal analysis of how signification and representation function, eschewing heremeneutical interpretation of ideological content for a more formal and structuralist type of analysis.

Some postmodern theory indeed claims that in the contemporary society of simulacra, images are by nature flat, one-dimensional, and glitzy, referring only to themselves or to other images (a strong version of this thesis is found in Baudrillard 1983a while a weaker version is found in some of the essays in Gitlin 1987; see the critique in Best/Kellner 1987).[3] Such a formal postmodern image critique, then, would content itself with describing these images, much as Susan Sontag (1969) urged in her strictures "against interpretation"—which anticipated postmodern positions and the postmodern sensibility, the ironic, erotic, and playful. Such a formal and anti-hermeneutical temptation will be resisted here. It may make our critical activity easier and cleaner while yielding new insights and ways of seeing, yet it also is too restrictive and one-sided for certain pedagogical tasks, such as the one which I shall undertake here.

Indeed, I find Derrida's method of deconstruction (1976) more suggestive for the process of reading images critically. Just as Derrida finds texts to be saturated with metaphysical oppositions and positions, so too are the images and scenes of mass-mediated culture. In the following reading of some familiar advertisements, I shall show that their images contain precisely the sort of metaphysical oppositions that Derrida finds in texts and that the images serve to cover over or occlude the metaphysical oppositions which often turn out to be social contradictions. Advertising metaphysics are linked, as I shall try to demonstrate, to dominant ideologies, thus deconstructive critique of advertising and other artifacts of mass-mediated culture is also a critique of ideology.[4]

READING ADVERTISEMENTS CRITICALLY

As a test case for a critical pedagogy of images, I will take advertising, that prolific and potent source of cultural imagery. Elsewhere, I develop a general theory of advertising and fashion, and review new critical perspectives on advertising (Kellner 1989c and Harms/Kellner in press). Here I will focus on developing tools to decipher, interpret, and criticize those ubiquitous advertising images that saturate our culture. The phenomenon of advertising and importance of learning to read advertisements critically is far from trivial, as U.S. society invests over $102 billion a year into advertising, fully two percent of our gross national product, far more money than in education (Association of National Advertisers 1988, 4). This is a crime and a national scandal which alone should concern educators.

Postman argues that before the twentieth century advertising tended to be generally informative or at least used the media of print, rational argumentation, and verbal, rhetorical persuasion to induce consumers to buy the products offered (1985, 60). By the 1890s, however, advertisements began to make increased use of photographs and illustrations and their text degenerated into slogans, jingles, and simple rhymes, with image replacing discursive rationality. In a sense, advertising became a dominant public discourse of the twentieth century with its portrayals of commodities, consumption, lifestyles, values, and gender roles displacing other forms of public discourse. In this way, imagistic discourses of the private life, of commodity gratification eroded more discursive political discourses and constituted a radical displacement of the public sphere which postmodern theorists claim has been destroyed in the contemporary consumer and media society (compare Habermas 1989 with Baudrillard 1983b).

Furthermore, the significance of advertising for education is many-sided. Advertising constitutes one of the most advanced spheres of image production with more money, talent, and energy invested in this form of culture than practically any other in our hypercapitalist society. Advertising itself is a pedagogy which teaches individuals what they need and should desire, think, and do to be happy, successful, and genuinely American. Advertising teaches a worldview, values, and socially acceptable and unacceptable behavior. Advertising as Jules Henry (1963) argued contains a morality and a view of truth which stresses self-indulgence, instant gratification, hedonism, and relativism. Henry argued that advertising constitutes an entire philosophical system which incorporates the values of our most powerful social force, corporate capitalism, itself a major pillar of consumer capitalism.

Moreover, advertising is an important social text and social indicator which provides a repository of information concerning social trends, current fashions, contemporary values, and what really concerns the denizens of consumer capitalism. Much can therefore be learned from studying advertising. It may also be a major force in shaping thought and behavior. I shall bracket, however, the debate concerning whether advertising is or is not a powerfully efficacious force in directly shaping consumer behavior and simply assume that advertising exists as a major sector of the cultural industry whose products a critical pedagogy should engage. Far from being merely flat one-dimensional exemplars of a postmodern image culture, I shall argue that advertisements are multi-dimensional cultural texts with a wealth of meaning which require sophisticated decoding and interpretation. As an exercise in this direction, let us take up the task of learning to read and criticize some familiar cigarette ads and to discern what this critical process tells us about ourselves and our society.

Symbolic Images in Virginia Slims and Marlboro Ads

In order to provide an introduction to reading the symbolic images of ads critically, I shall examine some print ads which are readily available for scrutiny and which lend themselves to critical analysis. Print ads are an important section of the advertising world with about fifty percent of advertising revenues going to various print media, while twenty-two percent is expended on television advertising (Association of National Advertisers, 1988, 4). Although apologists for the advertising industry claim that advertising is predominantly informative, careful scrutiny of magazine, television, and other imagistic ads indicate that it is overwhelmingly persuasive and symbolic and that its images not only attempt to sell the product by associating it with certain socially desirable qualities, but they sell as well a worldview, a lifestyle, and value system congruent with the imperatives of consumer capitalism.

To illustrate this point, let us look, first, at two cigarette ads: a 1981 Marlboro ad aimed primarily at male smokers and a 1983 Virginia Slims ad which tries to convince women that it is cool to smoke and that the product being advertised is perfect for the "modern" woman (see figures 1 and 2).[5] Corporations like the tobacco industry undertake campaigns to associate their product with positive and desirable images and gender models. Thus in the 1950s, Marlboro undertook a campaign to associate its cigarette with masculinity, associating smoking its product with being a "real man." Marlboro had been previously packaged as a milder women's cigarette, and the "Marlboro Man" campaign was an attempt to capture the male cigarette market with images of archetypically masculine characters. Since the cowboy Western image provided a familiar icon of masculinity, independence, and ruggedness, it was the preferred symbol for the campaign. Subsequently, the Marlboro Man became a part of American folklore and a readily identifiable cultural symbol.

Such symbolic images in advertising attempt to create an association between the products offered and socially desirable and meaningful traits in order to produce the impression that if one wants to be a certain type of person, for instance, to be a "real man," then one should buy Marlboro cigarettes. Consequently, for decades Marlboro used the cowboy figure as the symbol of masculinity and the center of their ads. In a postmodern image culture, individuals get their very identity from these figures thus advertising becomes an important and overlooked mechanism of socialization as well as manager of consumer demand.

Ads form textual systems with basic components which are interrelated in ways that positively position the product. The main components of the classical Marlboro ad is its conjunction of nature, the cowboy, horses, and the cigarette. This system associates the Marlboro cigarette with masculinity, power, and nature. Note, however, in figure 1 how the cowboy is a relatively small figure, dwarfed by the images of snow, trees, and sky. Whereas in earlier Marlboro ads, the Marlboro Man loomed largely in the center of the frame, now images of nature are highlighted. Why this shift?

All ads are social texts which respond to key developments during the period in which they appear. During the 1980s, media reports concerning the health hazard of cigarettes became widespread—a message was highlighted in the mandatory box at the bottom of the ad that read "The Surgeon General Has Determined That Cigarette Smoking is Dangerous to Your Health." As a response to this attack, the Marlboro ads now feature images of clean, pure, wholesome nature, as if it were "natural" to smoke cigarettes, as if cigarettes were a healthy natural product, an emanation of benign and healthy nature. The ad, in fact, hawks Marlboro Lights and one of the captions describes it as a "low tar cigarette." The imagery is itself light, white, green, snowy, and airy. Through the process of metonomy, or contiguous association, the ad tries to associate the cigarettes with light, natural, healthy snow, horses, the cowboy, trees, and sky, as if they were all related natural artifacts, sharing the traits of nature, thus covering over the fact that cigarettes are an artificial, synthetic product, full of dangerous pesticides, preservatives, and other chemicals.[6]

FIGURE 1

Thus, the images of healthy nature are a Barthesian mythology (1972) which attempt to cover the image of the dangers to health from cigarette smoking and to naturalize cigarettes and smoking. The Marlboro ad also draws on images of tradition (the cowboy), hard work (note how deeply in the snow the horse is immersed; this cowboy is doing some serious work), caring for animals, and other desirable traits, as if smoking were a noble activity, metonomically equivalent to these other positive social activities. The images, texts, and product shown in the ad thus provide a symbolic construct which tries to cover and camouflage contradictions between the heavy work and the light cigarette, between the natural scene and the artificial product, between the cool and healthy outdoors scene and the hot and unhealthy activity of smoking, and the rugged masculinity of the Marlboro Man and the Light cigarette, originally targeted at women. In fact, this latter contradiction can be explained by the marketing ploy of suggesting to men that they can be both highly masculine, like the Marlboro Man, and smoke a supposedly healthier cigarette, while also appealing to macho women who might enjoy smoking a "man's" cigarette which is also lighter and healthier as women's cigarettes are supposed to be.

The 1983 Virginia Slims ad (figure 2) also attempts to associate its product with socially desired traits and offers subject positions with which women can identify. The Virginia Slims textual system classically includes a vignette at the top of the ad with a picture underneath of the Virginia Slims woman next to the prominently displayed package of cigarettes. In the example pictured, the top of the ad features a framed box that contains the narrative images and message, which is linked to the changes in the situation of women portrayed through a contrast with the modern woman below. The caption under the boxed image of segregated male and female exercise classes in 1903 contains the familiar Virginia Slims slogan "You've come a long way baby." The caption, linked to the Virginia Slims woman, next to the package of cigarettes, connotes a message of progress, metonomically linking Virginia Slims to the progressive woman and modern living. In this ad, it is the linkages and connections between the parts that establish the message which associates Virginia Slims with progress. The ad tells women that it is progressive and socially acceptable to smoke, and it associates Virginia Slims with modernity, social progress, and the desired social trait of slimness.

In fact, Lucky Strike carried out a successful advertising campaign in the 1930s which associated smoking with weight reduction ("Reach for a Lucky instead of a sweet!"), and Virginia Slims plays on this tradition, encapsulated in the very brand name of the product. Note too that the cigarette is a "Lights" variety and that,

FIGURE 2

like the Marlboro ad, it tries to associate its product with health and well-being. The pronounced smile on the woman's face also tries to associate the product with happiness and self-content-ment, struggling against the association of smoking with guilt and dangers to one's health. The image of the slender woman, in turn, associated with slimness and lightness, not only associates the product with socially desirable traits, but in turn promotes the ideal of slimness as the ideal type of femininity.

Later Capri cigarettes advertised its products as "the slimmest slim!" building on the continued and intensified associa-tion of slimness with femininity. A 1988 Capri ad pictures its happily smoking woman as more stylishly and modly attired than the more conventional and conservatively attired 1983 Virginia Slims woman, replicating the increased emphasis on expensive clothes and high fashion in the yuppie era where high consump-tion as a way of life has become a much advertised goal. A 1988 Virginia Slims ad (figure 3), in fact, reveals a considerable transfor-mation in its image of women during the 1980s and a new strategy to persuade women that it is all right and even progressive and ultramodern to smoke. This move points to shifts in the relative power between men and women and discloses new subject posi-tions for women validated by the culture industries.

Once again the sepia-colored framed box at the top of the ad contains an image of a woman serving her man in 1902; the comic pose and irritated look of the woman suggests that such servitude is highly undesirable and its contrast with the Virginia Slims woman (who herself now wears the leather boots and leather gloves and jacket as well) suggests that women have come a long way while the ever-present cigarette associates a woman's right to smoke in public with social progress. This time the familiar "You've come a long way, baby" is absent, perhaps because the woman pictured would hardly tolerate being described as baby and because indeed women's groups had been protesting the sexist and demeaning label in the slogan. Note, too, the transformation of the image of the woman in the Virginia Slims ad. No longer the smiling, cute, and wholesome potential wife of the earlier ad, she is now more threatening, more sexual, less wifely, and more mas-culine. The sunglasses connote the distance from the male gaze which she wants to preserve and the leather jacket with the mili-tary insignia connotes that she is equal to men, able to carry on a masculine role, and is stronger and more autonomous than women of the past.

VIRGINIA SLIMS

Virginia Slims remembers how the woman of 1902 pulled herself up by the bootstraps.

Fashions: Azrex, U.S.A.

© Philip Morris Inc. 1988

Lights: 8 mg "tar," 0.6 mg nicotine—100's: 14 mg "tar," 0.9 mg nicotine av. per cigarette, FTC Report Feb.'85. 120's: 14 mg "tar," 1.0 mg nicotine— Ultra Lights: 6 mg "tar," 0.5 mg nicotine av. per cigarette by FTC method.

SURGEON GENERAL'S WARNING: Quitting Smoking Now Greatly Reduces Serious Risks to Your Health.

FIGURE 3

The 1988 ad is highly anti-patriarchal and even expresses hostility toward men with the overweight man with glasses and handle bar mustache looking slightly ridiculous while it is clear that the woman is being held back by ridiculous fashion and intolerable social roles. The new Virginia Slims woman, however, who completely dominates the scene, is the epitome of style and power. This strong woman can easily take in hand and enjoy the phallus, i.e. the cigarette as the sign of male power accompanied by the male dress and military insignia, and serve as an icon of female glamour as well. This ad links power, glamour, and sexuality and offers a model of female power, associated with the cigarette and smoking. Ads work in part by generating dissatisfaction and by offering images of transformation, of a "new you." This particular ad promotes dissatisfaction with traditional images and presents a new image of a more powerful woman, a new lifestyle and identity for the Virginia Slims smoker.

Although "Lights" and "Ultra Lights" continue to be the dominant Virginia Slims types, the phrase does not appear as a highlighted caption as it used to appear and the package does not appear either. No doubt this "heavy" woman contradicts the light image and the ad seems to want to connote power and (a dubious) progress for women rather than slimness or lightness. Yet the woman's teased and flowing blonde hair, her perfect teeth which form an obliging smile, and, especially her crotch positioned in the ad in a highly suggestive and inviting fashion code her as a symbol of beauty and sexuality, albeit more autonomous and powerful. In these ways, the images associate the products advertised with certain socially desirable traits and convey messages concerning the symbolic benefits accrued to those who consume the product.

The point I am trying to make is that it is precisely the images which are the vehicles of the symbolic meanings and messages. Therefore, critical literacy in a postmodern image culture requires learning how to read images critically and to unpack the relations between images, texts, social trends, and products in commercial culture. My reading of these ads suggests that advertising is as concerned with selling lifestyles and selling socially desirable subject positions, which are associated with their products, as with selling the product themselves—or rather, that advertisers use the symbolic constructs with which the consumer is invited to identify to try to induce her to use their product. Thus the Marlboro Man, i.e. the consumer who smokes the cigarette, is smoking masculinity or natural vigor as much as a cigarette, while the Virginia Slims woman is exhibiting modernity, thinness, or female power when she lights up her slim.

Making these connections enables individuals to discern the hidden compulsions and enticements behind certain forms of consumer behavior. Enabling individuals to gain critical literacy in regard to advertising and other forms of popular culture provides emancipatory competencies which enable individuals to resist manipulation by consumer capitalism; beyond that, it also provides us with skills which enable us to read current trends in society and to note significant changes. For example, the two Virginia Slims ads suggest that at least a certain class of women (white, upper-middle and upper class) were gaining more power in society and that women were being attracted by stronger, more autonomous, and more masculine images.

A comparison of a 1988 Marlboro ad (figure 4) with its earlier ads also yields some interesting results. While the ads once centered on the Marlboro Man, and in the early 1980s continue to feature this figure, curiously, by the late 1980s, human beings disappeared altogether from some Marlboro ads which projected pure images of wholesome nature associated with the product. The caption "Made especially for menthol smokers," the green menthol insignia on the cigarette package, and the blue and green backdrops of the trees, grass, and water all attempt to incorporate icons of health and nature into the ads, as if these menthol "Lights" would protect the buyer from cigarette health hazards. In particular, the prominent use of water provides a purifying and refreshing paleosymbolic aura to the totality of the scene, attempting to wash away fears that smoking might indeed damage one's health.

Undoubtedly, this transformation in the Marlboro ads was a response to the growing concern about the health hazards of cigarettes which required even purer emphasis on nature. Indeed, the mandatory warnings on the ads are becoming larger and even more threatening with the Marlboro ad telling the customer that "Cigarette Smoke Contains Carbon Monoxide" and recent captions on woman's cigarette ads warning the "Smoking Causes Lung Cancer, Heart Disease, Emphysema, and May Complicate Pregnancy" and "Smoking by Pregnant Women May Result in Fetal Inquiry, Premature Birth, and Low Birth Weight." Against these dire warnings, recent Marlboro ads have therefore abandoned the human figure, the familiar Marlboro Man, featuring instead images of pure nature. The romantic uses of nature in these ads

FIGURE 4

codes nature as a site of innocence and tries to appropriate such images for the hardly innocent cigarette. This nostalgia for innocence is arguably a feature of a fallen postmodern culture and shows the magical ways that advertising attempt to produce another world, a transformed utopia. Such advertising seeks to blot out the dystopia of modern technological society with its dangerous products and health hazards and spoil-sport government regulatory apparatus which forces advertisers to warn consumers that their products may well kill them.

Yet the absence of the Marlboro cowboy might also point to the obsolescence of the manual worker in a new postmodern information and service society where significant sectors of the so-called new middle class work in the industries of symbol and image production and manipulation. The prominent images of the strong and energetic horses, however, point to a continued desire for power, for identification with figures of power. The actual powerlessness of workers in contemporary capitalist society make it in turn difficult to present concrete contemporary images of male power that would appeal to a variety of male (and female) smokers. Eliminating the male figure also allows appeal over a wider range of social classes and occupational types, including both men and women who could perhaps respond more positively to images of nature and power than to the rather obsolete cowboy figure. Further—and these images are clearly polysemic, subject to multiple readings—the new emphasis on "Great refreshment in the Flip-Top box" not only harmonizes with the refreshing images of green and nature, but points to the new hedonist, leisure culture in postmodern society with its emphasis on the pleasures of consumption, spectacle, and refreshment. The refreshment tag also provides a new legitimation for cigarette smoking as a refreshing activity (building on the famous Pepsi "pause that refreshes"?) which codes an obviously dangerous activity as refreshing and thus as health-promoting.

Other readings are, of course, possible. The absence of human figures in the recent Marlboro ads could be read as signs of the erasure of the human in postmodern society, giving credence to Foucault's claim that in a new episteme the human itself could be washed away like a face drawn on sand. Or, more mundanely, the absence of the Marlboro Man might be an effect of the death by cancer of one of the men who posed for the ad who, in fact, appeared before his death in videotapes warning individuals against the dangers of the product that he had once represented.

Thus, these ads are multi-dimensional, polysemic, and open to variety of readings. A Freudian reading of figures 1–3 might focus on the phallic images of the cigarette, with the white, phallus figure standing up firm and erect in figure 1 while in figure 2 the Virginia Slims woman firmly yet daintily holds the icon of phallic power. Note by contrast that in figure 3 she holds it more casually and ambiguously, glove on hand and dark sunglasses over her eyes, raising the question: what will these women do with the phallus!? A Freudian reading might note that although the phallic cigarette protrudes more hesitantly from the Marlboro package in figure 4, the horses can also be read as strong images of virility and phallic power. Yet the cigarette image can also be read in the ads as an example of humans dominating and controlling nature, or as an example of how humans can use a synthesis of nature and culture for their own pleasures.

Any number of readings of these multivalent texts are possible. Combining Marxist, feminist, structuralist, and other critical methods could show how the ads present certain images of women, work, class, and power which serve as vehicles for certain ideological messages. Such analysis could indicate how the ads and images attempt to resolve ideological contradictions as well as contradictions between nature and culture. More systematic semiological readings could show how these ads fit into the system of contemporary advertising and exhibit certain dominant codes, models, and rules. This sort of exercise thus helps show how gender and socially approved behavior are constructed and puts in question certain dominant models and types of behavior.

CRITICAL LITERACY, MEDIA, AND CONSUMER IMAGE CULTURE

In the previous section, I drew on several methods of interpretation to provide examples of a critical reading of contemporary image culture, mixing postmodern analysis with ideology critique and hermeneutical readings. Such mixed methods are justified, I believe, because we are now on the borderline between modernity and a new society and culture which many theorists are labelling postmodern. Because we are still living, however, in a capitalist and patriarchal society Marxist and feminist modes of thought continue to be relevant in analyzing the contemporary social situation. Likewise, because cultural texts continue to be saturated with multi-layered social and political messages, the sort of depth-model interpretive readings associated with modernity are still relevant.

Postmodern pedagogy, however, requires obliteration of the division between "high" and "low" culture and intensified attention to reading images, to gaining critical literacy in the domain of mass-mediated culture. Advertising is merely one part of the culture industries which include radio, television, film, music, cartoons, comic books, and the other artifacts of so-called popular culture. Critical methods of reading have been developed in several of these domains and the teaching of critical media literacy should become a standard part of a progressive educational curriculum. The artifacts of the cultural industries have assumed tremendous cultural power; they are a part of a cultural apparatus which has produced increased privatization, commercialization, and reification of our culture that has led to a decline of individuality, community, citizenship and democracy (Giroux 1988; Kellner 1989a). Developing critical literacy helps to reverse the trends toward growing powerlessness by empowering individuals—by providing them with competencies to resist the power of the culture industry and to learn to begin remaking culture, to produce a more democratic and participatory culture and society (Giroux 1988).

Attaining critical literacy in the domain of learning to read popular and media culture critically involves learning the skills of deconstruction, of how cultural texts work, how they signify and produce meaning, how they influence and shape their readers. In teaching this activity, I have experienced over and over the empowerment of students who learn to comprehend and critically evaluate taken-for-granted aspects of their culture. Invariably, they quickly take to the activity of attaining critical literacy and quickly become adept decoders and critics of their culture. I disagree, however, with McLuhan 1964), who argued that critical media literacy is a natural asset possessed by denizens of the postmodern media culture. On the contrary, I have found that media literacy must be acquired through learning methods of reading cultural texts.

I have suggested there that it is precisely "modern" methods of criticism (Marxian and feminist ideology critique, structuralism, myth-symbol criticism, etc.) in conjunction with postmodern focus on the image and popular culture that provide important contributions to developing critical literacy. Following Freire's

model of an emancipatory pedagogy, developing critical literacy
should empower individuals through enabling them to learn to see
through the mystifications of their environment, to see how it is
constructed and operates, and to see how they can free themselves
from dominating and oppressive aspects and learn to remake
society as a mode of self and social activity. Dialogue is important
in this process and I suggest that teaching critical media literacy is
an excellent means of getting students to talk about their culture
and experience, to articulate and discuss cultural oppression and
domination. For students familiarity with advertising, exposure to
television, film, music, etc. enables them to engage more readily
with the artifacts of their culture than more traditional book
culture. Analysis of familiar cultural artifacts can demonstrate the
socially and culturally constructed nature of subjectivity and
values, of how society constructs some activities as valuable and
beneficial while devaluing others. Studying popular culture critically can teach students to refuse and resist the imposition of
certain activities (smoking, drugs, aggressive competition, etc.), of
role and gender models, and of sexist and racist behavior by
showing that such activity and models are not natural, are not
beneficial, are not even arguably good. Such analysis requires
careful use of the language of value and of discriminating between
competing value systems and social valuations. Finally, study of
media and consumer culture links individual experience to public
policy and the language of critique to the language of pubic life. To
illustrate this point, I conclude with discussion of how analysis of
advertising can lead to concern with public policy and progressive
social change.

Implications for Education and Public Policy

I indicated that in 1988 more than $102 billion or roughly
two percent of the U.S. gross National Product was spent on advertising. Advertising expenditures in 1950 were about $6.5 billion a
year while by 1970 $40 billion a year was squandered, an by 1980
$56 billion was wasted. Advertising expenditure almost doubled
from 1980 to 1986, pointing to an alarming expansion of advertising during the 1980s. When one considers that an equal amount of
money is spent on design, packaging, marketing, and product
display, one grasps that a prodigous amount of money is expended
on advertising and marketing. For example, only eight cents of the
cosmetics sales dollar goes to pay for ingredients; the rest goes to

packaging, promotion, and marketing (Goldman 1987, 697).
Consequently, consumer capitalism constitutes a tremendous
waste of resources, and forces consumers to pay high prices for
products that they are induced to think that they need for success,
popularity, self-esteem, and other socially desirable qualities.

This vicious process of waste and manipulation during an age
of growing scarcity of resources is a national scandal and raises the
question of what can be done to combat the excesses of consumer
capitalism. Such questions make advertising a public policy issue
and a contested terrain subject to critique and struggle with. The
question of cigarette advertising immediately raises the issue of
whether all cigarette advertising should be banned, as television
cigarette advertising was banned in the 1970s. The very fact of
cigarettes, a highly addictive and potentially dangerous uncon-
trolled substance, raises questions concerning how to deal with
this public health menace. While the Surgeon General has been
helping to publicize the dangers of cigarette smoking, surely
stronger actions could be taken.

In the light of the massive federal deficit, heavy user taxes on
cigarettes, alcohol, and other "sin" products might, in conjunction
with a public health campaign, reduce the harmful effects of
cigarette smoking, drinking, drug use, and so on. Considering the
social effects of advertising also raises the issue of whether advertising should be subject to taxation; currently, it is written off by
corporations as a business expense, thus passing off advertising
expenses to the taxpayer, as well as the consumer. Congress could
also consider disallowing tax writeoffs for advertising and could
also tax advertising expenditures and advertising agencies at a
higher rate, given the dubious impact of advertising on U.S.
society and the massive waste of resources, talent, and human
energies.[7] At the very least television advertising could be taxed as
could print advertising for cigarettes, alcohol, and other socially
undesirable products. The question of advertising also raises the
question of the effects of advertising on our media system and
whether a commercial media system really provides the best
model.[8]

In these ways the language of critique can be linked to the
language of struggle and change. As Giroux (1988) argues, this
requires educating students to become active citizens, participants
in the making and remaking of society. A critical pedagogy plays a
crucial role in this process and to some extent certain postmodern
political positions can be of use here in their emphasis on local

plural struggles. Radical politics needs to be redefined to encompass the politics of everyday life, ranging from developing critical literacy to achieving more equitable gender relations. While some postmodern theory promotes cynicism, pessimism, and despair, a radical pedagogy need not fall prey to these temptations however easy it may be to succumb to despair during this period of conservative hegemony. Now is not the time to despair or give up. The linking of critical literacy with attempts to change the direction our political system remains a challenge for a new radical politics that has yet to be produced.

SHARON WELCH

Chapter Two

An Ethic of Solidarity and Difference

How can the differences that create our particular identities, differences of race, ethnicity, sexual orientation, class and gender, best be recognized, affirmed and understood? The preoccupation with difference is as central to political activism as it is to current theoretical debates. While mainstream politicians, both Democratic and Republican, deny the validity of difference in their critique of "special interest groups," a resolute embrace of difference marked the populist Rainbow Coalition of Jesse Jackson. Iris Young, for example, contrasts the Enlightenment ideal of the civil public "in which persons unite for a common purpose in terms of equality and mutual respect" with the public created in the Rainbow Coalition.[1] While the Rainbow Coalition "includes commitment to equality and mutual respect among participants, the idea of the Rainbow Coalition specifically preserves and institutionalizes in its form of organizational discussion the heterogeneous groups that make it up."[2] The aims of equality and respect are met by *highlighting differences*, not by transcending them or looking beneath them for a common foundation.

Debates over the necessary ingredients of a basic curriculum also reflect these concerns with difference. Allan Bloom's and William J. Bennett's call for a return to an emphasis on the "classic texts" of Western civilization is matched in urgency and *critical power* by the growing attention to the literature and history of the majority of humankind, an attention seen in Women's Studies, African-American, Asian, African, Latin American, Hispanic, and Asian-American Studies. Philosophers, literary critics, ethicists, and those involved in developing critical pedagogies all address the intellectual and moral imperative of recognizing the diversity and particularity of cultures and intellectual traditions. Yet we who advocate a critical pluralism still have much work to do. As Henry Giroux reminds us, the crisis in education is largely due to the "failure of radical educators to match neo-conservative educational politics with a corresponding set of visions and strategies."[3]

In this essay I hope to contribute to the visions and strategies of critical pedagogy by presenting an argument for the ethical imperative of highlighting differences, and claim that a careful exploration of difference offers an alternative to both the appeals to reason of modern philosophers and ethicists and the denial of grounded ethical and political critique by some postmodern theorists.

While many activists and theoreticians applaud the postmodern critique of Enlightenment claims to universality and inclusivity, many of us are doubtful of its adequacy as a positive account of ethically challenging and politically transformative difference. Daryl McGowan Tress, for example, questions whether "the postmodern attitude," with its "denial of depth to the self...and to legitimate grounding to claims of any kind" can offer the understanding of self and society women need in our struggle against oppression.[4]

> There is no one who persists, who remembers, whose experience and suffering counts; there *is* no one to emancipate. Without the possibility of subtle meaning, insight and self-understanding become trivial, irrelevant.[5]

The postmodern valorisation of difference does not have the same meaning as the political emphasis on difference. Part of the difficulty for many theorists of politically transformative difference is a confusion *between* differences between groups and the assertion in postmodern theory of a self lost in the play of differ-

ence.[6] The use of French theorist Luce Irigaray to understand the
differences between groups of women is especially misleading. The
difference extolled by Irigaray is the fluidity and difference of the
individual self.[7] She does not discuss the differences between
various groups of women, for her focus, although unacknowledged,
is the fractures and ambiguities of the self of the Western elite. As
Barbara Christian reminds us, the analysis of postmodern theorists
is culture specific and not true of the dynamics constitutive of language and self-formation in all peoples.[8]

The confusion is understandable. Irigaray, for example, in her
two most influential books, does refer to themes central to the politics of difference. In *Speculum of the Other Woman* she criticizes
the Freudian construction of woman and her sexuality arguing
that woman "is reduced to a function and a functioning whose historic causes must be reconsidered: property systems, philosophical, mythological, or religious systems."[9] There is a complementary acknowledgement of historical specificity in *This Sex Which
is Not One*. Here Irigaray affirms the importance of the dual task
of exposing "the exploitation common to all women" and finding
"the struggles that are appropriate for each woman, right where
she is, depending on her nationality, her job, her social class, her
sexual experience, that is, upon the form of oppression that is for
her the most immediately unbearable."[10]

These affirmations lead one to expect a modulation of claims
by Irigaray, a recognition that the construction of Woman she so
carefully criticizes is a Western, elite phenomenon, and a recognition that the subversive, fluid "self" she extols is similarly culturally specific. Unfortunately, that is not the case. In the work of
Irigaray there is nothing from working class women or women of
color and precious little about the concrete political and cultural
differences that shape women's lives. In sharp contrast to Irigaray's
work, the political debates central for many feminists focus on the
understanding and mediation (through conflict and/or coalition) of
differences between groups of women, each group asserting a fluid,
complex, multilayered yet particular identity. Irigaray's claim that
"woman never speaks the same way. What she emits is flowing,
fluctuating. *Blurring*" while undoubtedly characteristic of the
speech and experience of some women does not describe the fierce
affirmation of self and community that funds feminist political
work throughout the world.[11]

How best to describe the claims to truth of fluid, yet describ-
able, particular identities? A too hasty return to the Enlighten-

ment foundations of a shared reason and human nature misses the challenges and opportunities posed by a thorough exploration of difference. Tress, for example, argues that the only means of combatting injustice is "the primacy of reason."[12]

> It is *only reason*, at work in any person, that would have some measure of ability to stand apart from the practices of injustices and to identify them; *reason alone is independent of contingencies* and is universal and available to everyone (emphasis mine). [13]

While Tress's fears are shared by many activists and theoreticians, her solution, a universally available and historically transcendent reason, seems increasingly suspect. Surely there are other grounds for compassion, justice, and liberation than an elusive and illusory shared reason. In her reply to Tress, Jane Flax mentions other political and social constituents of justice:

> There are many ways in which such qualities [liberation, stable meaning, insight, self-understanding, the self and justice] may be attained—for example: political practice; economic, racial, and gender equality; good childrearing; empathy; fantasy; feelings; imagination; and embodiment.[14]

In this essay I provide a theoretical framework that unites many of these diverse practices, describing them as the necessary prerequisites of ethical judgment and liberating political activity. I describe an alternative to both poststructuralist thought and liberal political theory, a form of ethical practice in which the recognition and understanding of difference is central to ethical and political critique. The foundation for ethical judgments is neither a shared reason nor a common human essence but the practice of communicative ethics.

Communicative ethics are an alternative to the communal ethics of Alistair MacIntyre and Stanley Hauerwas. Unlike theorists who argue that the prerequisite of solid moral reasoning is a cohesive community with a shared set of principles, norms, and mores, I argue that material interaction between multiple communities with divergent principles, norms, and mores is essential for foundational moral critique. A cohesive community, such as the Aristotelian polis, lacks the means to criticize constitutive forms of injustice, forms of exclusion and limitation (like the Athenian institutions of slavery and the oppression of women) central to the operation of a given social system. The moral critique of structural forms of injustice emerges, rather, from the material interaction of different communities. In contrast to Jürgen Habermas, I argue that morally transformative interaction requires far more than conversation between different groups and peoples, and that "genuine" conversation presupposes prior material inter-action—either political conflict or coalition or joint involvement in life-sustaining work.

While I agree with the liberal critique of much postmodern philosophy, seeing in it the inability to make principled distinctions between various interests, I find Alistair MacIntyre's influential conception of an alternative basis for ethical judgment, what he calls the communal position, equally inadequate. MacIntyre argues that we should pursue historical and anthropological investigations of systems of morality, learning about a wide range of "moral practices, beliefs, and conceptual schemes."[15] MacIntyre sees in one such community, the cohesive Aristotelian *polis*, the solution to the "moral calamity" of our day—the impossibility of appealing to shared moral criteria.[16] In contrast to MacIntyre, I would argue that the moral calamity of our day lies not in the lack of shared moral criteria but in the inability of most communities to engender or accept a thorough critique of their "own purposes" and their "terms" of implementing those purposes. From this perspective, the Aristotelian *polis* appears to be fundamentally flawed in the same way that many contemporary communities are flawed—unable to see as unjust the inequality crucial to its functioning.

As Foucault has demonstrated in this study of classical Greek culture, the ethics of the Aristotelian polis were intrinsically an ethic of exclusion, an ethic limited to the activity of free men.[17] MacIntyre, in sharp contrast to Foucault, notes only the exclusion of slavery, and ignores the exclusion of women. While he argues that Aristotle's justification of slavery is "indefensible," he claims that it is unrelated to the adequacy of his ethics, stating that it "need not carry any large implications for our attitudes to his overall theory."[18]

I would argue that what led to Aristotle's defense of slavery is what is most dangerous in our own society: the assumption that one's own community and social class possess the prerequisites for moral judgment and that other groups are devoid of those same prerequisites. As MacIntyre states, Aristotle dismisses non-

Greeks, barbarians and slaves as "incapable" of political relationships, and thus incapable of participating in political forms which
are necessary for the existence of virtue.[19]

He (Aristotle) seeks to be the rational voice of the best citizens of the best city-state; for he holds that the city-state
is the *unique political form in which alone the virtues
of human life can be genuinely and fully exhausted* (emphasis mine).[20]

The confidence in the superiority of the Aristotelian *polis*
precludes being challenged by either the political systems and
ethical standards and experiences of other communities or by the
ethical standards of other groups (women and slaves) within the
same community. Communicative ethics, on the other hand,
avoids the dangers of isolation and self-justifying ethical systems
by its involvement in political coalitions and its openness to political conflict. *Foundational ethical critique requires difference.*
Foucault has argued that we can see a system of logic as partial,
and not as reason itself, only because we participate in alternative
systems of making and validating truth claims. The same is true of
ethics. We can see foundational flaws in systems of ethics only
from the outside, from the perspective of another system of defining, and implementing, that which is valued. In order to determine
which interests or positions are more just, what is required is pluralism, not for its own sake, but for the sake of enlarging our moral
vision.

Communicative ethics combines, therefore, pluralism and
social responsibility. From this perspective, Euro-American feminists are justified in criticizing the oppression of women in other
cultures, criticizing Indian suttee, for example, and African genital
mutilation. We must remember, however, that critique goes both
ways. Genuine communication has not occurred until we become
aware of the flaws in our culture that appear quite clearly from the
vantage point of Indian and African societies, taking seriously, for
example, an Indian critique of the Western treatment of children
and a traditional African critique of our extreme individuality and
valorization of symmetry and order.[21] From the perspective of communicative ethics, we cannot be moral alone. The discernment of
both norms and strategies requires the interaction of different
communities.

A communicative ethic takes as its standpoint the interaction between "concrete others."[22] Seyla Benhabib has described the challenge of feminism to liberal political and ethical theory in terms of our redefinition of the other selves involved in making social compacts and adjudicating competing interests. She criticizes the idea that we should approach social policy or make ethical judgments with the idea of a common humanity, affected in the same way by mores or policies. The idea that there is a common interest, shared by all, reached by transcending our special interests, is fundamentally ideological. We all are radically different. Given past and extant systems of exclusion and oppression, the experiences and even the needs of different groups of people are radically diverse. Nancy Fraser has argued that we cannot take into account the differences of each individual in making political and/or ethical judgments, but we can take into account the needs of the collective concrete other.[23] We can be cognizant of the fact that women often have different needs than men, that people of color are often affected in a different way by policies than are Euro-Americans.

The ideal situation for moral discernment is thus a collective, historical process. Moral reasoning cannot be carried out by any one theorist but requires dialogue with actual members of different communities.

Beverly Harrison makes a similar claim, arguing that "objectivity," or freedom from subjective bias in moral decision-making, requires conversation with people from different groups.

> "Objectivity" here means openness to others' history and to the critical claims that history bears and also the ability to learn from others' historical experience.[24]

Harrison reminds us of another significant aspect of taking the standpoint of the collective concrete other. For not only are we members of different groups, but also our groups are related to each other within networks of hierarchy and exploitation. The Euro-American women's perspective, or the perspective of African-American women and men cannot be simply added to that of privileged Euro-American males. Even the feminist imperative to tell our own stories requires telling the stories of white women's participation in the systemic oppression of women of color. Harrison advocates, therefore, a critical history. The collective telling of stories is the foundation for seeing, and then challenging, patterns of systemic injustice.

"Official" history suppresses the stories of resistance and dissent against the status quo and presents the past either as the triumph of the deserving or as inevitable. Critical history breaks open the past, in its full complexity, and re-presents that past as bearing a story of human struggle against domination. Even failed resistance bears powerful evidence of human dignity and courage that informs our contemporary vocations.[25]

From the standpoint of such a critical history, there is an epistemological privilege of the oppressed. Those of us who are oppressed, while not having an ontologically given primacy, do have a point of view essential to moral critique. Sandra Harding describes the preference for the viewpoint of the oppressed as a "standpoint epistemology."

The logic of the standpoint epistemologies depends on the understanding that the "master's position" in any set of dominating social relations tends to produce distorted visions of the real regularities and underlying causal tendencies in social relations—including human interactions with nature.[26]

As Harding points out, since men are in a master position in regard to women, the knowledge of women is particularly valuable. Harding criticizes what I criticize as well, the tendency among some feminists and social critics to reify a particular standpoint as the only standpoint productive of significant social critique. She argues that the logic of standpoint epistemologies entails greater attention to the knowledge of those who are oppressed at many levels—by reason of gender, sexual orientation (gays and lesbians), race, class, nationality, and degree of physical limitations.

CONSENSUS, MATERIALITY, SOLIDARITY

The goal of communicative ethics is not merely consensus, but mutual critique leading to more adequate understandings of what is just and how particular forms of justice may be achieved. When such critique occurs, we may well find that more than our definitions of what is just are challenged. The prerequisites of acting justly may also be redefined.

What are the prerequisites of moral judgement and moral action? Jürgen Habermas locates the foundation of ethical action in the claims implicit in human speech. In the exercise of communicative ethics, I find myself both dependent upon the work of Habermas and departing from his project. As feminists search for a form of individuation outside the categories of abstract individualism, the work of Habermas offers many possibilities for critical reflection and political action. Within his theoretical perspective one can imagine interaction between groups that are different, and his work is an exploration of the grounds for that interaction within the nature of speech itself. He also claims, in contrast to Foucault, that there is the possibility of significant social transformation and emancipation.

> Forms of life are totalities which always emerge in the plural. Their coexistence may cause friction, but this *difference* does not automatically result in their *incompatibility*.... Convictions can contradict one other [sic] only when those who are concerned with problems define them in a similar way, believe them to need resolution, and want to decide issues on the basis of good reasons.[27]

Habermas has tried to explain and ground the emancipatory potential of social analysis. He describes a type of social interaction—communicative action—in which the goal is to reach, without force, a mutually acceptable understanding:

> The goal of coming to an understanding is to bring about an agreement that terminates in the intersubjective mutuality of reciprocal understanding, mutual trust, and accord with one another.[28]

Habermas's exploration of communicative competence leads him in directions similar to that of many postmodern critiques of objective reason. He criticizes the modern reduction of rationality to the "cognitive-instrumental rationality" of a technocratic society, and finds three levels of rationality relevant to social analysis.[29] The critique of logocentrism is not found only in postmodern philosophers such as Derrida; Habermas, too, writes that "logocentrism means neglecting the complexity of reason effectively operating in the life-world, and restricting reason to its cognitive-instrumental dimension (a dimension, we might add, that has been noticeably privileged and selectively utilized in processes of capitalist modernization)."[30]

Habermas's vision of the self is also complex. As Giddens states, he "does not posit a self-sufficient subject, confronting an object-world, but instead begins from the notion of a symbolically structured life-world, in which human reflexivity is constituted.[31]

Habermas tries to ground non-coercive dialogue in the nature of speech itself, arguing that in each sentence we claim that our words are understandable, that they are accurate in their descriptions of reality, that our words are appropriate to a particular situation and that we intend to speak without deception.

> In action oriented to reaching understanding validity claims are "always already" implicitly raised. These universal claims (to the comprehensibility of the symbolic expression, the truth of the prepositional content, the truthfulness of the intentional expression, and the rightness of the speech act with respect to exiting norms and values) are set in the general structures of possible communication. In these validity claims communication theory can locate a gentle, but obstinate, a never silent although seldom redeemed claim to reason, a claim that must be recognized de facto whenever and wherever there is to be consensual action.[32]

Although Habermas is most noted for this "linguistic turn," his work also includes attention to the material dimensions of consensus and emancipatory dialogue. In *Knowledge and Human Interests*, he recognized the necessity of first instituting the social conditions that allow mutual communication, and he has continued to acknowledge the psychological and institutional matrix of actually living out the decisions reached through "the force of the better argument."[33]

> The cognitive capacity to justify moral actions norms has to be supplemented if it is to become effective in the context of ethical life...Without the capacity for judgment and motivation, the psychological conditions for translating morality into ethical life are missing; without the corresponding patterns of socialization and institutions, i.e. without "fitting" forms of life to embodied moral principles, the social conditions for their concrete existence are missing.[34]

I find Habermas valuable for his recognition and affirmation of interactions between groups in which power can be redistributed and social barriers can be removed. I am interested, however, in searching for more adequate models of the structures of thought and action that enable the breaking of class barriers and race and gender hierarchies. It is in this regard that I find Habermas's use of conversation as the mode of mutually transformative, socially emancipatory relation problematic.

Habermas's goal of consensus is shared by liberal feminists, who have argued that the political and philosophical task of feminism is to extend to women the basic rights articulated by male liberal theorists. But to focus on the ideal of conversation, and the extension of that ideal to include women as participants, elides a material reality that prevents such inclusion. If the inclusion of women and minorities is simply a matter of extension, why has it been so long in coming? This query has immediate relevance for the work of Habermas. He is faulted by Giddens for his failure to extend the bounds of conversation to include cultural traditions that are in clear opposition to, or highly different from, that of the Western intellectual and economic elite.[35] Giddens poses the question quite sharply:

> I was somewhat surprised to see that the section of your book concerned with myth in oral culture amounts to only a few pages. If you are going to demonstrate that oral cultures—and agrarian civilizations—operate at a lower stage of rationality to Western or modernized culture, surely a more detailed treatment is called for?[36]

While Habermas may be right to fault the reliance on tradition in some oral societies, he fails to recognize the possibility of mutual critique. While the West may offer one way of producing social change, oral cultures can offer models of the social self that Habermas himself values, and while not providing as Habermas does a critique of the autonomous isolated self, they do exhibit practices that constitute a collective, larger self.

In his two-volume work, *Theory of Communicative Action*, Habermas engages in a thorough and carefully nuanced conversation with other theorists. The insights of oral cultures are, however, summarily dismissed. He dismisses the Zande tribe for its cognitive inadequacy, its closed worldview and lack of means of testing validity claims that enables change and modification.

According to Giddens, Habermas fails to recognize that gaining education as a condition of conversation is itself a preclusion to genuine conversation. The attainment of literacy destroys the fabric of an oral culture. The condition, then, of conversation is conquest. Habermas has not imagined the search for alternative modes of conversation and interaction in which not only the validity claims but the substantive proposals of each culture could be fairly explained.

The work of Richard Katz serves as a helpful alternative.[37] In his examination of an oral culture, the Kalahari Kung, he describes aspects of that culture that challenge Western notions of agency and subjectivity. He describes a process of psychological and physical healing. All members of the tribe participate in a collective dance, in which healing power, or "boiling energy" is raised. While some people circulate among the group as "healers," actually being filled with boiling energy and touching the people who are afflicted, they are not viewed as the only healers. The dancers, drummers, and all the other participants in the ritual are fully seen as healers, for their activities are necessary to raise the energy that the healers then direct. Katz sees there a recognition of a collective self, and the creation of collective power that he describes as a serious challenge to Western notions of the autonomous individual actor.

Genuine conversation with other cultural traditions leads to a further fundamental challenge to Habermas. If other cultures are to be included, assessment of the criteria of successful conversation and of the norms for that conversation must be joined. While Habermas poses the norm of the force of the better argument, I find it equally plausible to assert the appeal of the more richly textured narrative as a criterion of description, and, as a criterion of strategies, those which create the most possibilities for further emancipatory responses. Barbara Christian, for example, argues that there are forms of understanding reality and making judgments that cannot be reduced to the canons of Western logic.

> For people of color have always theorized—but in forms quite different from the Western form of abstract logic...[O]ur theorizing is often in narrative forms, in the stories we create, in riddles and proverbs, in the play with language, because dynamic rather than fixed ideas seem more to our liking.[38]

The logic of narratives, proverbs, and riddles, with the implicit criteria of complexity and evocativeness may have a ground in human experience as basic as that of consensus. Giddens poses a thought provoking alternative to Habermas:

> "Our first sentence," you once wrote, "expresses unequivo-cally the intention of universal and unconstrained consen-sus." Why not say that our first gesture of recognition of another person promises a universal solidarity of human beings?[39]

The intention of solidarity is potentially more inclusive and more transformative than is the goal of consensus. Consensus is best understood, not as the end of dialogue, but as one of the ele-ments of ethical action. Taking as an example the interaction of groups from different strata in an unjust social system, what is the meaning of the goal of consensus? Imagine a conversation between Euro-American feminists, African-American womanists, African-American men, and Euro-American upper class men. What would consensus mean in such a situation? Much more is required than a common analysis of oppression. It would be transformative if the Euro-American men and women could be convinced by the African-American men and women of the pervasiveness of racism, and become convinced that its costs are intolerable. Similarly, the women involved would want the men to recognize the myriad manifestations of sexual oppression and become actively involved in trying to eradicate this form of injustice. The group identified as the oppressor in each case would work for a recognition of their good intentions and sensitivity to the difficulties entailed in their own transformation.

Even if we accept an understanding of consensus that means a common recognition of social ills and the need for the rectifica-tion of those ills, solidarity is presupposed as a prior step. In order for conversations of this depth to occur, there must be the presup-position of solidarity. Solidarity has two aspects in this case: grant-ing each group sufficient respect to listen to their ideas and to be challenged by them; recognition that the lives of the various groups are so intertwined that each is accountable to the other. These forms of recognition assume working together to bring about changes in social practice.

I agree with Habermas that conversation is valuable, but claim that transformative dialogue occurs only as the fruition of more foundational interchanges. I want to examine the material base of consensus and the materiality of the movement of emanci-patory conversation. From the point of view of the women's movement, I will argue that Habermas's model of communicative action requires the inclusion of materiality at two points.

The goal of a conversation in which the only force is that of the better argument presupposes material transformation. Let me take as my example the entry of women into the mainstream of theological education. Women can be part of shaping the theological tradition most fully if certain material conditions are met. There is, for instance, the simple matter of numbers. The differences posited by women are apt to be taken more seriously when they are asserted by many women, and the women attempting to bring a different point of view into dialogue are able to do that with more facility if there are many women in the conversation. Many women with differing perspectives can create a fuller explanation of the feminist critique of the adequacy of self-sacrifice, for example, as a positive model of love. Also, transformations in understandings of basic values can be entertained and evaluated more easily if one is not the only spokesperson of one's group, but has the actual physical presence of women who can also assess the extent to which one is being either co-opted or challenged to a more adequate understanding of basic values.

There is a second aspect of the materiality of conversation. What leads to the attribution of equal weight in dialogue, what enables the acceptance of formerly oppressed or ignored others into conversations? Given that there are substantial power imbalances between different groups, and given that there are substantial conflicts in terms of values and political strategies as well, what leads to mutually challenging conversation between these groups?

As is evident in Habermas's dismissal of oral cultures, we are not merely rational actors. The imperatives present in speech do not insure that all others will be included as participants in conversation. It is essential that we examine the ways in which excluded groups are not seen as fully human, the exclusion itself is not seen, and the pain of exclusion not recognized.

In the work of African-American women I find richly textured narratives of these processes of exclusion. Paule Marshall's work *The Chosen Place, The Timeless People* is an excellent case in point.[40] She depicts the racism of well-meaning whites, and the way in which material factors, i.e., structural imbalances in power, poison even genuine attempts to provide material help to blacks who are oppressed. She describes the cultural mechanisms by which efforts at emancipation are thwarted by the inability of those in power, despite their willingness to help, to admit the extent of the damage done by racism. She describes the ways in which those who are in power inure themselves to the actual costs of oppression by the simple fact of shutting down, of not hearing what is said when it is said in an angry tone. Conversation is stopped at the point when deep pain or rage is expressed. Efforts at reform inevitably fall short, for the extent of the wound is not seen. Also, a material power imbalance is maintained in that those who come to help hold on to the privilege of leaving the fray. They choose to help those who are oppressed but hold on to the possibility of leaving, of going back to life as usual. As long as some people think they can leave, the trust necessary for genuine conversation is impossible. Those who are being "helped" cannot trust either that they will be heard, or, that if they speak honestly, that the group that has more privilege will stay in the conversation.

Another way in which an unacknowledged power differential thwarts transformative interaction is the extent to which the changes sought by those who have been victimized are seen to entail only loss for those who are more privileged. For some sharing power seems like death, a loss of self rather than the invitation to explore an alternative construction of selfhood. For some, explorations of alternative structures of persuasion and self-critique seem like the abandonment of reason rather than the entry into a larger conversation in which the nature of rigorous thought is carefully assessed.

An adequate model of transformative relation thus includes far more than "the force of the better argument." Giddens's alternative goal of solidarity is more inclusive of the material complexity of transformative relationships: "our first gesture of recognition of another person promises a universal solidarity of human beings."[41] When mutual transformation occurs there is the power of empathy and compassion, of delight in otherness, and strength in the solidarity of listening to others, bearing together stories of pain and resistance. Paule Marshall also provides a rich depiction of this process in the same novel. She describes the transformation in action, thought, and empathy of another liberal reformer who enters a mutually transformative relationship with those he is helping. Transformation occurs as the reformer feels the pain of the people who are oppressed. He is open to examining different standards of justice, thus understanding why certain development projects were rejected by the oppressed group. Also, listening to the pain of others requires that the person who is the oppressor acknowledge his or her own pain, no longer accepting it as a necessary cost of a civilized social order, but evaluating again its necessity and its implications for a cultural and political system. And finally, there is the dimension of the enlargement of the self. Genuine conversation occurs as one finds joy in listening to others, and even as previous and present worlds of meaning are challenged, experiences delight in the complexity of what emerges.

Habermas acknowledges that the claims to reason of the ideal speech situation are rarely met. There is a political reason for such frequent failures. Conversation alone is not enough. Emancipatory conversations are the fruit of work together; the result of alterations in relationships between groups. In work we create as much as we affirm the rational principle of shared humanity. We share our humanity in work and then can move to the conversations that explore the nature of this humanity and the political imperatives it entails.

By work I mean material interaction at the most basic level. For those whose differences are large, working together is often possible at only the most basic level: preparing food together, cleaning, building houses, making clothing. In working together the alienation of class is challenged: one can see the physical effort required for sustenance and has the option of a different sort of conversation, recognizing the wisdom of the use of the body and the humor that often accompanies such material effort. The travesty of the collectivization of labor is as much the isolation of workers from one another in the factory (isolated by the sheer level of noise and by the division of labor) as in the appropriation of the value created by that labor.

For those with more areas of commonality, a different sort of work enables genuine conversation to occur. A genuine conversation between those who are privileged by way of class, gender, race and those who have experienced oppression or discrimination on the basis of those characteristics is possible when those who are privileged work to end the oppression or discrimination they denounce. As we do more than vote for those opposed to racism, challenging racism directly in our workplaces, in our families, in our own lives, we can be trusted in a way that enables those oppressed because of race to speak with us more honestly. In our work, we see more clearly the costs of racism, and the intransigence of structures of oppression. Men who work against rape or domestic violence, who are involved in challenging the value systems that lead to such violence, are able to hear the voices of women, and women are able to trust them in a way impossible if the only form of relation is a dialogue.

Communicative ethics presupposes, and sustains, political transformation. The process of dialogue, mutual critique, and political action is dynamic, a spiralling movement in which rudimentary practices of political action enable further critique and evoke more adequate forms of political practice.

LINDA BRODKEY
MICHELLE FINE

Chapter Three

Presence of Mind in the Absence of Body

We commonly tell stories about what happens to us and what we make of our experience. In a sense, then, the stories documenting our lives tell what we find worth remembering and contemplating and sharing with others. It is of course the "others" who complicate the telling of stories, for stories are not usually told to ourselves alone, but to those we hope will understand our construction of events. The stories included in this essay concern the sexual harassment of students by professors. We have tried to reconstruct the historical and institutional circumstances of the telling along with the stories told because the transformative potential of the narratives cannot be understood apart from the context in which they were written and read.[1]

The sexual harassment narratives were written by undergraduate and graduate women at the University of Pennsylvania in response to an open-ended question on the *Penn Harassment Survey*.[2] These students are of the generation of women for many of whom, as Annette Kolodny recently put it, "feminism is either outdated—because of the naive belief that 'there aren't any problems any more'—or a distorted melange of media images and Reagan-era backlash" (461). For some of them, Kolodny adds, "feminism is both personal and problematic" because their mothers "tried to reject traditional family roles in a society that offered their offspring no compensating structures and amid a movement too new to prepare us all for the consequences of such radical change" (461). Yet the women who wrote these narratives know what sexual harassment is. Their narratives confirm the findings of survey research on college and university campuses: women students are routinely harassed; postsecondary institutions have been egregiously hesitant to address harassment (much less write, publish, and enforce sexual harassment policies); and remedies for reporting and grieving sexual harassment favor, if not harassers, their institutions (Robertson, Dwyer & Campbell 1988). After reading and reflecting on these narratives, we have come to believe that the future of academic feminism is activism and that activism begins in pedagogy.

The narratives clarify the findings of the Penn survey, namely, that women are reluctant to report sexual harassment and reticent when they do because they suspect that institutional indifference will lead to reprisals of one sort or another. We think their fears are justified and in turn warrant feminist curriculum intervention. What we have learned from women's narratives of their experiences of harassment, however, suggests that we will need to encourage all students and women in particular to explore not so much the fact but the complexities of harassment. After all, harassment sits at the nexus of gender, power, and sexuality in the academy—as it does in all institutions. Exploring it will take the students and us far outside the boundaries of legal definitions and institutional remedies and it will even take us outside current feminist analyses of gender and sexuality, for most women students judge sexual harassment to be beyond the reach of law and feminism.

To teach this new generation is to try to understand that they encounter sexual harassment as women whose civil rights have been guaranteed since birth, and hence as women who have believed themselves to be protected by those laws—and have only recently found that they are not. And to work with them is also to realize that even as their narratives reveal the partiality of their visions of gender and sexuality, they critique the partiality of our more seasoned feminist analyses of gender inequity and sexual violence. We are arguing for feminist pedagogies to accompany what

Donna Haraway calls "situated and embodied knowledges," the partiality and plurality of which contest "various forms of unlocatable, and so irresponsible, knowledge claims" (1988, 583). Partial perspectives exert a sobering influence on feminist pedagogies, privileging self-conscious acts of critical vision and imagination that are openly hostile to the already established vantage points of either relativism or totalization, which Haraway sees as "promising vision from everywhere and nowhere" (584). Yet she is also suspicious of all "innocent" positions, including what can be seen from the vantage points of subjugation, and offers positioning as a responsible political and epistemological feminist practice for continuing the conversation on gender already in progress in the academy. The pedagogical and political project then is to interrogate the ways in which the sexual harassment narratives undermine the transformative potential of narration by effectively withdrawing their narrators from the conversation we had hoped they would enter.

TELLING IT LIKE IT IS/WAS AND LIKE IT ISN'T/WASN'T

Given that the Penn Harassment Survey focused primarily on sexual harassment, and given the demographics of students at Penn, the narratives written by undergraduate and graduate women raise almost exclusively the concerns of white women from the middle and upper social classes. Yet their narratives confirm the findings of other campus surveys and hence frustrate any hopes we may have had that knowledge of civil rights defends women against their harassers. Of particular concern here are the narratives written in response to Questions 21:

> It would be helpful to us if you would describe this experience in detail. Please do so omitting any incriminating information, (e.g. names, courses, etc.). You may include a separate piece of paper if necessary.

Ignoring for the moment the likelihood that the proviso to omit incriminating information may have also discouraged many women students from including details of any kind and the fact that the quarter-inch allotted for response was inadequate, we offer the narrative below as typical, inasmuch as the woman provides a markedly attenuated description of the event itself relative to the elaborate explanation of both her professor's behavior and her decision not to report him.

> When the incident happened, his attention lasted about one month. It did not occur to me that it was sexual harassment per se because I don't tend to think in terms of deviant behavior.
> I perceived a troubled man experiencing a mid-life crisis, and more important, a colleague with whom I genuinely shared intellectual commitments and interests. Unfortunately, he saw a young, bright cutsie who could help him with this work and who could potentially serve as an escape route from his unsatisfactory marriage. Basically, all I had to do was make my "No" repetitive and very clear, but the situation was so muddled and in many ways, not so cut and dried as sexual harassment. Things occurred on a very subtle level and are not reported for this reason. All professors have to say is "She's unstable, paranoid, imagining things or lying, etc." Graduate women don't have a leg to stand on. (File 403-31)

Many statements in this account warrant commentary. She refers to "the incident" but never describes what her professor actually did. We're not then certain if she considers the "attentions that lasted about one month" sexual harassment and hence "deviant behavior" or if, as she later asserts, "the situation was so muddled and in many ways, not so cut and dried as sexual harassment." She contrasts her complex view of him, "I perceived a troubled man experiencing a midlife crisis, and more important, a colleague with whom I genuinely shared intellectual commitments and interests," with his simple view of her, "Unfortunately, he saw a young, bright cutsie who could help him with his work." Here lies her conflict. And it matters because she has located the danger in his gendering of her, that is, in being turned into a woman. For she goes on to explain that his professional abuse is but a preface to an attempt to transform her into a woman whose body "could potentially serve as an escape route from his unsatisfactory marriage." She tells us that she dealt with her harasser as one might an unruly child, "Basically, all I had to do was make my "No" repetitive and very clear," and then explains that she and all the others have no other recourse, since "all professors have to say is "She's unstable, paranoid, imagining things or lying, etc." And her last words, "Graduate women don't have leg to stand on," summarize both her own situation and her position on the gendering of women by their male professors.

LEAVING YOUR BODY TO SCIENCE

We have a good deal of sympathy for this graduate woman's rendering of the academic world she inhabits, where her experience of gender has been reduced to slut and madwoman. While we delight in her refusal to take her professor's extracurricular forced-choice exam, we are, nonetheless, troubled by the argument that she and other women students use to represent their strategies for resisting harassers, for it certainly looks as if their practice is to transcend their bodies and deny that women students are women. We say this because of the stunning regularity with which women students position themselves in their narratives as disinterested bystanders who have been asked not to describe what happened to them, but to explain why professors harass their women students.

> This behavior increases when his wife leaves town, if we are in a situation involving liquor or if we are in the presence of other individuals who find this behavior entertaining. (File 947–31)
> Male faculty in a department in which I conduct research make suggestive comments, joke and tease most of the time. There are no female faculty members of the department and my assumption has always been that they were simply ignorant of how their behavior was affecting the females who are associated in this department. (File 431–61)
> He was drunk which I'm sure contributed to the problem. (File 344–51)

What troubles us about the women's explanations of the extenuating circumstances surrounding acts of harassment is the extent to which each has positioned herself as a narrator who, because she has personally transcended the experience, is "free" to evaluate her harasser's behavior from the vantage point of an expert witness. She does this by assuming a clinical posture with respect to sexual harassment, treating the event as a mere symptom of a disease she must diagnose. Instead of a personal narrative recounting her own anger, sorrow, pain, or even pleasure, she impersonally catalogues his motives: he drinks; his wife is out of town; his colleagues egg him on; he's socially maladroit; he's old; he doesn't know any better. She's taking good care of him. That wouldn't concern us much except that the narrative positions women assign themselves suggest that they understand their own survival to depend on the ability to cleave their minds from their bodies. This mind/body split reproduces in each of them the very cultural ideology that has historically been used to distinguish men from women and justify gender oppression. By severing mind from body and then privileging the "mind's" dispassionate, even clinical, explanation of events, each woman materially reproduces in her narrative the very discursive dichotomies that have historically been used to define a seemingly endless string of culturally positive terms (male/mind/reason/culture) in contrast to a negative string (female/body/intuition/nature) (see Caplan 1986).

We take such representations of self as mind by women students as pleas to be seen by professors as *not* women. In poststructural terms, the women attempt to achieve unity and coherence as writers in an academic discourse, often called science, that has in recent history offered a few privileged white males the comforting belief that they and they alone legislate reality. These men reside in a world in which "mind over matter" means that what counts is what each individual man can know, understand, and represent as empirical. While poststructural theories argue convincingly that the unity afforded our divided sense of ourselves as discursive subjects is an illusion (Belsey 1980; Brodkey 1989), we are presumably most attracted to discourses that promise to represent us to ourselves and others as empowered subjects—as the agents who speak the discourse rather than the objectified subjects of which it speaks. For many faculty and students, scientific discourse regulates academic speech and writing. And we think the women students are trying to reproduce a version of scientific discourse by positioning themselves as narrators who, having transcended their bodies, are then entitled to use their dispassionate observations as the bases of their clinical explanations of men's motives and cynical speculations on institutional reprisals. What happened to their bodies (sexual harassment) is not problematic and hence plays little part in the narratives; why it happened (his motives) and what would happen (reprisals), however, remain problematic long after the event and hence the narratives tell the story of a torturous struggle to represent themselves as genderless.

We see each woman student as offering to pay an exorbitant, not to mention impossible, price for the coherent self represented in her narrative. In exchange for her "mind," she leaves her body to science. Such a strategy for resisting harassment, however, uncritically accepts the illusory coherence of scientific discourse and presumes that human subjectivity is essentially rather than multiply determined (overdetermined) in democratic societies. Yet there is overwhelming evidence in theory, research, and practice that mind, body, gender, sexuality are not facts we must live with but social constructions we have learned to live by.

LEARNING TO STAND TOGETHER

Our goal in this essay is to discern the potential for a liberatory pedagogy of political analysis in the sexual harassment narratives. We understand such inquiry to be transformative, that is, intellectual work in which students and teachers think in terms of both epistemology (ways of knowing the world) and activism (ways of acting in the world). To this end, we have found it useful to review the narratives first in light of feminist standpoint theory (Hartsock 1985), and then in light of critical pedagogy (Giroux 1988) for educational projects of possibility that pose teachers and students as intellectual and political agents.

In *Money, Sex, and Power* Nancy Hartsock argues that because women experience themselves as continuous with the world and men experience themselves as discontinuous with the world, they stand in materially different relationships with themselves, other people, and the world of objects. Thus, women and men view the world from entirely different and indeed opposing standpoints. Hartsock traces the construction of these opposing and gendered epistemologies to early childhood experiences of body and boundary as described in the work of Nancy Chodorow (1978) reasoning that girls, "because of female parenting, are less differentiated from others than boys, more continuous with and related to the external object world" (238). Such a division of labor in parenting, argues Hartsock, means that "girls can identify with a concrete example present in daily life" while "boys must identify with an abstract set of maxims only occasionally present in the form of the father" (238). Relationality is particularly useful in explaining how women reason from experience. And it is plausible to conclude, as Hartsock has, that designating women as the

primary caretakers of children might result in gender-differenti-
ated epistemologies, in which even harassed women would tend to
see, create, and value relationality.

While Hartsock's notions inform us about what women
might have been trying to do in their narratives, the idea that a
single feminist standpoint could account for all women is not
plausible. It obscures the complexity and diminishes the importance of differences, such as race and class, in women's lives.
Further, the theory does not address the extent to which personal
development through "object relations" is confounded by the cultural hegemony that affects the way women think about, talk
about, and organize against harassment in the academy. In other
words, the struggle toward standpoint cannot be abstracted from
the struggle against the distractions and attractions of dominant
ideology (Gramsci 1971). It is, after all, inside an academic hierarchy of asymmetrical relations between students and teachers that
women students answered question 21 like "good" students,
thereby representing their personal experience of sexual harassment in the same disinterested terminology used in the survey.

Saturating standpoint theory with the understanding that
cultural hegemony is also determining, we are better able to
understand how women students might have independently
arrived at similar political stances in their narratives of sexual
harassment. Instead of *describing* what happened, their narratives
try to *explain* what happened by imagining what might have moti-
vated their harassers and what might have happened had they
reported the harassment. A standpoint of relationality may
account for the formal structure of the narratives, but the contents
spell hegemony. The transcendent narrator is a standpoint from
which a writer can relate the concerns of harasser and harassed
alike. But the motives and reprisals women name come out of
that dreary stockpile of conclusions/premises/arguments that individualism and proceduralism commonly use to explain why "you
can't fight City Hall" and why men can't be held accountable for
harassment.

The political potential of the standpoint of relationality as an
activist epistemology is severely tested by the content of the
sexual harassment narratives, inasmuch as it becomes clear that
when women link the incident to men's motives and institutional
reprisals, they are left standing alone and wishing they were not
women. Their analysis of motives and reprisals leads them to
believe that since men harass women for untold reasons, women

who report harassment will be subjected to more of the same arbi-
trary treatment from the institution. The dispassionate language
in which graduate women speculate on institutional reprisals is
academic and this strikes us as all the more eerie not only because
it reproduces the mind/body split, but because their fears are far
from academic. Consider, for instance, the way in which this
student juxtaposes form and content in the following passage:

> *I think* female graduate students *probably* bear the brunt of
> sexual harassment at the University. *Most* of the guys who
> harass you or *just make life difficult* are your teachers and
> dissertation committee members. Graduate students here
> have no power. We're dependent on our departments for
> financial aid, and are afraid that these professors *could* black-
> ball us in our future careers. (File 344–51; emphases ours.)

Because sexual harassment is woven into the very fabric of
faculty-student relations, women do not as a matter of course
appeal to legal remedies; institutional procedures only further
jeopardize their professional lives. Student complaints about
sexual harassment are not likely to be taken as seriously by the
institution as allegations of capricious grading or irregular office
hours. While the modulated phrasing may mean that women students are confronting irrational behavior from their professors by
responding rationally, and relationally, this very act of using their
heads effectively preempts taking an activist stance.

Hartsock understands the epistemology of standpoint as
liberatory:

> Because of its achieved character and its liberatory potential,
> I use the term "feminist" rather than "women's standpoint."
> Like the experiences of the proletariat, women's experience
> and activity as a dominated group contains both negative and
> positive aspects. A feminist standpoint picks out and ampli-
> fies the liberatory possibilities contained in that experi-
> ence.(232)

We do not see relationality in the sexual harassment narratives as liberatory or even potentially so, and think it could only
become so if feminist educators were willing to work with students to imagine liberatory possibilities not raised when analysis
fetishizes individual men's motives and institutional reprisals. In

other words, we see relationality as an epistemology that helps to explain the reasoning of women students who experience inequity, bypass their outrage, and rationalize that the way it is is all there is.

A subjugated standpoint does not necessarily facilitate collective activism on behalf of women who, in the absence of support, have individually devised ad hoc strategies for deflecting harassment. With such strategies, a particular woman may be able to prevent or protect herself against individual acts of harassment. Such strategies, however, neither interrupt nor disrupt the material and ideological gender asymmetries organizing the academy. Such strategies do not call public attention to sexual harassment as simply the most overt and explicit of those practices reminding women that we are not card-carrying members (pun intended) of the academic club (and again).

What we've learned from reading these narratives is that if the women appear not to have said "what really happened," that was because we were only listening for the legal categories that count as sexual harassment: that is, evidence of social transgressions that are specified by the EEOC guidelines and that can be documented empirically in terms that the court understands. The voices of women students in the sexual harassment narratives speak of a pervasive, routinized, and institutionalized sexual intimidation calling for a far more radical institutional project than heretofore suggested by either adversarial law or positioned feminism.

The violent behaviors that feminism and law bracket as sexual harassment and that institutions then treat as exceptional practices do not begin to capture the sense of danger lurking in the women's narratives. The unspoken oppression strikes us as all the more brutal when, as in example below, difficulties with language suggest that the author may also be a foreign student:

> I went to private office to visit this person. He greeted me at the door, closed the door and locked it. He leaned over me, standing very close and started unbuttoning my overcoat. I fumbled with coat buttons trying to make light of/ignore his behavior, and trying to dissipate his sexual attention. He helped me remove my hat, coat, scarf and hang them up. He took my hand and led me over to couch in office. We had often sat in that part of the office before to chat, with him on couch (often lounging) and me on chair facing him. He sat

down on couch and pulled me by my hand to sit next to him. I pulled to try to sit in chair as per usual; he would not let go. He lay down on couch and pulled me down to sit next to him. I pulled to try to sit in chair as per usual; he would not let go. He lay down on couch and pulled me down to sit next to him on edge of couch, near his hip level. He released my hand and I moved back to far end of couch. There were no chairs nearby. I could not move to sit elsewhere without drawing tremendous attention to my action: 1) I would be overtly rejecting him if he was seriously pursuing me sexually; 2) I would be quite rude if he then decided to pretend he had no sexual intentions. My first thought was not to provoke him since the door was locked and the office quite soundproof. He kept urging me to sit closer to him and I declined. He finally took my hand and pulled me, I resisted but moved closer as a last resort before an outright struggle and possible scream. He kept holding my hand. He then tried to pull me down on top of him, coaxing me verbally. I refused. I stayed upright and using as much strength as necessary and shook my head no, looking him straight in the eye. Luckily, he wanted to seduce me, not assault me violently. (File 1974–31)

Her narrative reminds us that even though legal categories account for his behavior, she appeals not to law but popular psychology to explain her professor's motives: "I felt that this incident was due more to an ego-attack of older man (mid-sixties) rather than the machinations of a sexual psychopath." If a stranger had attacked her on the street, no doubt she would have seen it as an assault. But she casts her professor's "strange" behavior in the most benign light possible—by comparing him to a psychopath— presumably so that she can imagine completing her studies:

We have resumed our usual interactions. In this case, there was enough of a personal friendship to use as a basis to deal with the incident on a person-to-person way. Had that not been the case, however, I would have risked losing the support of an internationally renowned scholar with impressive professional contacts and influence. That's quite a bit of leverage to have over someone, isn't it? (File 1974–31)

This narrative is unusual because its extensive analysis is grounded in a description of the event itself. To be sure, she offers the usual explanations of motives, but she elaborates the harassing incident in tandem with her many modes of resistance before stating her ambivalence about the institutional vulnerability of graduate student women.

When oppression is normalized, privatized, and rooted in a powerful and pervasive institutional ambivalence toward the oppressed, a woman student is more likely to pose and resolve the conflict in her narrative by glossing the incident and concentrating on explanations:

> A mutual sexual attraction grew between myself and a professor. It was in part physical—in many settings and to people at large, the professor projects his sexuality—but was also based upon the discovery of shared values. This bond struck a chord with me, as I felt very lonely and isolated, for the usual—and institutionalized—reasons that graduate students feel this way. (File 1851–31)

Her seeming calm is soon belied, however, by a catalogue of fears iterated in many of the narratives: "I shortly grew alarmed both at the power of my own feelings and the increasing power of the professor's feelings"; "Although I did not feel physically threatened—that seemed unlikely—I became afraid that he would begin to manipulate me by using the power of my own feelings and my need for him"; "This fear arose as I learned how he was irrationally competitive with us [graduate students]"; "I felt that I had lost both his respect and his important professional support"; "I knew if needed he would not 'go to bat' for me in the personally influential ways that professors have to work for their students" (File 1851–31). In a later, more sustained passage, she explains why the fears that simmer internally are not to be expressed formally:

> It seemed impossible to resolve the situation by talking it over with him—the relationship always had an unspoken nature about it, and he very likely would have stonewalled me, making me feel totally responsible for what had happened. I did not feel that it would be helpful to speak to any other faculty members given my own involvement and the provocative and controversial nature of a sexual and political relationship which is not even supposed to exist. I also feared discrediting myself and I felt that the faculty's personal loyalties rested with this professor. (File 1851–31)

The women who wrote the narratives know they've been treated unfairly by their professors. And while they do not blame themselves, their reluctance to insist that professors are responsible leaves women students recognizing harassment but transfixed rather than transformed by their knowledge of oppression (see Fine 1986). The fact that personal knowledge does not necessarily become grounds for political action is clear not only from the narratives, but from the survey. Even though 45 percent of graduate and professional women students reported some sexual harassment over the past five years, over 80 percent handled it "by ignoring or going along with it or by avoiding contact with the offender." And, indeed, only between 0 percent and 6 percent of graduate students (depending on the type of harassment) report filing a formal grievance in response to an incident of harassment (de Cani, Fine, Sagi & Stern 1985, p. viii).

Feminist interpretation means reading these stories as true but partial accounts of sexual harassment. But feminist pedagogy strives to recover the intellectual and creative energy dispersed when women try to transcend their bodies and find themselves standing alone against their harassers. This is a pedagogy that would transform that wasted individual energy into a collective desire to identify and examine the institutional practices that succor sexual harassment and begin to institute counterpractices that do not. The possibilities for pedagogy in the next section arise out of our analysis of the narratives and pose a feminist project in terms of transforming the scene of institutional harassment so that women in the academy are free to study and teach—with our bodies and minds intact.

LEARNING HOW TO SPEAK IN THE ACADEMY

In this section we set out to amplify in pedagogy some political projects that we now think may have been attenuated in the sexual harassment narratives. We do this realizing that the survey itself may have encouraged harassed women to resolve prematurely the tensions and complexities their narratives posed. The designers of the survey had hoped that open-ended questions would offer women students an opportunity for both critique and empowerment. Instead, women respondents commonly took this opportunity to consolidate experiences about which they were seemingly quite ambivalent and effectively returned all responsibility for advocacy to the committee. At least this is how we have come to understand the lengths some women went to in thanking the committee:

> Thanks for your concern over this issue. I realize that I was less than responsible to my fellow students for not pursuing a formal complaint but I'm glad to help with the survey. (File 1799–11)
>
> I do appreciate being able to tell someone about this who will take this information seriously. (File 1851–31)
>
> I thank you for conducting this questionnaire. I hope you publish the results and information on the procedure for reporting situations. (File 1486–11)
>
> Thanks for listening! (File 1418–31)

We take seriously Giroux's reminder that "oppositional political projects...should be the object of constant debate and analysis" (69). We recommend basing the curriculum on a *negative critique* of these and/or other individualistic and futile attempts to interrogate or interrupt forms of institutional oppression organized around gender, race, and social class. Central to this project is the demystification of institutional policies and practices that cloak social inequities. We need to engage young women and men in exploring how our analyses of the causes and consequences of social inequities construct not only our understandings of the present, but our images of what is possible in the near or far future. Unable to imagine institutional change, the women who wrote the sexual harassment narratives default to reworking relationships with faculty, or, even more consequentially, to reworking or denying their bodies.

Feminist pedagogy begins by animating the policies and procedures that contribute to harassment. The faceless image of authority sustains the illusion that institutions are immutable and hence oppression inevitable. This is the illusion feminists must first seek to dispel if we hope to enable young women and men to see oppression as mutable through critical and collective reflection and action. A pedagogy intentionally remote from political activism incidentally fosters the very alienation, individualism and cynicism we confronted in these narratives. We were heartened to find young women who grew up in the wake of civil rights legislation and witnessed the victories and losses of feminism in the courts and state legislatures struggling against harassment. Their collective narrative however, is a story of despair, for each woman encounters the lechery of professors alone, with little hope that law can, or that the institution will, intercede on her behalf. And so she tries to rise above the scene of harassment in narratives reminding us that the halls of academe are littered with the bodies women students leave hostage in their flight from professorial treachery.

We could set an intellectual and political process in motion by asking students to imagine how a series of university representatives might respond to the narratives. What would the university counsel, the lawyer whose job it is to subvert grievances and suits against the institution, make of a narrative about the institutional threat of violence rather than an actual act of violence? How might the director of the Women's Center respond? Or a feminist professor? A nonfeminist professor? A faculty member who has been or thinks he may be named in a sexual harassment suit? The editor of the student newspaper or the alumni magazine? And what about the dean of the school? The man or woman chairing the department? The president of the university? The president of student government or the faculty senate? The counseling staff? What changes if we know that the narrator is white, black, straight, gay? The harasser white, black, straight, gay? While the list is far from complete, it points out that since institutions speak not one but several "languages," students need to apprise themselves of the range of "dialects" representing their university.

At any given moment in its history, the representatives of a university will be unevenly committed to preserving the status quo which means that the possibilities for political change are always contingent on revealing heterogeneity within what only appears to be a single voice to outsiders. While it is nearly always the case that the university lawyer will not hear such a narrative, the other representatives are not nearly so predictable in their responses. The related narrative task suggested by the first is, of course, revision. Having imagined what university representatives might do with the narrative as written, how might a particular narrative be rewritten to secure a hearing from each of the representatives? We are not suggesting an exercise in writing for audiences, but recommending that students do this kind of imaginative work before they meet and interview representatives concerning their jobs and their positions on harassment of women and/or minority constituencies on campus. This collaborative work requires students to take careful notes, report back to peers and faculty, and compare findings and impressions; they should do this before making any decisions about who and what to write, and before making plans for more sustained collective action. We see what can be learned from representatives of the institution as a first lesson in understanding how power is or is not dispersed locally and as a first step toward interrupting the illusion that institutional authority is literally anonymous.

What happens next is of course contingent on what students and teachers are willing to deem appropriate under the circumstances. Students might go on to write a white paper on the status of women students on their campus, a series of articles for the student or a city newspaper, a pamphlet for entering students and their parents, a broadside for students, faculty, and staff. Or they might decide that their preliminary research warrants additional studies of the institution and its relations with students on a number of issues that include but are not bounded by sexual harassment. The point is that it would be pedagogically irresponsible to set up an intellectual exploration such as we are suggesting and assume that students will have succeeded only if they reproduce familiar feminist analyses, that is, execute what we have already conceptualized. There is no feminist standpoint they must find. There is instead a feminist project, struggling to find the crevices in the institutional facade that glosses over oppression of students, staff, and faculty across lines of race, class, and gender.

The unevenness of commitment to the status quo does not mean that any particular strategy meant to engage university representatives in a conversation will result in desired/desirable political change. We have only to review the recent political successes of the New Right in the academy and elsewhere to realize that heterogeneity is itself no guarantee that discussions will move administrations to more progressive policies. While speaking is certainly a form of action, institutional representatives often understand talk as a way of appeasing and defusing student, faculty, and staff activists. Students as well as educators need to bear in mind that talking and writing to representatives may not be enough unless they are also willing to enlist support from institutions that are (or have representatives who are) interested in their university. Included among the possibilities are: the press, professional organizations, legislators, community activists committed to gender and race equity, alumni, well known political "radicals" willing to visit campus and speak out for students, and parents who thought that education would support, not undermine, their children. While political networking is as difficult to learn as to maintain, such a network is critical both as a lever for starting conversation inside the institution and as an alternative if or once a conversation breaks down. Outside the boundaries arbitrarily set by the academy, moreover, young women and men are sometimes better positioned to notice and interrupt the institution's version of reality and protectionism, and so better positioned to represent themselves as informed and critical agents of change.

LEARNING WHAT TO DO WHEN TALK IS JUST TALK

Women have been known to contemplate and even commit outrageous acts when conversation fails. The most dramatic example we know of happened at the University of Pennsylvania in the early 1980s. Once a week, with great regularity, the campus was secretly decorated with photographs of prominent male faculty, whose pictures were captioned WANTED FOR CRIMES AGAINST WOMEN and signed by The Women's Army. Along with others, we presumed this to be the work of a small group of undergraduate women who, distressed that conversations with the provost, university government, and individual faculty failed to draw sufficient attention to problems of sexual harassment, resorted to extraordinary methods for naming the problem.

University officials and many faculty were alarmed that The Women's Army was irresponsibly accusing men. Which it was. Yet we also read these actions as evidence of the women's despair over adamant institutional refusal to listen and act. At the time Penn had an elaborate set of mechanisms for voicing student dissent, but "listening" was revealed as a way to appropriate such dissent, that is, appease "angry young women." We have heard that at some other institutions, young women on campus welcome parents on Parents Day with the gruesome statistics of the likelihood that their daughter will be harassed and/or raped during her four years at college.

We are not recommending these strategies. They are not attempts to alter the conditions of women's lives. They are the voices of despair that institutional indifference provokes. People have been known, however, to throw caution to the wind when institutions refuse to talk, or when they intentionally set out to confound by offering talk in lieu of policy. Women are particularly vulnerable once engaged in conversation, since the willingness to talk is considered the most important evidence of growing trust and cooperation. And most of us, needless to say, find it excruciatingly difficult to break frame and go public, even when it becomes evident that the official conversation is fruitless.

While The Women's Army and their sisters elsewhere do not provide models of political projects aimed toward transformation, the outrageous is nonetheless of untold pedagogical value. Worst-case scenarios stretch the sense of possibility even as they terrorize the imagination. Images of the irrational strategies we may want to avoid help us to imagine how to insist that institutions take seriously their conversations with women.

FEMINIST ARCHIVES FOR INTELLECTUAL ACTIVISM

This analysis suggests the need for an archive of feminist intellectual activism to chronicle the varied ways of identifying, analyzing, interrupting, and, under exceptionally perverse circumstances, disrupting gender-based power asymmetries in the academy. Feminist activism must reposition itself inside a larger politics of solidarity with "other self-conscious political projects" (Harding 1988, 163), which at the very least would also include struggles around race/ethnicity, class, disability, and sexual orientation. Such an archive could already be stocked with: reports of the re-emergence of women's consciousness raising groups on campus; core curricula which mainstream feminist, African-Americanist, and Third World scholarship (and organized efforts to marginalize or eliminate them); charters for establishing women's centers; arguments for developing gay men's and lesbian women's studies programs; policies of professional organizations that monitor the use of sexist language in presentations and publications (Conference on College Composition and Communication) or the presence of African-American studies and women's studies courses within accredited programs (American Psychological Association).

As impressive as we find this list, the narratives caution us that far more is needed. This new generation of women is equipped with a striking sense of entitlement and yet beset by fears that their female bodies are liabilities, their minds male, their professors likely to corrupt their intellectual relationships, and their legal rights hollow. We can't anticipate what they will contribute either to the archive or the struggle, but social history assures us that it will not be precisely what we added. After all, they inherited rather than advocated for the gains of the 1970s, yet they share the threat of stunning disappointments in the 1980s and 1990s.

Perhaps the lesson we most need to learn is that it is as important for students as it is for teachers to become researchers —students as well as teachers are intellectuals and need to see themselves as informed political agents. We have learned that teachers and students need to collaborate critically across generations, histories, life circumstances, and politics to create curricula and pedagogies that seek to transform institutions not by reproducing or resisting the practices of oppression, but by confronting the institution on intellectual grounds. Only thus can we imagine a context in which every woman's story could realize its full liberatory potential, and no woman would decline to tell her story because "Any information would be incriminating" (File 2174 C31).

MARIAMNE H. WHATLEY

Chapter Four

Raging Hormones and Powerful Cars: The Construction of Men's Sexuality in School Sex Education and Popular Adolescent Films

INTRODUCTION: WHY IS A FEMINIST STUDYING MEN?

As a feminist educator who has been teaching women's health and biology, as well as education courses on health and sexuality, my work has primarily focused on the construction and presentation of women's sexuality in the health care system, in formal education, and in popular culture. Along with others who teach women's studies, I have frequently been asked, "What about men's studies?" While this can be dismissed with the obvious answer that the entire university teaches men's studies, an examination of the interests underlying this question is important. The question may arise from an antifeminist "men's liberation" perspective which views women's power, particularly sexual power, as oppressive to men, while ignoring ways in which men benefit from gender-based inequalities. Other men have developed an alternative antisexist perspective which, while recognizing that current gender structures can be oppressive to men as well as women, identifies the ways all men collude in and benefit from these arrangements. Thus, depending on the perspective, men's studies can serve to attack or support and complement women's studies. Oppressed groups have always studied the oppressor in order to survive. People of color, for example, are in a sense experts on white behavior while women have long examined men's attitudes, foibles, behaviors. Given the two manifestations of a "men's movement"—antiwoman or antisexist—my decision to bring a feminist perspective to issues of masculinity serves two purposes: know the enemy (as people of color may study white supremacist groups), and to return support to those who identify as allies.

Feminist studies of men's sexuality are particularly important because not only does men's sexuality impinge so directly on women's lives, but also women have been expected to take responsibility for men's sexuality. Sexuality education, both inside and outside schools, reinforces the notion of women's responsibility for male sexuality. Young children are being taught in sexual abuse prevention programs that they can and should identify potential abuse, say "no" forcefully enough to stop it, and then report it to an adult who will believe them. A five-year-old, boy or girl, is expected to be able to control the sexual behavior of the abuser, who is usually an adult man (Whatley and Trudell, in press). At adolescence, as men begin to assume their socially-constructed adult power, they move from the position of victim to that of potential aggressor. The discourse around women's sexuality, at the same time, continues to focus on potential victimization by men's sexuality (Fine 1988). Adolescent women are encouraged to "solve" the "problem" of teenage pregnancy by just saying "no" to presumably unwanted intercourse. A major market for condoms (for example, see the "Would you buy a condom for this man?" advertisement for Today Condoms) is women, who, it is assumed, will extend their traditional responsibility for contraception into prevention of sexually transmitted diseases. A biological rationale for women's responsibility is often given in either case—not only are women the ones who get pregnant, but HIV, the AIDS virus, is more easily transmitted from men to women during intercourse then vice versa. However, nothing inherent in biology justifies the dominant cultural norms that make women responsible for men's sexuality.

Even though it has become less acceptable to place the blame for rape on a woman—what she wore, how she walked, where she was, her previous sexual experience—sexual assault prevention efforts are still primarily aimed at women, who are now expected to screen out potential rapists among dating partners and to learn some form of self-defense. There has even been some backlash against the antiviolence movement. Recently, a "male liberation" proponent received extensive publicity for his "dating contract," a signed agreement between a woman and her date (Braun 1988). Under this agreement, if a man pays for a date, the woman must consent to any sexual contact he demands; therefore, there would no longer be date rape. In addition, if she pays for the date and initiates any "sexual interest," she cannot deny her partner "intimate" enjoyment. Given this trend, it is critical that attention be focused on men's sexuality with the ultimate goals of making men responsible for their own sexuality and defining women's sexuality independently of masculinist constructions. A feminist analysis of the construction of men's sexuality and how it serves to define women's sexuality is a necessary step in the process of altering power dynamics around gender and sexuality.

OVERVIEW

The first section of this paper draws on previous work (Whatley 1985, 1987) to discuss issues of men's sexuality and biological determinism in the context of school sexuality education curricular materials, while presenting an overview of some basic issues in sexuality education. In the second section, I extend the analysis to units on human reproduction in secondary biology texts, because biology classes often provide the only formal sexuality education in a school. These two sections serve to define official school knowledge about men's sexuality and critique it from a feminist perspective. In the third part of the paper, in order to provide an alternative form of knowledge about adolescent sexuality, I examine some of the progressive books on human sexuality, development, and reproduction, which are more likely to be used outside a school setting. The fourth section of the paper is an analysis of the presentation of men's sexuality in six films, popular with adolescents, which are produced, directed, and/or written by John Hughes. These films provide evidence of student knowledge about sexuality against which to compare official school knowledge.

Understanding the knowledge of students as it is both presented and constructed in popular culture can be seen as crucial
in understanding the knowledge with which students enter formal sexuality education. As Henry Giroux and Roger Simon
(1988) argue:

> Educators who refuse to acknowledge popular culture as a
> significant basis of knowledge often devalue students by
> refusing to work with the knowledge that students actually
> have and in doing so eliminate the possibility of developing a
> pedagogy that links school knowledge to the differing subject
> relations that help to constitute their everyday lives.

In an attempt to forge these links, I have analyzed Hughes's
films in relation to official school knowledge about men's sexuality. Examining the construction of men's sexuality in both formal
and informal sources of adolescent knowledge reveals the overlap-
ping and contradictory discourses that adolescents negotiate in
defining and redefining men's sexuality.

SEXUALITY EDUCATION AND BIOLOGICAL DETERMINISM

The presentation of sexuality education in the schools is
often constrained both by the fear of controversy and school organizational factors (Trudell 1988). Teachers and texts may minimize
both constraints by reducing topics to the facts of reproduction;
for example, the most frequently taught topics in school sex
education programs are anatomy and physiology, pregnancy and
childbirth, sexually transmitted diseases, and teenage pregnancy
(Kenney and Orr 1984). Discussions of masturbation, sexual
pleasure and desire, and homosexuality, are almost completely
absent. Secondary sexuality eduction, often hidden under titles in
which the sexuality is deliberately left out, such as "Family Life
Education" or "Human Growth and Development," may appear as
part of a health eduction course (which may be linked to physical
education) or as subunit in a biology course. Sexuality and reproduction then form a small unit among many others, safely identified as part of biological science or health science, with the
assumed neutrality of science deflecting potential criticism.

Sexology, the research area from which sexuality education
information is derived, has struggled to earn credibility as a scientific field. William Masters and Virginia Johnson, who are consid-

ered largely responsible for developing sexology as a laboratory science, wore laboratory coats in their early speaking engagements to create the impression of scientific expertise. There have been numerous contemporary critiques of scientific "objectivity" and "neutrality" which examine ways in which scientific research is politically and socially constructed and can be used as a political tool to reinforce the status quo in terms of social inequalities (see Bleier 1984 and Gould 1981). However, this critique has had little impact on sex education or sexology (Pollis 1988). The texts and curricula in the area of sexuality education are often written by "scientific" sexologists, whose scientific view of sexuality is then carried over into school sexuality education. While giving complete accurate biological information is necessary, this approach eliminates many areas of student interest and also reinforces biological determinist notions about sex roles, sex drive, and the role of hormones (Whatley 1987).

Biological determinism is firmly embedded and unchallenged in texts used in college level sexuality classes and in teacher education courses about human sexuality, as well as in sexuality education curricular materials (Myerson 1986; Whatley 1985, 1987). Even though sex educators often distrust biological determinism and may have specifically questioned this view, they may be uncomfortable critiquing what appear to be strong scientific findings. As a result, they often teach about "sex" roles and male-female differences in sexual behavior as if there are strong genetic and hormonal determinants (Whatley 1987).

Information about sex hormones is particularly pervasive and misused. These hormones, androgens and estrogens, are generally referred to respectively as male and female hormones, a very inappropriate and inaccurate terminology since both androgens and estrogens appear in and play critical roles in normal development in both males and females. The imprecise terminology easily leads to the belief in hormonal causes for what are identified as inherent male and female differences. Though the arguments supporting socialization factors as explanations for apparent gender differences are even stronger, the belief in science and the desire for the most parsimonious explanation seem to create an easy acceptance of biologically determined sex differences in behavior. Reading the sexuality literature, one can find claims that the levels of these sex hormones affect such areas as: gender identity and sexual preference; levels of aggression, activity, and sex drive; interests in careers of parenting; tomboy behavior; gender-related roles and activities; and cognitive differences between males and females, particularly in math and visual-spatial skills. Sex education curricula and texts perpetuate this misinterpretation of the role of hormones and thereby reinforce the concept of limited and limiting sex roles (Whatley 1985).

The Hormonally-Driven Man

One of the consistent messages carried in the biological determinist misinterpretations of hormonal roles is that men, due to high levels of androgens, have a stronger sex drive. Androgens do play an important role in the biological component of libido, but their effect is dependent on a threshold level and is not dose-dependent (that is, increasing levels of androgen above a minimal level do not cause increase in sex drive). Women, who generally have lower levels of androgens than men do, actually have higher levels than minimally required for a healthy libido. Unfortunately, in sexuality education, the subtleties and complexities of the biological component of libido are ignored, as are the psychological, social and cultural components. Instead, the recurring theme in texts and curricular materials is that there is a powerful, innate, hormonally determined sex drive in men, with very little indication that there might be some equivalent in women. The message is that women, having little trouble overcoming their weak libidos, are responsible for saying no to men, who ideally should learn proper control but are often too strongly hormonally driven to be able to stop on their own. The responsibility for men's sexuality clearly falls on the woman, as she must be careful never to lead him on, to always resist his advances, and, if unsuccessful, to ensure that contraception is used. Many teenage men and women readily support this view of women's responsibility for men's sexual behavior: if he is sexually aggressive, it is her fault for dressing, walking, speaking, or acting in a way that triggered his uncontrollable drive (Fingler 1981). The author of the "dating contract" discussed earlier also suggests that an uncontrollable hormonal drive to have sex should be used as a defense in rape cases.

As the previous example implies, beliefs about the role of androgens in men's sexual behavior carry over into legal and medical policy. The simplification of the role of androgens in sex drive provides a biological explanation for rape, while ignoring the whole social and cultural context of rape, including all issues of power and dominance; the conclusion is that some men have such high levels of androgens that their sex drive cannot be controlled by any cultural, social, or legal restraints. In extreme cases, a biological treatment is suggested for what has been defined as a biological problem; Depo-Provera, an anti-androgen, is used to treat rapists and other sex offenders. The result is rapists without erections; the behavior may be stopped but not the underlying causes. However, some judges have offered Depo-Provera as alternative to incarceration for sex offenders.

School sexuality education leaves out any discussions of women's desire, sexual pleasure, and positive aspects of sexual exploration (Fine 1988). When this absence is combined with the view of men as under the control of their raging hormones a double standard is created which interferes with the possibility of students making thoughtful, responsible decisions about sexual behavior. When sexuality is presented in terms of "neutral" scientific knowledge, issues of power are obscured. In her study of sexuality textbooks, Marilyn Myerson (1986) found that what appears to be an interactionist approach—that is, acknowledging the complex interactions among biological, psychological, and cultural influences—is quickly reduced to essentialism, or biological determinism, by the assumption of the naturalness of certain aspects of sexuality. By making the man-woman double standard of sexual behavior seem biologically inevitable and natural, any need to challenge power issues in existing gender relations is eliminated, and the status quo is reinforced with so-called scientific knowledge.

Biology Texts and Men's Sexuality

Misinterpretations of biological information (always in a way that supports determinist views) are found throughout many of the texts used in sexuality courses taken by teachers-in-training; they are also found in sexuality curricula and resources teachers use in class preparation (Whatley 1985). Because the only formal sexuality education in some schools may be in biology classes, not in specific health or sexuality classes, high school biology texts are another potential source of sexuality knowledge. Sexuality education is often relegated to biology courses as a way of avoiding controversy and these courses may be more explicit about sexuality, particularly those aspects related to reproduction, because the aura of scientific neutrality shields them from attack. I examined the sections on human reproduction in five current secondary biology texts (G. Alexander 1987; P. Alexander 1987; Oram 1986; Schraer 1987; Wright, et al 1988), focusing particularly on male physiology and anatomy. Contrary to what I expected to find in a scientific text, there was little explicitness, and, in fact, a vagueness that could easily confuse students not already clear on the reproductive process. For example, the process of semen production was generally spelled out clearly but the process by which semen may enter the female reproductive tract was sometimes vague:

> The urethra runs through an organ called the penis. Sperm is transferred to a female's body through the penis (Wright, et al 1988, 388).
> The sperm ducts allow the sperm to pass from the testes to the outside of the male body through the penis (G. Alexander 1987, 329).
> The penis is the male organ through which semen passes to the outside of the body (P. Alexander 1987, 492)
> The vagina is the place where sperm enter into the body of the female (P. Alexander 1987, 492).

In the last example, how sperm move from outside the male body to the female vagina is not clarified. Only one of the texts uses the word ejaculation, explaining that "In human mating, or sexual intercourse, hundreds of millions of sperm are ejaculated into the vagina" (Schraer 1987, 379), while the remaining text explains human "mating" in a similar way, referring to sperm as being "ejected" (Oram 1986). There is, of course, no reference to semen being released from the penis during any activity other than mating. For example, adolescents may be very concerned about what happens to the sperm during heavy petting.

If students are confused at all about the process by which semen is transferred to the female, the illustrations will be of little help. Current secondary biology texts are lavishly illustrated, both with photographs and drawings; photographs of human genitals would not be expected in a book suitable for use in schools, but clear scientific diagrams would not seem inappropriately explicit. In the diagrams of the male genitalia and reproductive organs, three of the texts fail to include the scrotum and penis. These three show a front view, with urethra and testes labeled, but neither the urethra nor the testes are enclosed in any anatomical structures. Since most adolescents are aware of the location of the penis and scrotum but may be unsure of the relationship of the urethra and testes to these structures, such illustrations are both useless and unnecessarily coy. One of these three texts also contains a front silhouette of a male body, with brain, pituitary, and testes labeled. Unfortunately, since the scrotum and penis seem taboo, the testes appear to be located in the abdomen. Two texts, however, do show side views with scrotum, penis, and testes labeled. Identifying the penis and scrotum in a line drawing would certainly cause no problems for boys, who are well aware of these organs, and would probably clarify the relationship of other structures. The purpose then must be to keep adolescent girls mystified about male bodies, a purpose that seems out of keeping with either the presentation of scientific information or with the stated goal of many sexuality education programs of "informed decision making." The "correct" decision implied in many of these is, of course, sexual activity only in the context of monogamous heterosexual marriage, but even with that goal it would be useful for a woman to know more about men's bodies.

Alternative Resources on Sexuality for Adolescents

There are several excellent alternative resources for adolescents about human development, sexuality and reproduction which are explicit and clear. *Changing Bodies Changing Lives* (Bell, et al 1980) was written on the model of the women's health movement classic, *Our Bodies, Ourselves* (Boston Women's Health Book Collective 1971), with actual adolescent voices a key part of the text. Both books are written in a way that demystifies and makes accessible scientific and medical knowledge, while validating the experience and knowledge we have of our own bodies and health. Two other books I examined, *The Teenage Body Book* (McCoy and Wibbelsman 1978) and *The What's Happening to My Body? Book for Boys* (Madaras 1984) attempt to present information in an accessible way, particularly focusing on common questions boys have about sexuality and other issues of development. Both of these use a question and answer format as part of the text, similar to the question boxes some school sex educators use to ensure they are dealing with the real concerns of students. Though all three books deal with women's issues, I will focus solely on those sections about men.

The theme of all these books could be summarized as working to convey the message that "you are normal." For example, there is a strong emphasis on dispelling myths about penis size and allaying fears about the normality of spontaneous erections and nocturnal emissions. Explanations are given for penile discharges and genital pain, including clear discussions of such "problems" as retrograde ejaculation and "blue balls." Masturbation is presented as healthy and normal. There are numerous drawings of the genitals, side and front view, in different stages of development, erect and flaccid, circumcised and uncircumcised. It is often incorrectly assumed that men know a lot more than women about their own genitals, due to their greater visibility, and have fewer issues around normalcy (since, for example, penises are easily compared in a locker room setting). For that reason, among others, there has not really been an equivalent to the women's health movement in terms of educating men about their own bodies and health (Allen and Whatley 1986). These books then can form part of an important educational movement for young men.

Unfortunately, the strengths of these books also make them less accessible to teenagers. The explicitness, the willingness to deal with real concerns of adolescents, and their discussion of sensitive and controversial topics such as homosexuality, make them prime candidates for banning from the schools. They are certainly highly unlikely to be used as required texts. For the same reason that *Our Bodies, Ourselves* is one of the most frequently banned books in the United States, these books may also be missing from school libraries. Ironically, the value of these texts in sexuality education is limited by the lack of access students have to them.

ADOLESCENT MEN'S SEXUALITY IN THE FILMS OF JOHN HUGHES

Formal sexuality education in the schools provides only a small percentage of the sexuality knowledge students acquire. An examination of films popular with adolescents may provide some clues to the perceptions and views of men's sexuality circulating among adolescents in a particular social and historical context. My analysis is based on the premise that these films shape discourses, that is: "All representations are coded: they do not merely reflect a world outside the bounds of the text, but mediate external discourses, as it were rewriting and reconstructing them" (Kuhn 1985, 48).

The popularity of the films selected may be seen as an indication of the pleasure adolescents feel in seeing Hollywood films that present a view of their world that meshes with their own version. This pleasure, in turn, allows these films to be potentially powerful shapers of their perceptions and social practices. By examining the construction of men's sexuality in films popular with adolescents, I hope to identify some of the prevalent discourses and relate these to school versions of sexuality, as discussed previously in this paper.

Ann DeVaney (1987) analyzed five of the popular Hollywood films of John Hughes, who served as writer, director, and/or producer. She categorized these films as box office successes: they enjoyed long runs in movie theaters, and now are popular in video stores—especially among teenagers, who reportedly rent some of these films for two or three viewings each. Film critics attributed their popularity to the authenticity of the dialogue. This was validated in DeVaney's interviews with adolescents, but she found their ability to identify with or ridicule certain characters even more important to their popularity. Her work suggests that adolescents find specific characters in these films with whom they can identify strongly, an identification that is important for the viewer's pleasure. Positive identification can be shifting and mobile depending on narrative development (Neale 1983). For example, while a young man may laugh at a "nerdy" character at first, he may begin to strongly identify with him as the character gains power and revenge. Both film critics and adolescents have reported that adolescents not only view these films as true to life, but also encourage sympathetic adults to see them in order to understand this adolescent view of the world.

While these films depict adolescent behaviors and attitudes as envisioned by John Hughes, their popularity with and validation by teenagers imply that they offer certain adolescents opportunities for identification that they find meaningful and authentic. Ann Devaney (1987) analyzed five films for their representation of different groups (parents, teachers, jocks, etc.), particularly their depiction of women. I will use these five films, since she has established their popularity with teenagers, and add one other (released after her article) to examine their presentation of male sexuality. In order of release, from 1984–1987, these are *Sixteen Candles* (SC), *The Breakfast Club* (TBC,) *Weird Science* (WS), *Pretty in Pink* (PIP), *Ferris Bueller's Day Off* (FBDO) and *Some Kind of Wonderful* (SKOW).

It is important to note that these films all portray midwestern high schools, with populations that are overwhelmingly white (several exceptions are discussed later in this paper). If identification depends to any extent on sharing certain characteristics with screen characters, then the assumption is that white audiences would be more attracted to these. In terms of class, rich students are often portrayed negatively, but they can be redeemed, as are the two rich boys in SC and PIP. Several other central characters are wealthy, such as Wyatt in WS and Cameron in FBDO. Though all the films categorize students by class, there are only two that have class conflict as a central plot device, with only one clearly labeled working-class male central character, Keith, in SKOW. Outsider Keith wins support from a wide range of wrong side-of-town classmates when the girlfriend of a richie consents to a date with him. The men's characters in these films are categorized as athletes (jocks), brains (geeks), criminals (burners), richies (either villainous or redeemable), and heroes who can defy and cross categories. These categories are so well-developed in the Hughes films, that viewers need only small cues to locate a character in a category (DeVaney 1987).

While there has been much attention by feminist film theorists to the representation of woman in the cinema, little attention has been paid until recently to the cultural construction of man. After all, man is the norm against which woman is measured. In his article on masculinity in mainstream cinema, Steve Neale (1983) addresses this issue:

> There is an important sense in which the images and functions of heterosexual masculinity within mainstream cinema has been left undiscussed. Heterosexual masculinity has been identified as a structuring norm in relation to both images of women and gay men. It has to that extent been profoundly problematized, rendered visible. But is has rarely been discussed and analyzed as such (2).

While there have been increasing numbers of studies of masculinity in film, the issue of representations of men's sexuality in films aimed specifically at an adolescent market has not been explored.

Man and Virginity: Not surprisingly, loss of virginity is a common theme in dialogue and plot in these films. Virginity is viewed as an abnormality for normal, healthy males. It is assumed that the male central characters who are not nerds will be sexually experienced, though not promiscuous. In three films (SC, TBC,

WS), a young man's virginity is central to the plot. Incidentally, the virgin "brain" is played by same actor, Anthony Michael Hall in all three; his skinny gawkiness seems to represent both sexual inexperience and genius. In TBC, his character confesses reluctantly to being a "cherry," first having lied about his experience to the bullying "criminal." In SC, the freshman Geek (the name used in the credits) is trying to lose his virginity. After failing to seduce the heroine, he convinces her to give him her underpants so that he can win a bet with his friends. Later, when they are both drunk he does have intercourse with an older and highly desirable prom queen; however, he does not remember, asking her first if he enjoyed it and then if she did. In the fantasy WS, the central male characters are two virgin brains, who manage to create a beautiful living woman using their home computer. (This film presents a literal depiction of the masculinist construction of women's bodies, as the two feed cut-up pieces of *Playboy* centerfolds directly into their computer). While they do not have intercourse with their fantasy-made-flesh, her support and guidance help them link up with partners their own age from school. In contrast, in all these films, except SKOW, sexual experience is a given for the male romantic lead. Keith, the working class hero in SKOW, gets lessons in kissing from his best friend, who is a girl he grew up with, so it is assumed he is relatively inexperienced. The plot revolves not around whether he will gain this sexual experience but whether he will make the right choice in women.

While there are mixed messages in these films about women's virginity, it is clear that the only men who remain virgins are nerds and even they can be transformed into real men by sexual experience. In TBC, there is a discussion about the double messages girls receive: you're a slut if you do and frigid or a tease if you don't. However, there is no ambivalence at all about the importance of sexual experience for men.

Men's Sex Drive: The double standard of sexual behavior and sexual responsibility is partially a reflection of the view of men as hormonally driven, needing to release their powerful sex drive, a view that is in evidence in sexuality texts. Ways of expressing this drive besides intercourse are not acceptable. In WS, Lisa, the creation of the two main characters, speaks disparagingly of one of them having as his only sexual outlet "tossing off to magazines in the bathroom." There are several direct references to this view of the controlling sex drive. In SKOW, Watts, the main woman character says sarcastically to Keith, "It must be a drag to be a slave to the male sex drive." The virgin Geek in SC explains to the far more experienced hero that girls "know that guys are in perpetual heat. They know that shit and they enjoy pumping us up. It's pure power politics."

It is significant not just that men are viewed as in perpetual heat but that women know how to use this information. In TBC the criminal male character explains that a woman is "only a tease if what she does gets you hot." This belief about the manipulation of the biological weakness of men by women is a key argument in the antifeminist men's liberation arguments, the arguments that gave rise to the dating contract cited previously. In addition, it serves as justification for sexual assault, particularly date rape.

Penises—Metaphorical and Literal: Even though drawings and descriptions of the function of the penis are not well represented in biology texts, the presence of the penis is very evident in popular cultural representations of men's sexuality. In his book on men's sexuality, Bernie Zilbergeld (1978) discusses extensively the "fantasy model of sex," specifically how it is developed in popular culture and some sexuality education. The fantasy about the penis can be summed up in the title of his chapter, "It's Two Feet Long, Hard as Steel and Can Go All Night." Popular novels contain descriptions of these "fantasyland penises," which Zilbergeld points out, are not only larger than life:

> They also behave peculiarly. They are forever "pulsating," "throbbing," and leaping about. The mere sight or touch of woman is sufficient to set the penis jumping, and whenever a man's fly is unzipped, his penis leaps out (Zilbergeld 1978, 24).

One of the books about puberty, sexuality, and reproduction for boys, identified as "A Growing Up Guide for Parents and Sons," discusses the similar, though less explicit images from the Nick Carter novels popular with adolescent males at the time the book was written:

> It's always the hero's 'manhood' his 'organ,' his 'hardness' or his throbbing pulsating 'member' that so delights the ladies...never anything so clinical, explicit, or mundane as a 'penis' (Madaras 1984, 5).

These penises clearly are from the same fantasyland Zilbergeld described.

The progressive books for teenagers about sexual and reproductive issues include important sections which are designed to
allay fears about penis size and to present information about cir-
cumcision, wet dreams, erections, and problems such as retrograde
ejaculation (Bell 1980; Madaras 1984; McCoy and Wibbelsman
1978). The embarrassing problem of spontaneous erections in inappropriate situations is the focus of much of the more progressive
and sensitive educational materials for adolescent men. For
example, the popular puberty education film *Am I Normal?*
involves the attempt of a young teenage man to find out the truth
about hard-ons and wet dreams.

It might be guessed that penises would appear, not visually
but in references in the dialogues, in films such as Hughes's that
focus so much on adolescent sexuality. I only recall, however, two
references to erections: one a disparaging comment about "getting
a hard-on for trash" and other when the heroine of SC tells the
Geek, "I felt how much you like me....I felt it on my leg." The
only reference to nocturnal emissions is in the criminal's sarcastic
comment to the brain that he is "a parent's wet dream" in TBC.
One direct reference to a penis occurs in TBC when the criminal
threatens to urinate on the floor and the jock warns, "Whip it out
and you're dead." Perhaps, as with men's sexual experience, the
assumption is that a normal man has a healthy and active penis.
References to penises are generally derogatory, usually as part of
insulting epithets, such as "dickhead," "dickweed," "dickface,"
"you fucking prick," "I don't feel like a total dick." There are
important distinctions in the use of these terms. A "prick" is a
real man clearly possessing a penis and power; his ethics may be
called into question but not his masculinity. The word prick is
used in the films to address a powerful unpleasant man, as when
the jock calls the criminal a "fucking prick." Terms such as dickhead are used to refer to nerds; if a dickhead does have a penis, it is
in the wrong place. The presence of the penis in nerds is called
into question in a number of ways. For example, the criminal in
TBC, having hidden marijuana from the assistant principal by
shoving it in the brain's underwear, tells the other students that
"the dope is in Johnson's underwear," perhaps implying it is the
sole occupant or that Johnson's penis is a dope. In SC, two nerdy
younger men walk out of the school bus wearing jockstraps on
their heads (a visual representation of dickhead, also suggesting
they have nothing else to fill their jockstraps). In WS, when
Wyatt's older, brother, a cigar-smoking, duck-hunting, abusive

parody of masculinity is disgusted by his younger brother wearing a woman's underpants rather than suggesting Wyatt remove the pants, he tells him to cover up, handing Wyatt the towel which is the older brother's only garment. The older, clearly masculine brother obviously feels that to display his genitals is much better than to reveal what is missing under the woman's underpants.

While all of the central characters are white, in two of the films in which there are men of color, they are linked to sexual issues, especially penises. In SC, there is a Chinese student whose name, Long Duc Dong, is the basis of a running joke through the film. "The Donger," as he calls himself, is attracted to a big woman athlete, who is clearly viewed by all the other characters, and presumably the audience, as an inappropriate sex object. The running joke can be seen simply as a low form of a bilingual pun. The humor might also be seen as residing in the incongruity of having the name Long Dong without the matching equipment or of having the equipment but not directing his urges in an appropriate direction.

Racial stereotypes around penises and sexuality are played out much more in WS. The night the two brains create the beautiful woman, the three go out to a black club to party. When Wyatt goes into the men's room, the three black men standing at the urinals turn around and stare at him, whereupon he hesitates and then goes into a stall. As a young, nerdy white virgin, it seems he cannot measure up, literally as well as figuratively, to the black men. This scene draws on prevalent myths about powerful black male sexuality, which are often accompanied by myths about penis size. When Wyatt does step into the stall, after a brief pause, he exclaims, "Well goddam." A possible reading is that Lisa, who has managed to conjure up a car and new clothes for all of them, has also conjured up an improvement on his penis.

Besides these derogatory uses of the slang words for penis, the examples of the "missing" penis and the racist jokes around penis size, there is little explicit reference in these films to penises. For example, the young men do not joke about, insult, or even mention penis size. Given the frequent use of sexual slang in these films, enough to require frequent bleeping when shown on television, I do not think this absence can be attributed to either censorship or discretion. Since these are films for adolescent viewing, the ratings system would prohibit any actual depiction of either a limp or erect penis. However, the possible references in metaphorical or literal language are missing. On interpretation is that Hughes recognizes that adolescent men, uncomfortable with the newly grown penis, still at the mercy of wet dreams and spontaneous erections with no apparent erotic stimulus, would prefer not to have their masculinity and their sexual identity rest on this rather unpredictable organ. The absence of the penis is particularly notable because my personal observation suggests that adolescent women have become more openly interested in male crotches; some have rooms or lockers decorated with male pin-ups in briefs, including advertisements for men's underwear which often involve disembodied crotch shots. While some teenage girls may be reveling in their new-found role and ability to reverse the gaze, the focus on the penis and erections, no matter how prevalent in some literature, does not seem to be a major concern in these films.

The Function of the Penis: While references directly to the penis are uncommon in these films, there are references to its sexual function. However, from the language used to describe intercourse, this function does not involve pleasure for either men or women. "Nailing," the most common term for intercourse used in these films, makes intercourse seem mechanical for the man and painful for the woman. The man doing the nailing is dehumanized but strong, while the woman is completely passive and objectified. The criminal in TBC uses the phrase "slipping her the hot beef injection," which is as mechanical and painful as nailing. Of course most popular slang for intercourse is mechanical and man-centered. It is interesting that there seems to be no reference in these films to any possible pleasure for men or women from intercourse. If the function of the penis is mechanical and not pleasurable, then the role of women in these constructions of men's sexuality must clearly be examined.

Women as Objects of Status and Exchange: Women who are nailed then metaphorically become trophies nailed to the wall. Since intercourse does not represent pleasure and virgin men have low status in the adolescent culture of these films, then nailing a woman is a way to acquire status among peers. The possession of desirable women enhances the position of a young man among the other men. In WS, for example, the two nerds move to a position of some apparent power when Lisa tells the bad guys that she belongs to Wyatt and Gary. In SC, it is not the actual sexual experience with a woman that the Geek is trying to attain, it is just the proof (a woman's underpants) that he can show to his friends. The view of woman as trophy is emphasized by the language the Geek uses to confess his virginity, "I've never bagged a babe. I'm not a stud." In SKOW, the hero goes from outcast to a man respected by his peers—even if they are from the wrong side of the tracks—when news of his big date gets around. In PIP, the rich hero is threatened by his best friend with loss of status if he insists on dating the wrong woman. Women then become one of the ways by which men learn to measure each other; the woman as a person never really exists.

In addition, women, like any other valuable object, can be traded or given away. Disgusted by his drunken girlfriend, Caroline, and interested in pursuing the heroine, Samantha, the hero of SC lets the Geek drive the unconscious Caroline home in exchange for Samantha's underpants. The Geek first drives the borrowed Rolls to his friends' house so they can obtain the photographic proof because otherwise on one would believe him. The two villains in WS try to bargain with Wyatt and Gary for the "rights" to Lisa. For adolescent men, there is a clear message that a woman's value is in how much she helps a man measure up in the eyes of other men; if her value declines, she can be discarded and new property acquired.

The Phallus, Cars, and Power: The phallus is the symbolic expression of men's sexuality and power. As Richard Dyer points out in an article on the male pin-up, "The phallus is not just an arbitrarily chosen symbol of male power; it is crucial that the penis provided the model for this symbol" (Dyer 1982, 71). Reading Dyer's article helped me understand the significance of the de-emphasis on the penis in these films:

> For the fact is that the penis isn't a patch on the phallus. The penis can never live up to the mystique implied by the phallus. The limp penis can never match up to the mystique that has kept it hidden from view for the last couple of centuries, and even the erect penis often looks awkward, stuck on to the man's body as if it is not a part of him (Dyer 1982, 71–72).

The phallus in these films—the sign of male power—is predominantly the car. The possession of a powerful expensive car, even by borrowing, stealing, or magical creation, both causes and represents the transition from adolescent powerlessness to adult men's sexual power. These films can be read as presenting and reflecting both a cynical and sophisticated view of men's sexuality.

Men's sexuality is about power, about possessing expensive sports cars, and the penis and its erections are insignificant in this equation. In SC, the Geek unsuccessfully attempts to seduce Samantha, the heroine, in an immobilized car in the school shop; however, he finally does lose his virginity with the prom queen, Caroline, in a Rolls Royce belonging to the hero's father (incidentally, the Geek is too young to have a driver's license). The hero, on whom Samantha has a crush, rescues her after her sister's disasterous wedding, carrying her off on their first date in his sportscar. In WS Lisa creates a Porsche and a Ferrari, complete with personalized license plates, for Wyatt and Gary to drive their dates home after the first night they have each slept (I am using this term because it is unclear what else they did) with a woman. In FBDO, the hero Ferris borrows without permission his friends father's prized Ferrari. It is the borrowing of the car, which is totally destroyed by the end, that precipitates the friend's first attempt to stand up to his father. In SKOW, the hero Keith is chauffered on his big date in a Mercedes, illegally borrowed from the garage where he works. This is a continuation of a phallic battle between Keith and the rich villain, who has earlier driven his expensive sports car into the garage where Keith works, deliberately insulting him and warning him off his property, as he labels his girlfriend.

Women also have cars in these films but these do not have much phallic power. The heroine of PIP drives a small, old, run down car, while the heroine of SKOW dries a similar one which does not start when Keith wants to borrow it to drive his crush home from school. In SC, there is an exchange between Samantha and her friend which can be read as saying a great deal about cars, men's sexuality, and racial stereotypes. Her friend has described Samantha's dream as a pink Trans Am and a great looking guy, to which Samantha replies, "No, black."

Friend: "A black guy?"

Sam: "No, a black Trans Am and pink guy."

Based on the close association between phallic cars and men's sexual achievement, this confusion is not surprising.

While cars are the dominant phallic images in these films, in WS, Lisa does employ another one to help the two boys in their transition to sexual adult men. Gary uses a large handgun provided by Lisa to drive of a motorcycle gang that has invaded his party; this bravery wins Gary and Wyatt the adoration of the two women in whom they have been interested. These two men were so clearly lacking in power that they needed even more than a Ferrari to save them.

Power, Penetration, and Homophobia: A variation on the relationship of phallic power to the penis is the ability of older men with power to destroy the sexual power of the adolescent man, which can be read in simplistic psychoanalytic terms as fear of castration by the father. This is stated very clearly in several films, as when one of the male brains in WS says, "My Dad's gonna castrate me." Cameron, the uptight friend of Ferris in FBDO, worries about their high school dean of students, "This man could squash my nuts into oblivion." A similarly threatening and powerful hostile man is the assistant principal in TBC who warns the criminal, "I'm gonna knock your dick in the dirt."

Beside the castration threat, there is a threat of sexual dominance by the latter two authority figures. In FBDO, the dean of students has been obsessively trying to catch Ferris illegally out of school and finally sees someone he mistakenly assumes is Ferris. Coming up behind the person, he says, "Your ass is mine," only to have the person turn out to be a young woman. The assistant principal in TBC also is obsessed with asserting his power over all of the students in detention but particularly Bender, the criminal. While he calls all of them, three men and two women, girls, he repeatedly threatens Bender. Having given Bender Saturday detentions for two months, he gleefully says, "You're mine, Bender. For two months I've got you." As he says this, he points two fingers, in an unintentionally obscene gesture, at his victim.

In his discussion of the gaze as castrating or penetrating, Dyer (1982) writes:

> It is clear that castration can only be a threat to men, and more probable that it is the taboo of male anal eroticism that causes masculine-defined men to construct penetration as frightening and the concept of male (hetero)sexuality as 'taking' a woman that constructs penetration as an act of violence (66).

The threat from these authority figures is both the threat of castration and of penetration; the fear for the young man is to be feminized, to be taken in the same way women get nailed. However, as an adolescent male said of Hughes' work, "These films are a good revenge" (DeVaney 1987, 24) and there is appropriate revenge. In his crazed attempts to catch Ferris in FBDO the dean of students ends up having to hitch a ride on the school bus. He is filthy and battered, with torn clothing, and, perhaps most important, with this trousers split open in back. The threat in "your ass is mine" has been turned back on him. In TBC, after the assistant principal has delivered one of his many threats to the students assembled in detention, he turns around to leave, revealing a disposable paper toilet seat cover hanging out of the waistband of his trousers.

In WS, the villains of the film are two rich, powerful and popular male students in the same school as Wyatt and Gary. They are constantly humiliating the two brains, for example, by pulling down their gym shorts as they stand gawking at the girls gym class. When the two bad guys show up at a party given by Lisa, Wyatt, and Gary, one attempts to act tough and sophisticated in ordering a drink from the black bartender. (The bartender, incidentally became a friend of the brains the night they visited the black club.) The bartender threatens to shove the "bottle straight up your ass." This draws on the same myths about black men's sexuality as did the urinal scene. If black men are seen as possessing superior sexual power (though not necessarily other forms of power) then the threat of penetration is even stronger. The bad guy is effectively put in his place. It is at this party that Gary later wields a gun to drive off the motorcycle gang, while his former tormentors are completely ineffectual or, I suppose, impotent.

While it is possible to argue a psychoanalytic interpretation of these issues, more significantly I see these as a reflection of the prevalent homophobia in this society, a clear theme throughout these films. For a man to be perceived as feminine is the same as being identified as gay and is an indication of lack of masculine power. Two of the strongest insults to men in these films are to be called "girl" or "faggot." Throughout the films, men and women insult men with the term faggot. In WS it is reported that a girl kicked Gary in the nuts and called him faggot. Later, when Gary, phallic gun in hand, orders the leader of the motorcycle gang to leave, he refers to the gang as "your faggot friends." He has successfully moved from the castrated, feminized weak man to this powerful position. In SC, the Geek tells his friends not to be "such faggots." The term faggot is not reserved for those seen as weak or nerdy but can be used to attack even the most masculine. For example, in TBC, there are a number of confrontations between the jock (who is a wrestler), and the criminal Bender, including exchanges of faggot insults. At on point, Bender says sarcastically that he has "deep admiration for guys who roll around on the floor with other guys," which changes the masculine sport of wrestling into a homoerotic encounter. When Brian, the brain, finds out the wrestler's uniform includes tights, the jock loses masculine status even in the eyes of this low-status virgin.

In contrast, the only remark about lesbians occurs when the central female character of SKOW is asked by a hood, "How long have you been a lesbian?" He says she has "too much up front to be a guy" so she must be a lesbian. She plays the drums, wears cut-off jeans to school, has short hair, but she is clearly heterosexual in her crush on Keith, with whom she does end up at the close of the film. Since there are no other references to lesbianism or use of slang terms such as "dyke" as insults, homophobia in these films is clearly much more focused on males. This is not surprising given the relative invisibility of lesbians, compared to gay men, in popular cultural images of homosexuality. In addition, there seems to be more adolescent concern about sexual preference among men than among women. For example, Sarrell and Sarrell (1981) interviewed over 4000 university students about issues of sexuality. In discussing resolution of conflict about sexual orientation, they point out that women rarely questioned their sexual orientation while men often did. The experiences that led men to worry about their sexual orientation included: adolescent same-sex sex play; delayed onset of sexual maturation and behaviors; more intense sexual response from self-stimulation as compared to intercourse; being a virgin at an age when he thinks everyone else has had intercourse; sexual inadequacy or dysfunction. Given the likelihood of adolescent men's experiencing some of the above, as well as other reported problematic experiences, such as erections in the locker room in the presence of other men, a man is likely to question at some time whether he is homosexual.

Certainly, in the Hughes films, the sexuality of the virgin men is questioned by other characters. However, there are no characters in these films who are actually identified as being gay. Rather than portraying gay students, homosexuality is raised only as an insult or as a fear of what a man might be if he does not prove his heterosexuality by loss of virginity with a woman. Even though some of the men characters may be called faggots, in the end they prove themselves to be real men, through sexual encounters with women. Unfortunately, this attitude is also reflected to some extent in sex eduction literature. Even in some of the more progressive materials, a major message is what Katherine Whitlock and Elena Dilapi (1983) call "The Homophobic Disclaimer," defined as: "The explicit or implicit message that while many young people may have homosexual thoughts, feelings, experiences, and so on, these probably are (or should be) only passing phases through which adolescents will move on their way to normative heterosexuality" (21). In the same article, these authors point out that many of the sexuality books for adolescents use a conversational "you" throughout except when discussing homosexuals who are a distant "they." While many of these books try to present homosexuality as an acceptable alternative for some people, the heterosexual assumption is so strong that any positive aspects of this message are undermined. As in these materials, gay people in the films are a very distant "they" and all the characters will safely pass through the phase of being an unproven heterosexual to a proven one.

IMPLICATIONS FOR SCHOOL PRACTICE

As a feminist educator, challenging sexist and antifeminist sexuality discourses circulating both in the schools and in popular culture is a focus of my work. At the same time these challenges can be supportive of antisexist men whose analysis involves a recognition of the ways they benefit from inequalities in gender relations. If the portrayal of men's sexuality in the adolescent films is an active shaping force of adolescent sexuality discourses, there are important implications for those educators who wish to challenge the status quo.

Perhaps the most significant and disturbing messages of these films are the equation of men's sexuality with power, particularly economic power, and the homophobic construction of "normal" men's sexuality. While we might expect that adolescents would view men's sexuality in terms of the body (the penis, erections), sexuality instead is seen to reside in the possession, even temporarily, of symbols of adult men's power, such as an expensive car, and in the possession of a woman. Lack of sexual power is represented by virginity, the feminized man, and the lack of a high-status car. Part of this message is that possession of a desirable woman enhances a man's status and power among other men. Seeing other men as those who judge and measure status and power prevents men from communicating openly and honestly with one another. This view also lends support to the homophobic construction of men's sexuality.

In spite of clear issues of power it is interesting that the only time the word power is used in these films is in reference to women's sexual teasing of men—"pure power politics." While men's power is represented, it is never named. This denial of the reality of men's power in this culture and the identification of women's sexuality as the site of oppressive power over men are central to the antifeminist "men's liberation" arguments. To challenge this view involves identifying and naming the social, economic and cultural power men have. The school sexuality curriculum does not deal at all with issues of power, as the presentation of neutral, objective knowledge obscures issues of power and gender, while lending scientific support to the status quo. Physiology and anatomy are presented as the explanation for contemporary gender relations. This approach makes the double standard of sexual behavior appear inevitable and constructs sexual assault as a biological issue, not an issue of power. Alternative sources are much more willing to be explicit and to deal with controversial topics, providing valuable information about the body and sexuality not usually found in the formal curriculum. However, these too often fail to grapple with issues of power and sexuality.

In helping students make the transition from childhood sexuality to adult sexuality, education should include the recognition of the existence of cultural and social dynamics of power, gender, and sexuality, combined with a value system of none-exploitation (Whatley and Trudell, in press). It is difficult to encourage nonexploitative behavior, however, if the cultural construction of men's sexuality as hormonally driven and linked to power is accepted as natural, and if that power remains unnamed as such.

These films can serve as stimulating starting points for challenging this naturalness and for identifying various sites of power. While many adolescents view these films with pleasure, they also may find analyzing them equally pleasurable. Challenging the presentation of gender roles, sexual behaviors and the categorization of students into narrow groups does not seem to ruin the films for the viewers (which feminists are often accused of doing). A discussion of the forms of power the adolescent men and women each seem to have in these films, as compared to the lived experience of the students, can be useful in deconstructing gender roles and sexual power. Comparing men's and women's interpretations of who has the power in dating relationships and how far that power carries over into other aspects of their lives can bring to light some interesting misunderstandings on both sides. For example, one classroom exercise involves having men and women, in separate small groups, list ranked characteristics of an ideal partner. A useful variation is to ask men to identify what they think women want in an ideal partner and vice versa. When I have tried this in college classes, men consistently rank money or a good job at the top of what women want in men. The women, however, do not usually even include any financial consideration in the top five characteristics they would actually like in men. (While this assignment does not specify the gender of the partner, heterosexism always results in the assumption that the partner of a man is a woman.) This masculinist misunderstanding of what women want is certainly in keeping with the message in the films that the expensive car makes the man. An exercise such as this combined with an analysis of a Hughes film can help identify ways in which these films, perceived as authentic by adolescents, may be presenting a very limited view. This may then allow students to identify alternate readings of those films.

Educators should be challenging the biological determinist and heterosexist models that predominate in school sexuality education, at the same time recognizing that to challenge these is to challenge dominant discourses circulating outside the schools. By critiquing with students both the scientific neutrality of sexuality information and the popular cultural constructions of sexuality, the naturalness of the status quo in gender relations can be challenged. Young men do not have to grow up feeling constantly measured by their peers, viewing women as objects of exchange, and having all sexual pleasure linked to power and domination. A goal for educators is to help liberate young men from the construction of their sexuality as controlled by raging hormones and expressed in powerful cars.

Chapter Five

Schooling the Postmodern Body:
Critical Pedagogy and the Politics of Enfleshment

—self-alienation has reached such a degree that
it can experience its own destruction as an
aesthetic pleasure of the first order.
>   Walter Benjamin, "The Work of Art
>   in the Age of Mechanical Reproduction"

CRACKS IN THE HISTORICAL MOMENT

While educators in the United States are witnessing a reactionary and ultimately fatuous rearguard defense of the alleged transcendent virtues of Western civilization, a neo-corporatist assault on the New Deal welfare state, and what Jim Merod calls the "guiltless counterrevolutionary violence of state power" (1987, 191), they are also experiencing a new vitality in the realm of educational theory. The cultural/moral hegemony of mainstream approaches to curriculum, pedagogy, and epistemology are being fissured—and in some cases torn asunder—by new deconstructive postmodern strategies.

Largely imported from literary theory and influenced by continental poststructuralism, postmodern strategies e.g., Derridean grammatology and Foucaultian discourse analysis, have systematically problematized, if not dismantled, the epistemological certainty and transcendent claims to truth that characterize dominant strands of modernist discourse.[1] Suffice it to say that there exists a "crisis of representation" and a steady and sometimes vehement erosion of confidence in prevailing conceptualizations of what constitutes knowledge and truth and their pedagogical means of attainment.

Keeping in mind the conceptual inflation of the term "post-modernity" and its unwieldy semantic overload—which has come to designate a vast array of artistic, architectural, and theoretical practices—I want to make clear that I am using it in a severely delimited sense. While postmodernism crisscrosses numerous regions of inquiry, I am using it to refer to the material and semiotic organization of society, primarily with respect to what Stanley Aronowitz (1983) calls *visual culture* and the homogenization of culture (1981). That is, I am referring to the current tendency toward desubstantialized meaning or "literalness of the visual" in which students seem unable to penetrate beyond the media-bloated surface of things, thereby dismissing concepts such as "society," "capitalism," and "history," which are not immediately present to the senses (Aronowitz 1983). According to Aronowitz, "In the last half of the twentieth century, the degree to which mass audience culture has colonized the social space available to the ordinary person for reading, discussion, and critical thought must be counted as the major event of social history in our time" (468).

Our media culture has become a "buffer zone," a "paradoxical site" at which youth lives out a difficult if not impossible relation to the future (Grossberg 1988, 148). The former structuring principles of identity—family, peers, institutional life—have now taken on a vertiginous flux.[2] Situated as we are in the twilight of modernity, it is becoming more obvious that old forms of production and consumption have given way to a new universe of communication which celebrates the look, the surfaces, the textures, and the uniformization and commodification of the self. Cornell West notes that "the commodification process has penetrated cultural practices which were previously relatively autonomous" (Stephanson 1988, 274).

Postmodernism has now been absorbed into advertising; the image—which no longer points to some extramundane transcendence or physical outsideness but simply refers back to itself—has now superseded reality with the latter dissolving into the artificial reality of the image. It is a world—a "teledemocracy"—"symptomatic of Reagan's America in its unquestioning materialism"

(Kaplan 1987, 30), a terrain which Hassan describes as populated by "simulations rather than representations, intolerable to both Rightists and Leftists because it renounces the fiction of concealed truth, because it undermines the exercise of power—how does one punish or reward simulations of crime or virtue?" (1987, 228). Dick Hebdige offers a similar description of postmodern culture as "a parodic inversion of historical materialism [in which] the model precedes and generates the real-seeming" (1986, 84).

History is only glancingly recognized, and then only as an artifact of the past, as the temporal narratives which structure our political unconscious are replaced by the tyranny of the sign (Lash & Urry 1987, 292). The seductive symbolic power of goods has caused signs rather than products to become the primary mode of late capitalist consumption (288).

Postmodern representation in the mass media has the effect of transporting meaning through the circulation of signs, the churning out of an apocalyptic hemorrhage of signifiers, thick with borrowed or rented meanings, all interchangeable, all bleeding into one another so profusely that any distinction between them is all but cancelled out. It is this fragmented and hazardous aspect of postmodern culture which provokes Hassan to proclaim: "The message no longer exists; only media impose themselves as pure circulation" (1987, 221).[3] The postmodern subject is reduced in this process to a semiotic orphan, clinging to the underbelly of consumer society. This is not far removed from Fredric Jameson's pronouncement on postmodernism as "an alarming and pathological symptom of a society that has become incapable of dealing with time and history" (1982, 117). Time has become so discontinuous and unfixed that present and future merge together as images on a screen. The pulsating beams from the TV screen become the shifting and perilous ground from which we anchor our judgments and decisions that forge our communal vision, a ground in which desire is infantilized, kept separate from meaning, and maintained in a state of narcissistic equilibrium.

By locating the subject within the surface meaning of the image and by making our subjectivities so malleable, postmodern culture contributes unwittingly to the demise and depoliticization of the historical subject—literally suctioning out its capacity for critical agency, then filling the battered husk with consumer desire.[4] The subject is unable to look to the past or the future to secure itself within a unified identity, but itself becomes a site of struggle in the arena of the present. As Lawrence Grossberg explains, "this 'post-humanistic' subject...is constantly remade, reshaped as a mobilely situated set of relations in a fluid context ...struggling to win some space for itself in its local situation" (1986a, 72).

The current postmodern condition has not only witnessed the fracturing of the sovereign subject—which is, after all, a mythical product of enlightenment rationality—but also its reconstitution as a decentered text. Francis Barker explains that the modern body, having been separated from its previous unmediated carnality through textual representation, has become supplementary to written communication. In effect, desire and meaning are becoming detached as the modern body becomes more "de-realized...confined, ignored, exscribed from discourse" (1984, 63). Within these recent developments, existence is reduced more and more to a form of "eventfulness" which, to borrow a phrase from Klaus R. Scherpe, reflects "the subject's becoming unable to feel pain, a state characterized by the absence of pain, in which the individual's capacity to resist gives up its last line of defense" (1986/87, 124). Even the body, in the torment of its death throes, is remorselessly aestheticized in various forms of discursive representation (witness the growing number of documentaries about people dying of various illnesses such as cancer and AIDS).

The real danger facing the politics of signification in the present historical conjuncture is a shrinkage of the body's powers "as signs come to surpass the body [escaping] its sensuous control, dissevering themselves from the material world and dominating that which they are meant to serve" (Eagleton 1988: 97–98). In the regulated ignorance of today's commodity logic, which is inexorably tied to the profit motive, the codes of both signification and commodity partake of a general equivalence; that is, as Baudrillard has shown us, an abstract equation has now been operationalized in which all meanings are made equal. While all meanings are not created equal, or are certainly not equal in their effects, they are now at least consumed as if they were equal. The free circulation of the commodity system anchors the postmodern world's new regime of terror. Our bodies are now regulated by a fascist economy of signs, precisely because they are now so fully detached from the body's service. The body in this process has become reduced to a sign of itself. The body has been abandoned for a better version of itself. The body is now just another idea for com-

modity logic to terrorize. In the postmodern world of easy repro-
ductability and limitless circulation of signs, we are served up life
as a continuous series of jump cuts to different representations
with the same meaning.

THE POLITICS OF POSTMODERNISM

The ethical dilemma that has occurred as a result of this
crisis has created an ideological vacuum ripe for the ascendency of
a neo-conservative regime of truth. It is a regime which evinces a
persistent tendency to instrumentalize knowledge, strip it of any
serious socially emancipatory claims, and evaluate it in terms of
its immediate payoff in the capitalist marketplace and its efficacy
in transmitting a privileged "white man's" reading of Western
culture (McLaren and Dantley, 1990). This ethical dilemma which
postmodernity has brought to the fore is aptly summarized in a
question put forward by Andrew Ross: *"In whose interests is it,
exactly, to declare the abandonment of universals?"* (1988, p. xiv,
italics original)[5]
Social theorists on the left cannot easily claim immunity
from their complicity in the rise of the new cultural, political, and
moral closure that is currently plaguing the United States. They
have unwittingly helped this process along, not by advancing a
crypto-positivism, but by turning postmodern social theory into a
totalizing language of its own. On this point, Lawrence Grossberg
is worth quoting:

> The description offered by the postmodernists must be
> located within the broader social and cultural fields of every-
> day life and the struggles of power, domination, subordina-
> tion, and resistance that take place within them. Moreover,
> postmodernism's tendency to totalize its own descriptions, to
> slide from a description of a determining structure to the
> identification of that level with the totality of our lived and
> historical realities, must be resisted. (1988, 147)

Social theorists writing about postmodernity have often
elided the contradictions which occur in the lived experiences of
people who inhabit different class fractions and who are positioned
asymmetrically in society in terms of race, class, and gender. In
fact, the hegemonizing potential of forms of postmodern theoriz-

ing has prompted Ihab Hassan to remark that "the terms of our social discourse, its silent, constitutive metaphors, may now require reinvention" (1987, 227). It is a sentiment that is also shared by Barbara Christian, who decries the new critical literary discourse for being "as hegemonic as the world which it attacks" (1987, 55). The totalizing discourse that prevails in late capitalism often becomes a precondition for an alienated subjectivity since such language devalues individual experience and difference as a means of constructing resistant modes of subjectivity (Schulte-Sasse, 1986/87).[6]

Except for a few dialectical gestures to the contrary, Left educational theorists for the most part have displaced politics from the struggle of dispossessed groups and their "walking nihilism" to a narrow radical engagement with the text. This engagement is too easily detached from what West calls the "reality *that one cannot not know*" (Stephanson 1988, 277), what he describes as the "ragged edges of the Real, of Necessity, not being able to eat, not having shelter, not having health care, all this is something that one cannot not know" (287).

Left social theorists have not been able to effectively chart out points of resistance, counter-discourses, counter-identifications, and counter-practices in existing lines of forces, what Teresa de Lauretis calls "the blind spots, or the space-off of...representations...spaces in the margins of hegemonic discourses, social spaces carved in the interstices of institutions and in the chinks and cracks of the power-knowledge apparati" (1987, 24). Nor have Left social theorists been able to effectively challenge the disintegrating subject which haunts the theories of Jean Baudrillard (1983) and his disciples and haigiographers[7] and which also terrorizes some versions of poststructuralist and anti-essentialist feminist theories.[8] We are faced on the Left with theories of bodies without organs, shadow bodies which are merely discursive fictions, or fractured bodies composed of solitary links along a signifying chain. Rarely do we discover body/subjects who bleed, who suffer, who feel pain, who possess the critical capacity to make political choices, and who have the moral courage to carry these choices out.

Under these conditions, the New Right has encountered little opposition in its flooding of the public arena with a host of seemingly unstoppable authoritarian discourses which have had little trouble colonizing the moral void left by the deconstructive dismantling of the Enlightenment project.[9]

THE POSTMODERN BODY: BODY/SUBJECTS IN LIMBO

In the space remaining I want to make a case *against* some aspects of the Baudrillardian mode of postmodern theorizing *and* a case for the body as a site of resistance to the prevailing cultural and moral hegemony and to tease out some implications this might have for a critical pedagogy.

The term "body" is a promiscuous term that ranges wildly from being understood as a warehouse of archaic instinctual drives, to a cauldron of seething libidinal impulses, to a phallocentric economy waging war on women, to a lump of perishable matter, to a fiction of discourse. In this essay I will refer to the body as a "body/subject," that is, as a terrain of the flesh in which meaning is inscribed, constructed, and reconstituted. In this view, the body is conceived as the interface of the individual and society, as a site of embodied or "enfleshed" subjectivity which also reflects the ideological sedimentations of the social structure inscribed into it. Furthermore the body, as a form of socially inscribed intentionality, does not so much constitute a text as it does various modes of intertextuality (what I will refer to later as "modes of subjectivity").

THE DEMONIZATION OF THE EMPIRICAL REFERENT

Here I must sound my further hesitation with respect to the Baudrillardian tendency to dissolve the subject almost entirely into media text and the tendency of other critics of modernity to render the empirical world into complex strands of discourse. Both these positions are complicitous in the devitalization and derealization of the body and its reductive cancellation; furthermore, they solemnly strip bodies of intentionality and volition and their capability of resisting the image systems which help shape their subjective awareness. It is a position which maligns the lived body as a material referent for the construction of oppositional subjective forms, material practices, and cultural formations—what I call "zones of emancipation." In effect, postmodern culture has taken the body into custody where it has become liquidated to the currency of signs. It is as if the flesh has been numbed in order to avoid the unspeakable terror of its own existence. As Alan Megill warns:

All too easy is the neglect or even the dismissal of a natural

and historical reality that ought not to be neglected or dismissed.... For if one adopts, in a cavalier and single-minded
fashion, the view that everything is discourse or text or
fiction, the *realia* are trivialized. Real people who really died
in the gas chambers at Auschwitz or Treblinka become so
much discourse. (1985, 345)

Here, too, we are faced with the postmodern "loss of affect"
which occurs when language attempts to "capture the ineffable"
experience of the Other (Yudice 1988, 225). There is also a danger
of textualizing gender, denying sexual specificity, or treating difference as merely a formal category rather than having an empirical
and historical existence, problems which Teresa de Lauretis (1987,
25) has discovered in the work of Deleuze, Foucault, Lyotard,
and Derrida.

The warnings sounded by Megill and De Lauretis bring into
important relief the fact that we cannot—and should not—escape
the empirical referent. As Charles Levin points out, the body is
inescapable and cannot be deferred or lost in a chain of reference,
or split into signifier and signified; we cannot adequately capture
the reality of the body in terms of difference, indeterminacy, or the
ideological constitution of the subject (Levin 1987, 108). Levin
writes that "the body *is* the symbol; and while the relationship
between what constitutes meaning and the functioning of the
body can be separated out and arranged in the discrete markers of
temporal sequence, its actuality is never exhausted by this or any
other variation of linguistic meaning" (108).

Terry Eagleton (1988, 97) makes a similar point that while
discourse functions to broaden and intensify the body, the body
can never be fully present in discourse. Eagleton adds:

It is part of the very nature of a sign to 'abset' its referent.
The symbol, as Jacques Lacan once remarked, is the death of
the thing. In language we deal with the world at the level of
signification, not with material objects themselves (1988, 97).

It is important to acknowledge further the relation between
linguistic meaning and "real" bodies, a relationship explicated by
Kaja Silverman (1988, 146):

Not only is the subject's relation to his or her body lived out
through the mediation of discourse, but that body is itself

coerced and molded by both representation and signification. Discursive bodies lean upon and mold real bodies in complex and manifold ways, of which gender is only one consequence. Even if we could manage to strip away the discursive veil that separates the subject from his or her 'actual' body, that body would itself bear the unmistakable stamp of culture. There is consequently no possibility of ever recovering an 'authentic' female body, either inside or outside language.

Silverman recognizes that the body is "zoned and inscribed" in ways which have important implications for subjectivity. The issue here of course, is to recognize and redress the discursive conditions under which women, minorities, and other groups are demonized by patriarchy and the social relations of capital so that their presence as racial, cultural, and gendered subjects are effectively struck out of the archives and current narratives of history.

Yet bodies are always already cultural artifacts even before they are molded discursively. Since we cannot put on new bodies before we desocialize our old ones, the task at hand requires us to provide the mediative ground for a refleshed corporality. This means the creation of *embodied knowledges that can help us refigure the lineaments of our desires and chart the path towards the realization of our collective needs outside and beyond the suffocating constraints of capital and patriarchy.* This knowledge cannot be objectively known in advance but rather only from a subject position or perspective which is always partial (Haraway 1988, 585). This means that we cannot act in and on the world *as* others if we want to see from these positions critically (Haraway 1988; Giroux 1988). *But we can articulate a vision and a praxis in order to liberate others, to help them relocate meanings and their bodies.*

Haraway is arguing for a politics and epistemology of location, positioning, and situating where rational knowledge claims are based on partiality and not universality, what Haraway (589) refers to as "the view from a body, always a complex, contradictory, structuring, and structured body, versus the view from above, from nowhere, from simplicity." It is important to recognize that she is referring here to doing critical work in "unhomogeneous gendered social space" (what better description of the classroom can we get?) and in order to decode the conflicting discourses operative in such a space—or to liberate such a space—we must follow Haraway (589) in seeking an approach that "is always interpretive, critical, and partial...a ground for conversation, rationality, and objectivity—which is power-sensitive, not pluralist "conversation." This is what Haraway (589) refers to as "the joining of partial views and halting voices into a collective subject position." What this implies for critical educators is a sensitivity to the agency of the subjects' (students') generative bodies. Students as body/subjects are not passive biological resources to be mapped and manipulated by the latest advance in behavioral technology or from a subject position of moral certainty that exercises an authoritive closure on the meaning-generating abilities of the students in the name of a transcendent patriarch or imperial discourse.

THE POLITICS OF ENFLESHMENT

Either as a focus of theorizing or as part of a pedagogical strategy, the body carries little epistemological weight. Psychologist Howard Gardner conceptualizes bodily knowledge "as a realm discrete from linguistic, logical, and other so-called higher forms of intellect" (1985, 13). Largely as a legacy of Western Cartesian thought, such bodily-kinesthetic intelligence has been perceived as "less privileged, less special, than those problem-solving routines carried out chiefly through the use of language, logic, or some other relatively abstract symbolic system" (208). Other cultures do not draw such a sharp distinction between the active and the reflective. In fact, J.L. Hanna writes that "of all possible media of communication the body is the least removed from our associations of personal experience" (1983, 7).

Brian Fay argues that learning is not simply a cognitive process but also a somatic one in which "oppression leaves its traces not just in people's minds, but in their muscles and skeletons as well" (1987, 146). That is, ideology is not realized solely through the discursive mediations of the sociocultural order but through the enfleshment of unequal relationships of power; it is manifested intercorporeally through the actualization of the flesh and embedded in incarnate experience. Fay describes it as "transmitting elements of a culture to its newest members by penetrating their bodies directly, without, as it were, passing through the medium of their minds" (148). This is similar to Jacques Attali's concept of "autosurveillance" which, in Fredric Jameson's terms (1987 xiii), "marks the penetration of information technology within the body and the psyche."

Taking seriously Fay's insight, it is important to recognize
the essentially non-discursive penetration of flesh through both
the physical positioning and cultural tattooing of the body (in
schools an example of the former would be the panoptic space of
the school and the latter its dress codes). Culture in this sense is
inscribed both on and in the body by the sartorial extension of the
flesh according to the market-enforced logic of the fashion industry (which is no small matter in a youth culture in which stressed
leather bomber jackets become *couture* style, conjuring a "sons of
Yale" (see Higgs, 160–75) era of patriotic reverie: "flyboys" in
sheepskin and silk scarves and bush pilot adventurers emancipat-
ing us from the pressurized yoke of 1980s yuppiedom) and by the
inscription into the musculature and skeletal system of certain
postures, gaits, or "styles of flesh." This is our bodily knowledge,
the memory our body has about how our muscles should move,
our arms should swing, and our legs should stride. It is a way of
being in our bodies.

Enfleshment (the dialectical relationship between the material organization of interiority and the cultural forms and modes of
material production we inhabit subjectively) occurs not just at the
level of the materiality of the flesh, but through both the corporeal
embodiment of symbols and metaphors into the flesh and the
"fleshing out" of ideas at the level of cultural forms and social
structures. That is, the body *both incorporates ideas and generates them.* This process is, of course, a dialectical one. It is important here to recognize that words and symbols are physiognomic
and just as much a part of our bodies as our flesh (McLaren 1986,
1988b, 1989a). What this means is that language is not a disembodied mode of communication but rather constitutes what Denys
Turner calls "an intensification of the bodily powers" (1983, 17) as
well as an extension of these powers. By being inserted into the
abstractive power of language, our bodies become intensified and
extended. Ideas, therefore, have a "social materiality" (Turner
1983, 182); they are enfleshed in ideologies and historical and cultural forms of subjectivity. Enfleshment can be conceived here as
the mutually constitutive aspect (enfolding) of social structure and
desire. Discourses do not sit on the surface of the flesh nor float
about in the formless ether of the mind but are enfolded into the
very structures of our desire inasmuch as desire itself is formed by
the anonymous historical rules of discourse. It is in this sense,
then, that the body/subject becomes *both the medium and the
outcome of subjective formation.* Enfleshment, as I have been

articulating it, refers not only to the insertion of the subject into a pre-existent or preconstituted symbolic order (what Silverman calls "discursive interiority," 1988, 149) but also an investment on the part of the subject of what Grossberg (1986b) calls "affect". Affective investment transpires during the subject's insertion into or engagement with various fields of discourse. To be enfleshed is not only to appropriate symbols but it is to be identified with the symbol that one is appropriating; that is, it is to identify oneself with that selfsame symbol and also to arrive at a correspondence between the subject position provided by discourse and the subject. It is, in other words, to mistake authorship of such a position with the anonymous historical rules which have constituted it; furthermore, it is to fail to see (to repress, to forget) the contradictions between the body/subject and the discursive position or multiple positions one has assumed. To unproblematically identify with the symbol which one has appropriated or the subject positions made available within any discursive field, is to be in a condition of enfleshment. Resistance as a form of enfleshment can still be accounted for, in this case, not by the randomness of the signifier or the surplus of meaning (polysemy) attached to any symbol but rather because of what Colin McCabe (1983, 214) refers to as "the body and the impossibility of its exhaustion in its representations...the specific positioning of the body in the economic, political and ideological practices."

What I have been describing as enfleshment is similar to the process which de Certeau (1984) refers to as "intextuation" or the transformation of bodies into signifiers of state power and law. Schools become sites of enfleshment in the sense that they serve as discursive arenas in which the norms of class- and gender-based social power are intextuated into the student body, reflecting the wider body politic of the society-at-large (cf. Fiske, 1989).

It should be remembered that power is not simply oppressive but works relationally and schooling promotes a combination of relations of power—a certain "promotion of practices and techniques" which Michel Feher terms "a political regime of the body" (1987,160). The body then becomes both the object of power—"the actualizer of power relations"—and resistance to power. The exertion of and resistance to power does not happen outside the body but operates as a tension within the body (161). The question of disciplining the body becomes an ethical one: "What do we take our bodies for"? "What are our bodies capable of perceiving and doing"? "In the name of what are bodily activities disciplined or styled"? "What are the assigned goals of these ethical practices of the self-styling of the body"? In these four questions raised by Feher (162–163) we can see the fusion of an ethical typology of the body and the political regime of the body. It is by acknowledging such a fusion of politics and ethics that the body as a site of enfleshment takes on pedagogical importance.

The problem with schools is not that they ignore bodies, their pleasures, and the suffering of the flesh (although admittedly this is part of the problem) but that they undervalue language and representation as constitutive factors in the shaping of the body/subject as the bearer of meaning, history, race, and gender. We do not simply exist as bodies, but we also *have* bodies. We have bodies not just because we are born *into* bodies but because we *learn* our bodies, that is, we are taught how to think about our bodies and how to experience our bodies. And in a similar fashion our bodies invent us through the discourses they embody. We are not just male bodies or female bodies, but Afro-American bodies, White bodies, Chicano bodies, Jewish bodies, Italian bodies, Mexican bodies, and so on.

Many of us who write within the critical tradition have attempted to address the importance of radically reproblematizing the subject from its sovereign monocentrism to a subject that is historical, raced, classed, and gendered (Giroux 1988; McLaren 1989a). It bears repeating here that the consequences of excluding the voices of women, of minorities, of gays and lesbians, and "othering" of "occulting" them both in the discursive field of our pedagogies or in the specificity of our pedagogical practices carry serious political and moral effects. As Giroux (1988) has made clear in his discussion of voice, not all discourses carry equal weight and legitimacy in the classroom and critical pedagogy is only liberating to the extent that it palpably takes into account the patriarchal, class, and race-based interests which inform all forms of pedagogy, including those which claim to be critical. I would add here that we must be careful not to textualize marginalized voices by placing a fixed limit on the scope or means of their representation; nor must we posit a false equation among the various expressions of pain or modes of resistance that speak to the specificity of the oppression of Afro-Americans, Hispanics, White women, Afro-American women, etc. We need to construct in our classrooms those cultural spaces for the constitution of difference that test the limits of existing regimes of discourse, including our own. As Carolyn Porter (1988, 78) writes: "What we do not need is a criticism which re-others those voices which were and are marginalized and disempowered by these dominant discourses." Rather, we need to find ways in which we can intervene in dominant cultural and political formations so that we can be attentive to difference, while sharing a "common ethos" of solidarity, struggle, and liberation. In this way, different manifestations of critical pedagogy can speak to the specificity of race, class, and gender oppression and to the *differentia specifica* of various group projects while at the same time to the construction of new spaces of possibility, cultural justice, and human freedom.

MODES OF DESIRE, MODES OF PRODUCTION,
AND MODES OF SUBJECTIVITY

I want to argue that the constitution of the body/subject must be viewed as a complex process involving the production of subjectivity within various social and material practices. More specifically, it is a relationship which obtains among modes of desire, modes of production, and modes of subjectivity (Turner 1984). The term "modes of desire" refers to the different ways in which desire is socially constructed. It registers most acutely the fact that we cannot peel away the flesh to yield an unfettered access to some irreducible instinctual desire: the goals of desire are always kept in perpetual flight.[10] Unlike the Platonic notion of desire, desire is never wholly free-floating but is lived out in historically and culturally specific forms and is mediated by desires for and of the other. As John Brenkman notes, "The actual forms in which the dialectics of desire is played and lived are historical. These forms will open or close the play of satisfactions and recognition in specific ways which must, in turn, be related to the institutional framework of society as it organizes the satisfaction of human desire and the labor of others" (1985, 189).

For Jacques Lacan, needs are biological, and desire is the active principle of the physical processes which lies both *beyond* and *before* demand (Sarup 1989, 153). Desire may therefore be said to transcend demand because in essence it masquerades or conceals an absolute lack or unconscious desire for recognition by the Other. Madan Sarup (1989, 154) expresses Lacan's conception of desire as "the desire for desire." A desire is what cannot be specified by demand, since "the meaning of the demand is not intrinsic but is partly determined by the response by the other to the demand" (24). According to Lacan, demands cancel need but need then re-emerges on the other side of desire. As Sarup (25), summarizing Lacan, states: "Desire arises out of the lack of satisfaction and it pushes you to another demand."

Deleuze and Guattari support the conception that "lack" should not be seen as the universal prerequisite of desire but as a social construction within a particular historical configuration (1983, 25).[11] Objects of desire are shaped not in a value-free laboratory or homogenizing sphere but by the often conflictual social and cultural forms in which desiring takes place. Desire does not, as Deleuze and Guattari claim, directly invest the social field in a manner which makes it immune to mediation. We must avoid seeing desire as a form of vitalism that is produced by the will in combination with testosterone or the yearning for pre-Oedipal bliss, for this is the surest way to lapse into a naive essentialism, biological reductionism or form of naturalism.[12]

Ernst Bloch (1986) understood desire to be a form of dreaming, of searching for something beyond ourselves; he essentially rejected Freudian explanations of motivation and drives which he rightly pointed out were saturated with bourgeois assumptions. According to Bloch, Freud's understanding of desire tended to disembody human impulses and ignored their socio-economic aspects and historical mutability (Geoghegan 1987, 87–97). Capitalism engenders a socially constructed dialectics of desire—a libidinal economy of sorts—in which fantasy is mobilized in order to search for a substitute for a "lack," that is, to discover a material object to substitute for a mythical object we lack "in reality" and which we feel we *need* to complete our subjectivity (a notion which has its antecedents in the work of Jean-Francois Lyotard). It is important to recognize that forms of desire are linked historically and discursively to specific "modes of production" and "modes of subjectivity." Desire cannot be understood as a presocial or biological force. Desire and its social determinations, its cultural objects of desire, cannot be seen separately but must be understood as mutually constitutive. Similarly, desires which students express in schools cannot be understood outside the manner in which they have become institutionalized and socially legitimated, or without taking into consideration the ends and purposes—both, immediate and long range—for which they have been manufactured both in relation to established educational discourses and economies of power and privilege at work in the larger society. Turner notes that every mode of production has a mode of

desire and that the social relations of material production structure particular relations—or modes—of desire (1984, 13). This
amounts to saying that desire is always mobilized by the contingency of the social and its particular circuits of power which are
often tied to the economic requirements of dominant modes of
material and cultural production. Within capitalism, for instance,
modes of desire are linked to the production of surplus labor and
the process of consumption. In this context, consumer needs are
often superimposed on the desires of the body so that "the
subject's intention to satisfy the body must make a detour through
exchange value; the response to the demands of the body is
deferred, for the visible aim of laboring is the wage" (Brenkman
1985, 182).

MODES OF SUBJECTIVITY

I am using the term "modes of subjectivity" to refer to the
way in which postmodern culture has penetrated the constitutive
nature of our subjectivities. Jochen Schulte-Sasse (1987–88) calls
this a logical organization of sentiments that is beyond the control
of knowing subjects. It is a form of "psychological rearmament"
that is semiotically arranged and based on the "postindustrial colonization of the id" and "ideological organization of super-egos"
which have developed largely on the basis of new postmodern non-
linear narrative modes (1987-88, 127). By modes of subjectivity I
am also referring to the fact that modern capitalism tends to foster
modes of desire which contribute to what David Michael Levin
refers to as "a reduction of human beings to the dual states of sub-
jectified privatized egos and subjugated, engineerable objects"
(1987, 486). Within postmodern culture, we have witnessed an
erosion of symbolic processes that cathect body and communal
vision. This erosion of communal modes of subjectivity has
created pathologies conditioned by the duplicitous deterritorialization of the body under capitalist modes of production—what Levin
has called "historically conditioned pathologies of the will." He
writes that "the pathologies we are seeing today—the narcissistic
character disorders, the schizophrenias, and the depressions—are
pathologies distinctive of a society and culture in which the fate of
the Self has been hitched to the ego's increasingly nihilistic will to
power" (1987, 486). Grossberg echoes a similar theme when he
maintains that "Postmodernity demands that one live schizo-

phrenically, trying, on the one hand, to live...inherited meanings
and, on the other hand, recognizing the inability of such meanings
to respond to one's own affective experiences" (1988, 48).

I am not simply equating modes of subjectivity with pathologies of the will produced by particular modes of consumer desire. I
also wish to draw attention the the *moral technologies* which help
structure these modes of production and desire. The discerning literary critic Terry Eagleton describes moral technologies as "particular set[s] of techniques and practices for the instilling of specific
kinds of value, discipline, behaviour and response in human subjects" (1985/86, 96–97). Eagleton reveals how one such moral technology—that of English literature—serves to create a bourgeois
body/subject which values subjectivity *in itself.* What Eagleton
argues, convincingly in my view, is that within liberal capitalist
society the lived experience of "grasping literature" occurs within
a particular form of subjectivity which values freedom and creativity as an end in itself whereas the more important issue should be:
freedom and creativity *for what?* What the bourgeoisie body/
subject does not recognize in this process is *the enfleshment of
indifference to oppression.* Eagleton makes the important observation that "the shackling of the subject is from within—and that
shackling is itself nothing less than our very forms of subjectivity
themselves..." (1985/86, 100-101).

The point Eagleton is trying to stress is that liberal capitalism produces forms of subjectivity "free of any particular rigorous
ends" whose moral formalism e.g., creativity, sensitivity, and interiority for its own sake, draws attention away from the fact that
these very forms of subjectivity are colonized by specific capitalist
interests and modes of domination. I have described this process as
enfleshment.

THE RESISTING BODY: CRITICAL PEDAGOGY AND
THE POLITICS OF EMPOWERMENT

Without denying my own ambivalence towards postmodernity, I shall attempt in this section to establish some pedagogical
directions based on some of the insights provided to us by postmodernism with respect to the constitution of meaning and subjectivity. I have been arguing that the modes of subjectivity being
formed within the postmodern scene are precisely those which
give individuals the illusion of free choice while masking the

means by which the parameters that define such choices have been constituted by the social and material practices of consumer capitalist culture. If it is true that there is a connection between postmodern pathologies of the will and the constitution of the body/subject, then it is important to understand resistance to dominant modes of subjectivity, production, and desire, especially as this resistance is connected somatically to the formation of will, agency, and the construction of meaning. A critical pedagogy needs to counter the tendency of some critics of modernity to dissolve agency, claiming that we are always already produced and finalized as subjects within discourse. We must recognize that there also exist *modes of resistant subjectivity* which are more closely tied to the means of cultural production than the means of economic production and which develop as oppositional engagements with the dominant cultural hegemony.

It is one thing to say that individuals do not exist independently, as body/subjects, from surrounding social structures. Yet it is quite another to claim that they are simply the product of a monolithic engagement or identification with social texts. To mistake ourselves as merely products rather than producers of subjectivity is, in Lichtman's words, "to reify our alienation by having absorbed the mere facticity to which we have reduced the world into the very conception of ourselves" (1982, 257). Furthermore, Lichtman warns that "To hold that we do not deceive ourselves but that reality deceives us implies that we are absolved from struggling through the ambivalent vicissitudes of our own lived experience" (1982, 256). The body/subject is not simply the product of a homogenous totality of discourses but rather a terrain of struggle, conflict, and contradictions.

One of the central challenges of critical pedagogy is to reveal to students how conflictual social relations (society's social logic) are actively inscribed in human intentionality and agency without reducing individuals to simply the static outcomes of social determinations. While I agree with the poststructuralists who remorselessly decry the essentialist reading of the self and who claim that we cannot speak of the self as an essence or unmediated object of reflection, I disagree that the self is constituted only through background beliefs—both unconscious and conscious—engendered through enfleshment. That is why the important distinction must be made that human beings—bodies—*are self-conscious and not self-constituting*. That is, while individuals are constituted by background beliefs which are inaccessible to explicit self-understanding and knowledge (and which primarily lie outside of consciousness), their subjectivities are also informed by their *self-consciousness*. Self-consciousness and repression both play important roles in our subjective formation. Bodies cannot will their own subjective formation or determine their own significance by fiat. Unlike the self-conscious, self-present Cartesian body/subject, which claims the power to individuate consciousness by an act of will alone, individuals are not capable of intentional, transparent communication or unmediated actions in the world (Turner 1983). Yet it is necessary to acknowledge that the capacity of individuals to at least partially recognize the constitution of the self is what makes liberation possible. (This goes directly against Lacan's notion of the subject as a "vanishing point" which resists self-perception; see Larmore, 1981). It is also a precondition for *refleshment*, or forming a space of desire where we can assume self-consciously and critically new modes of subjectivity hospitable to a praxis of self and social empowerment. We must not forget that *we can act in ways other than we do.*

The task of critical pedagogy is to increase our self-consciousness, to strip away distortion, to discover modes of subjectivity which cohere in the capitalist body-subject and to assist the subject in its historical remaking. The project of placing desire into critical and self-conscious circulation necessitates a language that speaks to the lived experiences and felt needs of students but also a critical language that can problematize social relations which we often take for granted. It needs a non-totalizing language that refuses to strip experience from its contingency and open-endedness, that refuses to textualize oppression, and that refuses to dehistoricize or desexualize or degender the body or to smooth over difference in the name of justice or equality (Giroux 1988).

IDEOLOGICAL CONTRADICTIONS AND THE POLITICS OF PLEASURE

An important aspect of the production of pleasure within youth culture consists of what Grossberg terms *affective investment*—"the intensity or desire with which we invest the world and our relations to it" (1986b, 185)—in which different and often contradictory modes of desire and subjectivity are embraced which are generally absent in traditional school sites. Here, modes of desire may *consist of the very pleasure of participating in the act of desiring itself.* Bodies are produced which actively refuse the moral technologies, panoptic spaces, and modes of subjectivity produced in schools (Shumway, 1989).

While it is important to stress that individuals as body/subjects—as embodied or enfleshed subjectivity—constitute precisely the contradictory logic of the social world, it is wrong to assume that individuals remain passive within such a process of subjective formation. Students are inserted into culture in ways which are often arrestingly different and contradictory. For instance, what is often mistaken as youth conservatism or youth indifference is, in actuality, an active refusal to politicize reality. Youth often accomplish this by *entering the present more fully* as part of an affective rather than merely intellectual investment. Grossberg notes that "Youth's power lies in their ability to appropriate any text, to undermine the distinction between production and consumption and, in this way, to deny the power of ideology, and of the commodity" (1988, 140).

Consider the celebrated success of MTV. John Fiske writes that "MTV is read by the body, experienced through the senses, and resists sense which is always theirs. MTV is experienced as pleasure...The threat of the signifier is its resistance to ideology, its location in the sensations of the body, the physical senses rather than the mental senses. The plurality of meanings on video clips makes us talk of their senses, not of their sense (1986, 75). The pure materiality and overvaluation of the signifier, unattached and autonomous, freed from any secured signified, forms a seamless cultural surface of the present that resists ideological investment. In fact, to be confronted by the inherent ambiguity of this particular form of image production constitutes *a refusal of ideology.* Yet at the same time, to embrace such politics of representation is to inhabit most fully the bourgeois mode of subjectivity which believes that such an ambiguity of meaning represents a space offered for exercising the liberal humanistic freedom to choose one's own meaning. True, individuals can accept, reject, or choose particular meanings associated with free-floating images. But there is always an overdeterminate or "preferred" reading of images within the dominant culture. To believe that one can escape this sovereign or imperial reading by an exercise of critical reflection alone also presupposes that people make choices only on the basis of semantic understanding, and not through either the mobilization of desire and affect or a form of deintensification of experience David J. Scholle calls the "spectacle stance of the audience" (1988, 33). In their engagement with forms of media-generated images, viewers become the most vulnerable to the political agenda behind such images precisely when they feel they can intellectually distance themselves from their discursive articulation and persuasive power.

The New Right has most often benefited from the fact that the mass media communicates most effectively not to the faculties of logic but in mapping out our primary structures of affect. Consider the image of Willy Horton exploited by George Bush's ad men in the recent presidential election campaign. The Bush camp was able to compress its ideology on criminal justice into the negative image of Willy Horton, a Afro-American man who committed murder while on a prison furlough in Massachusetts. While most viewers more than likely understood this to be another sleazy ideological ploy (not to mention another historical violation of the Afro-American body) and felt that they still had free choice in the matter of accepting or rejecting what appears to be the intended effect of such an image, among large numbers of whites, the picture of Willy Horton nevertheless resonated *affectively* with previous socially induced fears of Afro-Americans. Here, an affective as opposed to ideological alliance was created with Bush's reactionary views on criminal justice (which would supposedly prevent more wild-eyed and teeth-clenching Willy Hortons from running loose and terrorizing whites by the abolition of prison furloughs). The success of such an alliance appears to confirm one of Adorno's major insights (1974) that cultural products are often accepted even though their ideological messages are understood by those who engage them (Scholle 1988, 33). Despite the fact that many viewers resisted the ideological message in the image of Willy Horton on a semantic level, they were nevertheless seduced by the affective play of the surface of the image—what Schulte-Sasse calls "the relatively unstructured semantic homogeneity of the world of images" (1986/87, 46)—and the Bush campaign was able to further advance its war of position. What is putatively a conscious refusal of ideology inscribed in televisual images often means that images from both the political left and right are accepted in a spectatorial detachment, as a chain of equivalent signified. Further, it suggests that electronic images are always already inscribed by the logic of the medium and overdetermined by it. Ideology in this case is not so much a form of cognitive mapping as it is the production of structures of affect.

A critical pedagogy must focus on popular culture and develop curricular strategies based on how student subjectivity is informed within it (Giroux & Simon 1988). For if we do not work with students in this area of their lives we deny them the very modes of subjectivity which give flesh to the meaning of their lives. If we want to take seriously the emancipatory possibilities inscribed within student resistance, then we must attempt to answer the following questions: How are the subjectivities, dreams, desires, and needs of students forged by the media, by leisure activities, by institutions such as the family, and by cultural forms such as rock 'n' roll and music videos? How for instance, is the practical ethics by which students engage everyday life inscribed within a contestatory politics of signification? How are images of male and female socially constructed (McLaren, 1989b)? How do the politics of signification structure the problemization of experience? How are the subjectivities of students constituted by the effects of representations which penetrate the level of the body? So it is imperative that as educators for the postmodern age we begin to examine issues such as the feminization and masculization of the body and the reification of the body politic. We need to study how our needs and desires as educators have been shaped in contradictory ways through dominant cultural forms, modes of subjectivity, and circuits of power (Giroux & McLaren, 1989). A critical pedagogy must grapple with the ways in which youth resist the dominant culture *at the level of their bodies* because in so doing the utopian moments to which such resistance points can be transformed pedagogically into strategies of empowerment. Jochen Schulte-Sasse writes that the empowerment of the imagination is inefficient as a culture-revolutionary project; what is more pressingly needed are "rhetorical strategies that break through the reign of the simulacrum and grasp, as adequately as possible, the linguistically and mentally receding structures of our id and of the global economy, and comprehend the inscriptions both leave on our bodies" (1986/87, 47–48).

A critical pedagogy must help us to distinguish our real needs and those of our students from fantasies in pursuit of artificial needs and to enunciate the demand for a new ethics of compassion and solidarity. I am speaking here about a praxis in which the knowing subject is an acting body/subject, a praxis which can empower us to take responsibility for history and for developing a vision of the world which is not yet (Giroux & McLaren, in press). This is not to deny the historicism of praxis but to embrace it more fully with a recognition that even in these postmodern times we are capable of seizing the stage of history in the unity of our thinking and doing, and bringing forth a new world at the command of our own voices and with the strength of our own hands. The prerequisite for such an enterprise lies in reclaiming the authenticity of the body and in formulating strategies of opposition whose primary referent consists of new ways of thematizing knowledge and subjectivity.

Such a project would culminate in a critical praxis of social transformation that works against the political horrors of our time. New communities of collective body/subjects must be shaped both by uncovering the subversive work of desire and by creating social and cultural forms in which new desires may be produced, and new modes of subjectivities formed based on compassion and reciprocity. We need to explore our self-constitutivity by using pedagogical strategies which allow us to testify to and enact the struggle of the oppressed rather than engage in strategies which demarginalize, decolor, degender, and aestheticize such suffering. Here, the unfixity and open-endedness which characterizes the postmodern condition can make possible "new enfoldings," what George Yudice describes as "unfixity delimited by the unboundedness of struggle" (1988, 229). In this way the guardians of the dominant culture can be deprived of the moral and political certainty they have taken as their refuge. Of course, in achieving such a goal we must never cease to retravel the road which runs from a negative dialectics to a critical hope. Nor must we ever give up becoming more theoretically vigilant on the basis that we are morally innocent. To claim immunity from our exercising domination over others on the basis that we have good intentions is to euphemistically dodge Michel Foucault's injunction that we judge truth by its effects and to deny our complicity in economies of oppression on the grounds of our theoretical ignorance.

CRITICAL PEDAGOGY: DIFFERENCE IN SOLIDARITY

A pedagogy of the postmodern body/subject can help educators better understand how the resistant body/subject attempts to signify beyond normative and available systems of signification, challenging and disrupting the discourses that create the space of subjectivity. Yet paradoxically, resistant body/subjects sign their own subjection by refusing to occupy the normative space of the body/subject—the socially encoded "proper" spaces of the "masculine," the "feminine" and the "citizen"—and by refusing to be semiotically engineered into the subjective mode of bourgeois "happiness." This is the case because it is difficult even for resistant students to escape reinscription as subjects into the consumer-driven codes of late capitalism. Within postmodernity it is more difficult to separate body/subjects from the languages which represent their desire. Lacking a language of resistance, resistant students simply become signs of themselves, and can only encode the anxiety of the present and apprehension of the future. Consequently, they remain in their resistance, dragged by images fleeing history, rather than forging symbols with the power to transform it. They enflesh the terror and not the promise of postmodernity. Fending off the fear of uncertainty, the horror of ambiguity, and the threat of difference requires body/subjects to construct a language that refuses its own limits, that is capable of locating gaps and fissures within the prevailing cultural hegemony. Such a language must enable its users to reflect on their own subjective formation and incorporation in the social relations of capital as well as participate in their own self-transformation.

Such a language must also help to transform critical pedagogy into a pedagogy of hope. It must move beyond the divisiveness of sectarian interest groups and beyond the various pluralisms of which Richard Bernstein (1988) is so eloquently critical: the "flabby pluralism" which constitutes a simple acceptance of the existence of a variety of perspectives and paradigms; a pluralism which regards different perspectives as virtually incommensurable; and the "decentered anarchistic pluralism" which celebrates uncertainty or lapses into a brooding and nihilistic retreat from life. We need to move beyond the great liberal Conversation and refuse to accept the constant deferral of meaning in any dialogue to the point where we choose only to speak to ourselves. The former position believes that by affirming difference unproblematically, liberation will ensue in a dance of pluralistic reverie. The latter believes that the tenuousness of all meaning inevitably places us in the thrall of never being capable of taking a position or speak from a space of authority or power. At its least dangerous extreme, the Great Conversation lapses into a silly relativism while the poststructuralist position becomes merely political foolishness. At their worst extremes, both positions lead to political inertia and moral cowardness where educators remain frozen in the zone of "dead" practice in which it is assumed that all voices are those which silence or which contain the "other" by a higher act of violence, and all passionate ethical stances are those built upon the edifices of some form of tyranny or another. Unable to speak with any certainty, or with an absolute assurance that his or her pedagogy is untainted by any form of domination, the "post critical" educator refuses to speak at all. This distressing position that has been assumed by some critical educators reminds me of a form of philosophical detachment of some social critics who, by constantly criticizing and radicalizing themselves on their path to universality, often fail to form a concrete praxis based on their own principles (see Michael Waltzer 1987).

For theorists like the ones I have been describing, pedagogy becomes a curse that can be abrogated only when all forms of persuasion, authority, rhetoric or self-assurance have been purged from the classroom discussion. In this view it is better to do nothing than engage in critical praxis because of the dominating interests that might lurk behind the lesson or the frames of reference with which the critical praxis takes as its ethical or conceptual starting point. It is one thing to ascertain in which ways the language of critical theory may be part of the oppressive unity of that which it attempts to liberate; it is quite another to banish such a language into the dustbin of history, as some "post-critical" groups are want to do.

We have arrived now at a watershed point in the development of critical pedagogy where we must ask the following: Are the various discourses of critical pedagogy capable of normatively grounding feminist and minority struggles for liberation? Only in an age which Cornel West (1988, 256) characterizes as being "obsessed with articulations of particularities e.g. gender, race nation" could such a question be raised with such a fervor. It is an important question which, of course, must be answered. But to answer "yes" invites some qualification. More specifically, to answer in the affirmative means to submit the various theoretical strands of critical pedagogy to both a constant ethical surveillance and self-monitoring and a rethinking of its conceptual edifice. This, of course, can be done without theoretical reductionism, and for the most part it has been the radical legacy of critical pedagogy, whose emancipatory project has always explored the preconditions of its own categorizations and assumptions. It is our responsibility to continue this legacy in our present and future theorizing. While much that currently passes for critical pedagogy bears the birth mark of a failed modernity, and while it may generate political contradictions and invite some confusion in the way it addresses questions of difference, it nevertheless provides an important and indispensable basis for a political and ethical revitalization of our schools as sites for self and social transformation.

Yet what is still not fully realized in the discourse of critical pedagogy is what I want to call a social-critical utopian praxis— critical action that is yet to be realized in history. Such a praxis is beginning to show promise in some of the ongoing critiques by critical educators of sexism, racism, economic exploitation, ecological violence, and militarism and in the ways revolutionary educators are forging a collaboration with Marxists, feminists, and social movements striving to uncover and confront the values and interests which are unknown but nevertheless are constantly operative in our pedagogies and liturgies of practical living—values which dehumanize and depersonalize. Social-critical utopian praxis calls for our unconditional withdrawal from inhumanity and for our movement towards what Agnes Heller (1988) calls the "common good," that is, towards a praxis which promotes the goodness of persons who prefer to suffer wrong than to commit wrong. In achieving the common good, we need to further develop a language of representation and a language of hope which together will allow the subaltern to speak outside the terms and frames of reference provided by the colonizer, whether or not the colonizer in this case happens to be the teacher, the researcher, or the administrator. We must acquire a language of analysis and hope that permits women to speak in words outside Name-of-the-Father vocabularies and does not prevent minorities and the excluded to speak their narratives of liberation and desire. Such a language must be able to uncover and transform the constructions of subjectivity. In so doing, the language of social-critical utopian praxis needs to de-authorize and rewrite the the master narratives of liberal post-industrial democracy and the humanist, individualist, and patriarchal discourses which underwrite it, while at the same time undermining and reconstructing the idealized and romantic conception of the subject which is shaped by Eurocentric and androcentric discursive power relations. Such a pedagogical praxis refuses the class subjection of the proletarian body through its sterile aestheticization by bourgeois categories of the flesh. It also refuses the inscription of patriarchy upon the female body and the intextuation of masculinist ideologies. We need to provide the marginalized and immiserated with power over the direction of their desiring. The project of critical pedagogy is positioned irreverently against a pedantic cult of singularity in which moral authority and theoretical assurance are arrived at unproblematically without regard to the repressed narratives and suffering of the historically disenfranchised.

We need to understand, as critical educators, that we are living in an epochal transition to an era of multiple feminisms, liberalisms, Marxisms which, on the one hand, hold the enabling promise of liberation, while on the other hand threaten to splinter the left irrevocably in a maze of often mutually antagonistic micro-politics. This calls for some form of totalizing vision—what I want to call an arch of social dreaming—that spans the current divisiveness we are witnessing within the field. This arch of social dreaming is meant to give shape, coherence, and protection to the unity of our collective struggles. It means the conquest of a vision of what the total transformation of society might mean. As Jameson (1988, 360) remarks:

> Without some notion of *total* transformation of society and without the sense that the immediate project is a figure for that total transformation, so that everybody has a stake in that particular struggle, the success of any local struggle is doomed, limited to reform.

Of course, the realization of this vision means that critical pedagogy must not become a site of further divisiveness among the left but rather serve as a forum which can generate an ethos of solidarity that speaks to what educators as critical agents— Hispanics, Afro-Americans, Anglos, feminists, gays, minorities and others—share in the common struggle against domination and for freedom while preserving the specificity of difference. Attali (1987, 143) catches the spirit of the creation of this new *groupe moteur* or "subject of history" to which I have been referring in his discussion of musical composition:

> ...in composition, it is no longer, as in repetition, a question of marking the body; nor is it a question of producing it, as in repetition. It is a question of taking pleasure in it. That is what relationship tends toward. An exchange between bodies—through work, not through objects. This constitutes the most fundamental subversion...to create, in common, the code within which communication will take place.

Those of us who work within the critical tradition in education would do well to look at what Cornel West (1989) has formulated as "prophetic pragmatism" as a "form of American Left thought and action in our postmodern moment" (239). Indebted to Marxism, structuralism, and poststructuralism, it also is an attempt to advance beyond "a Eurocentric and patriarchal discourse that not simply fails to theoretically consider racial and gender forms of subjugation, but also remains silent on the antiracist and feminist dimensions of concrete progressive political struggles" (215). Rejecting the Enlightenment search for foundations and the quest for certainty, prophetic pragmatism situates human inquiry into truth and knowledge in the social and communal circumstances under which persons can communicate and cooperate in the process of gaining knowledge (213). Prophetic pragmatism is a political mode of cultural criticism. It reflects Emerson's concepts of power, provocation and personality, Dewey's stress on historical consciousness, and DuBois' focus on the plight of the wretched of the earth. West recaptures Emerson's utopian vision, Dewey's conception of creative democracy, and DuBois' social structural analysis of the limits of capitalist democracy and links it all to the work of Niebuhr, C. W. Mills, and Gramsci. Prophetic pragmatism is not only an oppositional cultural criticism but "a material force for individuality and democracy" (232). Like Gramsci's organic intellectual and Mill's activist intellectual, prophetic pragmatism "puts a premium on educating and being educated by struggling peoples, organizing and being organized by resisting groups" (234). West summarizes this position as follows:

> Prophetic pragmatism worships at no ideological altars. It condemns oppression anywhere and everywhere, be it the brutal butchery of Third-World dictators, the regimentation and repression of peoples in the Soviet Union and Soviet-bloc countries, or the racism, patriarchy, homophobia, and economic injustice in the first-world capitalist nations. In this way, the precious ideals of individuality and democracy of prophetic pragmatism oppose all those power structures that lack public accountability, be they headed by military generals, bureaucratic party bosses, or corporate tycoons. Nor is prophetic pragmatism confined to any preordained historical agent, such as the working class, black people, or women. Rather, it invites all people of goodwill both here

and abroad to fight for an Emersonian culture of creative democracy in which the plight of the wretched of the earth is alleviated. (235)

Prophetic pragmatism is hardly unproblematic, but it does offer educators a philosophical approach that attempts to combine European Marxian and poststructuralist approaches with left thought that is distinctly American in origin and development and which speaks directly to the conditions for social transformation. It is, furthermore, an approach that avoids much of the self-annihilation and paralysis of the will that plagues many current postmodern theoretical perspectives.

Given the conditions of contemporary social life, its unleashing of collective desire with an absent center—a vacant theatre of the self built out of impotent illusions and hallucinated certainties which are in danger of collapsing under their own irreducible excess of signifiers, and which render our identities self-interested, insatiable, anarchic, and free-floating—prophetic pragmatism "gives prominence to the plight of those peoples who embody and enact the "postmodern" themes of degraded otherness, subjected alienness, and subaltern marginality, that is, the wretched of the earth (poor people of color, women, workers)" (237).

A PEDAGOGY VOICED FROM THE MARGINS

Critical pedagogy in its many diverse incarnations has been, since its earliest developments, on a collision course with the empowerment of the student as *Werkindividualitat,* or autonomous individual. Empowerment of the self without regard to the transformation of those social structures which shape the very lineaments of the self is not empowerment at all but a sojourn into a version of humanistic therapy where catharsis is coextensive with liberation. Critical pedagogy is more than a desacralization of the grand narratives of modernity, but seeks to establish new moral and political frontiers of emancipatory and collective struggle, where both subjugated narratives and new narratives can be written and voiced in the arena of democracy. These new narratives are not unified by objective and regulative moral principles but by a common ethos of solidarity and struggle for the realization of a deeper democracy and civic participation. The critical pedagogy which I have been describing is more than the exercise of imaginative sympathy or creative compassion. It is more than the luxuriant empathy of the liberal humanist or the formalized interest of the academic, an interest too often cleansed of history and struggle. Critical pedagogy does not refuse to take sides, balancing truth somewhere in an imaginary middle between silence and chaos. It does not domesticate indifference by ignoring the historical and cultural ruptures within Western industrial societies, or the imperial project of colonizing students' subjectivities in the interest of Western civility. Critical pedagogy works outside the inviolable boundaries of order, in the rift between a subversive praxis and a concrete utopia. Critical pedagogy recalls history not as a surrogate for experience but as a means of providing those memories which have been policed into silence with a voice, undistorted by the echoes of industry or the motors of progress.

The hope that is critical pedagogy rests with those educators who keep its languages and practices alive while taking account of changing historical contexts and the specificity and limitations of difference. The hope is with those who refuse to allow oppression of the mind and the body to become oppression of the spirit and who resist the grotesque identification of education with the economic interests of the dominant class.

Left to be swallowed by the darkness that exists outside the concreteness of historical and collective struggle, desire transforms itself into fantasy, endlessly in pursuit of what it lacks. Yet critical reason can give desire wings, so that thought can be lifted beyond the limitations of the present moment in order to be transformed into dreams of possibility. And with dreams we can do wonderful things.

Chapter Six

Women Dancing Back:
Disruption and the Politics of Pleasure

On the surface, going out dancing in clubs may be viewed as a set of practices that subordinate women in a male defined and controlled arena, where oppressive stereotypes of femininity and masculinity are enacted, and where sexist practices that demean women are tolerated and even expected.[1] Women often experience forms of objectification and repression, and a threat of violence in clubs that is taken for granted and naturalized. Rock music, an integral part of the dance scene and omnipresent in youth culture in general, often tends to lyrics that "perpetuate racist assumptions, glorify violence, and objectify, stereotype, trivialize, ridicule, and/or ignore women" (Dobkin 1985, 21). If rock music is, indeed, as Simon Frith and Angela McRobbie have argued, one way a "repertoire of public sexual behavior" is learned, then rock music is implicated in the constituting and experience of female sexuality on the club dance floor (1987/79, 3).[2] The very real practices of others—from door men to "cruising" men—and women's own self-regulation, as in the careful negotiation of the invisible and easily transgressed "good girl" line, work together to delineate women's experiences dancing in clubs.

Sexuality and the body often become the ground upon which women's social regulation in forms of popular culture takes place. At the same time women do find potent pleasures in going out dancing, and sexuality and the body become key to understanding those pleasures. As the sources of regulation are multiple, conflicting, and indeterminate in their effect, so are experiences of pleasure. Notions of pleasure and desire, refusal and resistance on the dance floor emerge as the appearance of women's consent to dominant practices is interrogated. This work is an investigation into this contradictory politics of pleasure: into women's bodies as a conflicting terrain of oppression and potential empowerment, liability, and pleasure.

To begin I locate myself in the research and place the research in context. I describe the multiplicity of pleasures that women may find in going out dancing, arguing that the way sexuality is allowed expression through dance contributes to the power of its pleasures. Stepping back to look at how popular culture in general functions as an ideological terrain, one where desire is courted and organized, I explore how dancing presents the possibility for embodied resistance to, as well as reproduction of, dominant practices and ideologies. I suggest that this occurs because of the way dancing is connected to the body and sexuality, and accesses the emancipatory powers of desire. I conclude with the paradoxes of women's resistance on the dance floor and the contradictions of resistance on the site of the body and I question the potential for form of popular culture to contribute to social change.

DOING (FEMINIST) RESEARCH:
WRITING ABOUT WITH PASSION

In the introduction to her collection of essays *Consuming Passions*, Judith Williamson wrote, "passion is another story. It is to be written *about* but not *with*: for the essence of all this academic work on 'desire' is to stay *cool*" (1986, 12). Sensual pleasures of the body, however, do not translate easily into either the written language of research or static image. To make clear the relationship that I have to going dancing means making clear the pleasure and passion that are my own—a sometimes awkward and

uncomfortable narrative of desire and not the requisite dispassionate academic discourse. Yet it is within the embodiment of the
pleasures of going out dancing, in the desires and passions evoked,
that the meaning which dancing has for women becomes evident.

Thus, within this academic work on women and desire I have
not remained cool. I do not pretend objectivity—I have tapped into
the history, pleasures, and passions of myself and others. The
images of myself interacting with others through dance are one
way I locate myself in my own history, in time and space. It is the
pleasure of memory that is physically recalled, of desires deeply
rooted in my body's memory. I need only hear the first bars of a
tune and feel a wooden floor beneath my dancing shoes to trigger
the "nostalgia for the real" that Dick Hebdige (1988) argues we
crave. Dancing precipitates an incredible longing. To recover the
pleasure—in the imagining and "re-membering," the connecting
again with my limbs, my breath, my body—is to ignite desire.
These are rare moments of realizing my body and mind as not distinct, and of feeling the power of creativity when embodied. This
is my history and investment in dance, always in the shadow of
the writing.

The project "going dancing" was a way to further my understanding of the intersection of desire and resistance for women in a
particular cultural practice. I chose a well-frequented dance club,
the Big Bop, a purple air-brushed warehouse on Toronto's trendy
Queen Street West.[3] There the black-clad artists, the pseudo-punk
teens, and the suburban pretenders dance, drink, smoke, talk, pose,
wait, stalk, primp, and party to recorded music. Two women
friends and I spent an evening at the Big Bop. My observations,
interviews the next day with Kerry and Seana, plus the stories
other women and men told me about going out dancing in the
clubs, form the backbone of this writing. Looking for ways to
extend these material practices beyond their common sense meanings, I interpret our stories through frameworks of theory, questioning the taken for granted assumptions about the meaning dance
holds for women and searching for alternative understandings.

It is important to note that the politics of pleasure that
follows is only one extended interpretation of the practices encountered in one specific location. Although I do not know how it
would differ elsewhere, and do not generalize to any other women,
I present this without hesitation, believing it is "important to
locate the potential, the renewal of the conditions for resistance
contained in everyday life" (Martin 1988, 40). Lived culture is a

terrain of contradictions, where dominant ideologies and practices are contested, as well as reproduced: the Big Bop is a graphic example of popular culture in all its contradictory possibility. In addition, this particular developing of women's experience into concept presents an acknowledgment of the body as critical in an oppositional politics—in any struggle against domination. I see the limitations of this work as the borders of territory for further exploration.

THE MULTIPLE PLEASURES OF GOING DANCING

Iain Chambers describes how in popular music,

> dancing is the fundamental connection between the pleasures of sound and their social realization in the libidinal movements of bodies, styles and sensual forms. It represents a social encounter...where bodies are permitted to respond to physical rhythms that elsewhere would not be tolerated; the moment where romanticism brushes against reality, and a transitory step out of the everyday can be enjoyed. (1986, 135)

It is here, in the physical, sensual, sanctioned, and embodied pleasures of dancing that I begin to outline an interpretation of its meaning. Pleasure is a key element in structuring the relationships of the individual to a cultural form. It helps to explain why we might engage in contradictory activities within forms of popular culture, appearing to consent to dominant, patriarchal practices and our own social regulation. Pleasure and desire, the "lack" in Lacanian terms that seeks fulfillment, are constructed, not outside, but from within history and the social world. Through forms of popular culture, desire is courted, mediated, organized, and embodied. We went out dancing at the Big Bop in order to engage our desires, to know pleasure, to feel the promise of possibility, and to realize the potential of our affective investments. Reproducing the social order was not on our agenda.

The desire to engage in popular cultural practices can be further connected to the way particular forms of pleasure are grounded in the body. The body is central to this affective power of the popular as field for emotion, and is evidenced in dancing where music and movement are written together on the site of the body. In her study of young women and girls out dancing in London clubs, McRobbie noted how dance and female pleasure were unmistakably connected: dance is one, although limited, site for many women to experience pleasure, sensuality, self-expression, and control (1984, 133). The way dance cuts across multiple discourses, signifying intertextually, means pleasure is rooted in many places. The promise of intersecting pleasures in a noncognitive domain, located in the body—in movement, dress, music, physicality—was explicitly shared by the three of us going dancing at the Big Bop.[4] Our pleasure was not pure, but tempered by the nearly disabling denseness of smoke, bodies, and sound and by the behavioral prescriptives of the club scene's unspoken code. Despite these reminders of the imperfection of this space (or any space) for dancing, the pleasure was undeniable, and multiple.

Music is a powerful part of that pleasure. One way music organizes emotions is through the genuine physicality of the sound waves vibrating—a concrete part of dancing's affective power, its "real" ability to make us feel (Grossberg 1986). The Big Bop offers two floors with recorded music: we spent the evening on the busy ground level where the retro-landscape of three decades of greatest hits was familiar to us. In the comfort of having grown up with these songs, we did not feel self-conscious although we were visibly missing some of the other forms that intersect with dancing in a Queen Street West Club—the Queen Street West clothes, haircuts, shoes, makeup, jewelry, and a certain youthfulness. The Big Bop may not have been wholly our style but it was our music.

Movement is the other obvious pleasure. There is a physical delight in dancing, in allowing ourselves to feel more than think, to move boldly through space experiencing muscle, blood, bone, and breath working. I treasured this opportunity to be somewhat more intimate with women I care for by sharing our playfulness, laughter, and creativity, as well as a physical nearness. We were self-confident, comfortable with our bodies and each other, exploring music, movement, space, and imagination in our dancing, interactively interpreting the variations in music from the full range of our dance skills, histories, and imaginations.

Writing Dance on the Body: Pleasure of Possibility in the Mobilization of Desire

The pleasures of popular dancing go beyond the exploration of music and movement. The dance floor is a rare public place where letting go of the tight rein women often keep on their sexuality is possible, where the pleasures of the body are embraced and privileged. It is one terrain where sexuality, "living gender in all its dimensions," in Frigga Haug's words, is not condemned (1987, 29). Thus, as dancing permits and frees the body to experience sensuality and desire, sexuality (frequently an area of silence and pain in women's lives) is allowed expression. This sexuality is not necessarily directed at another. As McRobbie argues, the relationship of dancing and pleasure for women "frequently seems to suggest a displaced, shared and nebulous eroticism rather than a straightforwardly romantic, heavily heterosexual "goal-oriented drive" (1984, 134). In other words, tapping into one's sexuality on the dance floor is pleasurable in it own right. And, as I noted earlier, heterosexual women may indeed delight in the company of other women.

Yet, at the same time, this eroticism agreeable for its own sake, in the immediate moment, is underlined by a more subtly understood but equally powerful sensation: the pleasure of unknown possibilities. The evening exists as a text with only the bare bones of the scene sketched in. The plot is unknown but prior experience suggests what the realm of potential stories might be. In Judith Lynne Hanna's (1988) comparative study of dance, gender images, and sexuality, she found that dance is consistently found to be a part of courtship behaviors across many cultures and times. At the Big Bop, too, there is implicit within dancing its potential as the preamble to other pleasures of the body, in the forms of flirtation, romance, and sex. In the anticipation of one, or all, of those unrealized possibilities is a palatable pleasure. It is the potential offer to be taken up with, or refused to, some perhaps exotic other. It is the danger of being swept up, and away, in desire, and in the pleasures of the body. It is also the danger of letting go of control that may result in being swept away by that unknown other. This active mobilizing of desire becomes linked with notions of potential intimacy as well as risk, and pleasure becomes rooted in its own further possibilities, in the realization of fantasy.

Attention to the role of others in constituting desire and the experience of pleasure is related to how popular dancing is constructed around notions of spectacle, of going out to see and be seen. The advertisements for the more popular dance clubs overtly offer ways to escape the static disco beat with the possibility of having the kind of time that cannot be had elsewhere. A space is opened that makes possible knowing oneself differently, outside of

the ordinary, but still within the everyday, and connects the pleasures of the particular dance scene with the presence of desirable
others. Being seen is a crucial part of the pleasure of dancing, and
if one does not provide one's own entertainment, one can be a
spectator, animated by the performance of others. As dancers
actively taking up space on the floor we were positioning ourselves
to be watched. Our responses to being the objects of both male and
female gaze varied widely. Seana told me she attempted to deny
being the object of the look: she immersed herself in her own
dancing, not wanting to be seen as performing. Kerry, aware of
how intensely we seemed to be watched by the onlookers, said she
hoped they were enjoying the energy of our dancing. The sense of
anonymity and protected performance the floor offered, mistaken
or not, allowed me to explore my own body in movement, in connection to Kerry and Seana, without concern that the sensuality of
it was too dangerous. Kerry spoke of the satisfaction of abandoning
rules and structures, but also voiced awareness of the risks of loss
of control, and did not want to dance too far out of line. An audience to note the creativity and breaking of rules enhanced the
pleasures of ourselves in movement.

There is an additional pleasure located in the naughtiness
that seems to have no place in the daylight. Naughtiness carries
with it the pleasures of child-like behavior—we savored a benign
sense of mischief without being genuinely wicked or disgraceful.
We enjoyed the sense of daring to be (potentially) "bad" by being
in the somewhat sleazy club, staying up late, flirting with
strangers, wearing short skirts, and allowing ourselves to feel
desire and desired, in addition to the fun of dancing expressively
and sensually. That popular dancing is connected to stepping
outside of "good girl" territory, and to the possibility of pleasure
and danger, is not new. In Sylvanus Stall's popular late 19th-
century *What a Young Man Ought to Know*, he inadvertently captures precisely some of the attractiveness of going dancing:

> That dancing deserves to be regarded as one of the amuse-
> ments which are most dangerous and destructive to virtue, is
> attested by the fact that recently a bishop in the Roman
> Catholic Church stated that the work of the confessional
> revealed that nineteen out of twenty women who fall,
> confess the beginning of their sad state to the modern dance.
> Late hours, expensive dressing, violent and protracted exer-
> tion, and other reasons might be named as a sufficient array

of arguments against the objectionable character of this amusement. To our mind, however, the insurmountable objection, and that which constitutes is real and by far its greatest attractiveness, consists in its appeal to the sensual nature. (1897, 243)

LINKING POPULAR CULTURE, IDEOLOGY, AND RESISTANCE

It is clear that dancing's appeal and power still lie in its sensual, affective qualities, its engagement of the body and desire. In the last section I argued how the presence of others and issues of control, danger and risk, intersect with expressions of sexuality and desire in the constitution of formations of pleasure on the dance floor. In this next part I look at how dancing can be understood as a site where dominant ideologies are both reproduced and resisted through women's accessing the powers of desire and their appropriation of pleasure and space for themselves. I begin by examining how popular culture can function as the ground for an individual's negotiated inscription into the social world.

As Tony Bennett suggests, "Culture consists of all those practices (or activities) that signify; that is, which produce and communicate meanings by the manipulation of signs in socially shared and conventionalized ways" (1984, 79). This viewing of culture as not a product but a *practice*, within a field of signification and ideology, offers a way to understand popular culture that moves beyond the often polarized images: the top-down imposition of low-brow junk for consumption by the masses versus the quaint emergence of "pure" culture from the folk below. Rather, popular culture is a set of signifying practices, where representations continually vie for ascendancy. However, dominant representations— images, popular sayings, common sense notions, taken for granted assumptions, and texts—are one way the terrain is already colonized (Haug 1987, 59). We are continually subjected to these dominant discourses, whose apparently fixed meanings reflect specific interests that are not necessarily our own; these discourses mediate reality for us, framing our experiences in a particular way. The process of signification, of attaching meaning to forms and practices, is an ideological one. Who creates culture, knowledge, and history, what is valued as culture, and how and with whom it is shared—all are dependent on the social and power relations that exist. Hence they always embody specific class, gender, and race interests and bias, that is, ideology (Wexler 1982, 286).

Individuals living their material relations to the dominant ideologies discover the contradictions between individual subjectivities and reality as presented. Michel Foucault (1983) argues that our subjectivities and investments form in relation to contradictory practices, that is, always in relations of power. We struggle against being tied to identities of self that subject us to domination and exploitation. As subjects we have multiple relationships to the dominant ideology. The self is constantly being re-organized, reconstituted within larger social relations. We make sense of our experiences in ways that attempt to resolve the contradictions of the self that are created and lived within dominant forms. An individual's inscription into the culture becomes a process of negotiated consent, not coercion, marked by moments of refusal. In other words, as Michael Apple writes, "The formation of ideologies...is not a simple act of imposition. It is produced by concrete actors and embodied in lived experiences that may resist, alter, or mediate these social messages" (Apple 1982, 159).

Thus, the definition and construction of reality, that is, how knowledge and meaning are created and organized, are always being challenged and struggled over. There is always contestation and resistance on the part of those who are subject to rule, hence "ideological hegemony is not monolithic and static, fully achieved and finished but constantly negotiated" (Alonso 1988, 48). The terrain of the contestation of ideology is often that of popular culture, as a contextualized, dynamic interrelationship, an arena of exchange and negotiated meaning between dominant and subordinate groups. Resistance and consent are not dichotomies but occur together, in the struggle over pulling pleasure and meaning from life. In Philip Corrigan's (1987, 2) words, the "cultural order includes both the rule and the transgression," that is, the dominant order and the competing ones.[5]

Desire and the Body: Locating Resistance in Dance

It is through people's involvements in forms of popular culture that investments in various meanings and identities are actively constructed. Going dancing, despite a relationship to a repertoire of mass-produced images and meanings, available through films, videos, advertisements, and fashion, produces and may be invested with a multiplicity of potential meanings and experiences.[6] As well, it is through forms of culture that desire is mobilized and invested. On the dance floor not only is desire present and active but the body is central as the focus of activity. It is this intersection of desire embodied and sanctioned, I shall argue, that contributes to the particular potential of dancing as a site of resistance for women.

Women's resistance historically has often taken the form of unsanctioned sexuality, with the body as locus, in "crimes" related to sexual immorality—prostitution, out-of-wedlock children, abortion, lesbianism, and I add with uncertainty, pornography and stripping (Rowbotham 1972, 33).[7] This locating of resistance in the body is possible, despite how the body is constituted within ideology and discourse and is often the site of oppression, because of the body's relationship to pleasure, desire, sexuality, and emotion.

The body, already "saturated" with desire, is better able to resist because of the paradoxical nature of desire. Desire not only contributes to our inscription into the social order, it fuels defiance as well and is a prime force behind oppositional activity (Aronowitz 1981). This force is a result of the power of desire to generate action in general, as Muriel Dimien puts it, "We wish, we want, we are in a state of longing—this is the experience of desire, the unconscious fount of activity, creativity, and subjectivity" (1984, 147).

The dance floor is one location where desire and pleasure are courted and orchestrated, where the body is central, and where sexuality, implicated in the production, limitation, and control of desire, is permitted expression. In the intersection of desire and sexuality and the body, dancing becomes a probable site for resistance. The release of sexuality from its usually rigid constraints accesses an additional power to resist the regulation of behavior and desire. As Audre Lourde tells us, "in touch with the erotic, I become less willing to accept powerlessness" (1984, 58). We experienced this empowerment in our dancing at the Big Bop: our willingness to risk, move boldly, and take up space increased as our passion for dancing began to emerge with our decreasing restraint. Annette Kuhn writes about how in film/images, "desire is fueled because in the final instance its object is unattainable—and unthreatening" (1985, 42). She is referring to the individual positioned as spectator. On the dance floor it is true for the "object" as well. Desire, and the pleasures of desire could grow, as we perceived the floor to be safe in relation to those watching. In allowing desire, the control of passion and the self-regulation that is oppressive to women is subverted and the power of the erotic is accessed instead.

Dance as site of resistance is argued most cogently in terms of its relationship to the emancipation of desire through the body. Although Dale McDonough speaks of performance-oriented, choreographed dance, the connection between movement of the body, desire, and resistance she makes is relevant for popular dance:

> The embodiment of vision and passion which dance inspires suggests that dance may be one powerful route towards promoting and activating social transformation....As activity, desire causes human agency. No wonder that in our detached, dislocated, abstract, disembodied groupings we have not made more headway to change. (1987, 5)

McDonough is suggesting our state of disembodiment, our lack of integration of and connection to our minds and bodies, is hindering our empowerment as women. Dance provides the possibility of embracing of body, a re-integration of mind and body that, according to Randy Martin, is precisely why the body is crucial to any oppositional politics:

> Culture in the West has been divided not simply by race, ethnicity, or other subcultural formation but also between an experience of mind and body. The attempts to control mind generate the conditions for opposition in the body. These divisions and the possibilities they create render culture the terrain of the expression and suppression of politics. (1988, 7)

Martin is arguing the body is not as colonized as the mind, which is no longer capable of truly critical consciousness precisely because the mind is the locus of the social control rendered in Western societies through consent and not coercion. The body, within forms of popular culture that sanction its presence, then holds possibility as a site of political "consciousness," notwithstanding society's constraints and regulation of the physical. The body, as the critical site of contestation, increases in importance as the split between mind and body intensifies, as "the representation of desire in commodified images gets farther and farther away from people's lived realities" (Martin 1988, 39). These representations generate desire without fulfilling it, laying the ground for the human agency invoked by desire. Resistance to regulation and refusal to be regulated become possible through the body. Larry Grossberg agrees, giving an example from one of the most pervasive forms of popular culture: "The popularity of rock & roll is rooted in the music relationship to a material body which is already worked over by lines of desire; this body is surprisingly able to resist hegemonic attempts to regulate its desire" (1986, 184).

But the pleasures and desires realized through popular dancing need to also be understood as socially mediated, organized and constructed within forms of popular culture, which are in turn constructed within hegemonic and ideological practices. As Henry Giroux and Roger Simon (1988, 9) argue, "the production and regulation of desire are as important as the construction of meaning." The struggle over meaning and the definition of reality, within forms of popular culture, is ultimately over the investment of desire. Thus, the mobilizing and controlling of desire becomes a contradictory politics of pleasure, subject to the processes of hegemony and ideology. Coward warns us how "our desire sustains us, but it also sustains a way of living which may not ultimately be the best and only way for women....The pleasure/desire axis sustains social forms which keeps things as they are" (1984, 13).

This has particular implications for women who—located within unequal relations of power, and weary from resisting the pervasiveness of oppression and the way our refusals are often themselves suppressed or turned around—may become resigned to hegemonic practices. Dimien believes that this is because "We suffer not from too much desire but from too little. One reason we fail to rebel, or have incomplete revolutions, is because our hopes have been truncated, particularly by sexism whose core is sexual oppression" (1984, 147). Thus, interpreting our experiences of going dancing at the Big Bop as resistance is tempered, always, by knowing that it can never be purely counter-hegemonic but is attenuated by notions of consent and the contradictions of refusal itself. In the following section I describe how we did refuse certain hegemonic practices at the Big Bop, while at the same time realizing that for every appropriation and refusal, for every rupture or contestation, we were supporting unnamed other practices.

THE DISRUPTION IN DANCING BACK

The ways dancing can contest dominant practices and forms are many. There is disruption of the dance floor scene when women take pleasure for themselves and with each other, when space is appropriated for women's use, when men are relegated to "unnecessary" status, when implicit and explicit rules are broken and control abandoned, and when the power of the erotic is accessed.

We ruptured the Big Bop scene by assertively taking up space, and by controlling that space. We never succumbed to dancing in the dominant mode—small and repetitious gestures in a circumscribed space—but filled the space that was available. The appropriating of space exclusively for women's pleasure, control, and solidarity is radical. In Leslie Saunders' introduction to *Glancing Fires*, her collection of essays by women on their experiences of creativity, she notes how the taking of space through these women's writing is "itself an act of resistance in a climate increasingly hostile to women's liberation from oppressive structures and to ordinary people's control over their own lives" (1987, 4). Amy Rossiter, in her work on women's experiences of early motherhood, notes how deconstructing those experiences means looking at the concrete, everyday ways in which power operates to maintain relations of domination. She suggests that one possibility for women's refusal to be subordinated lies on overcoming obstacles to occupying space, and learning to act in opposition to the discourse of femininity within which our bodies are constituted (1988).

Different clubs sanction different sexual preferences and screen and police the patrons to varying degrees. The heterosexual couple or gangs of men are the typical social units at the Big Bop: three women dancing together consistently is a somewhat unusual sight, a transgression of "normal" practices. Men felt obliged to rescue us with their company, questioned our ability to have a good time with each other, or attempted to undermine the obvious pleasure we were having. But, more importantly, our appropriation of space *together* as women constituted an interruption of the dominant practices and empowered us to continue to defy the heterosexual couple imperative. In Leslie Roman's research on the subcultural ritual of slamdancing, she noticed how young punk women seemed "covertly to challenge their sexual subordination as individual women by means of paired actions in relation to the dance...creating dyadic and so-called 'safe pockets' among themselves" (1988, 153). There, too, women find safety and contestation of accepted forms through collective action.

Desire plays an emancipatory role here, as it instigates this possession of space for women's experience. It is pleasurable to control through dance that small space in one's life that is not subject to total colonization yet is still within dominant cultural forms. Not everyone wants to risk being marginalized, given the investment we have in fitting in, being accepted and knowing our place. However, there is the need to be occasionally "out of the reaches of controlling forces," that is, beyond the dictates of hegemonic culture (McRobbie 1984, 136). McRobbie also argues for "forms of fantasy, daydreaming, and 'abandon' to be interpreted as part of a strategy of resistance or opposition." In other words, it is through being "temporarily out of control" as well as through the appropriation of control that the "small daily evasions" can take place (135).

One explanation of the power of disruption is in Kuhn's essay on cross-dressing as a narrative device in film (1985). She argues that men dressing as women confuses notions of sexual identity and calls into question the nature of gender. When Kerry, Seana, and I preferred dancing with each other, we disrupted the scene through the shaking up of popular dancing's taken for granted gender roles. Likewise, I will consciously undermine the symbolic significance of the "last waltz" (at traditional country dance events) as the prelude to (heterosexual) romance when I choose to do it with another woman. As Gillian Swanson writes, the result is to "denaturalize sexual identity, showing subjectivity to be constructed rather than natural, and therefore changeable rather than fixed" (1986, 23).

Taking control and upsetting taken for granted gender roles and practices undermines the structure of the scene, subverting the dominant male-female dynamics. We took the control into our hands, to be free from reliance on men to invite us to dance. We were able to liberate our own bodies on the dance floor. We enjoyed each other *in public*. (This contrasted to many of the younger women who spent large parts of their evening in the women's washroom in order to be together.) In that disruption there is a certain pleasure, a satisfaction, a rebellion that is empowering:

> The acts of analysis, of deconstruction and of reading "against the grain" offer an additional pleasure—the pleasure of resistance, of saying "no": not to unsophisticated enjoyment, by ourselves and others, of culturally dominant

images, but to the structures of power which ask us to consume them uncritically and in highly circumscribed ways. (Kuhn 1985, 8)

Although Kuhn is writing about literary or film deconstruction, the notion of resistance, as feeling good for its own sake, is part of the pleasure of dancing for some women. There is a certain pleasure of subversion, of deviance, and of rejection. The refusal to be as others expect us, or as dominant images suggest women are supposed to behave, is the refusal to be determined within a space that is perceived as an opportunity for creative expression. The flip side of "ought," Williamson (1986, 59) warns us, is "naughty" and in that naughtiness there is a pleasure, as I indicated earlier. There is also a sense of protection offered by being resistant, because it is not feminine and femininity means vulnerability. McRobbie, writing about young punk women, argues that punk, as an anti-feminine position, offers a certain empowerment:

> Punk might be risky, it might represent a steeping out of line, but on the dance floor and on the road home it inoculates the girls both against some danger by giving them a sense of confidence, and against the excesses of sexual discrimination by giving them a lifestyle which adamantly refuses the strictures of traditional femininity. (McRobbie 1984, 149)

THE CONTRADICTIONS OF RESISTANCE ON THE SITE OF THE BODY

The connection between desire and resistance, and the body and sexuality, is, however, riddled through with conflict. Historically, the inscription of individuals into the existing social order has been the task of the family, aided by a rigid sexual morality that ensured reproduction of the dominant structures and ideologies. Women's bodies and subjectivities and the parameters of their allowed activities have historically been regulated by men, whether through overt social legislation, or through more covert ideologies and the practices of individual men. In Sheila Rowbotham's (1972) Marxist analysis of the roots of women's oppression as a group and women's role in revolution, she outlines how one mode of controlling women has been to associate female sexuality with both nature and evil, to be mistrusted and denied;

female desire has been feared as a threat to masculinity. Amy Rossiter's work on mothering offers another example of the ways the social construction of femininity structures women's experiences of their bodies. She writes:

> The conjoining of medical discourse, which positions her as a diseased object, and individualism, which holds her to blame for her "bad" body, produces shame. Primitive, inner, continuously produced and reproduced shame structures women's participation in the various removals which constitute femininity: hair, smells, organ, babies, voices, spaces...Shame, as a layer of identity, is what compels her to define the experiences which produce Woman as "natural and normal." (1988, 34)

This kind of violence done to all women through historical, medical, legal, and extralegal channels means that women often experience their own bodies with mistrust, their desires and passions as dangerous, and their bodies and sexuality with shame and not pleasure.

Even when women do experience pleasure on the site of the body it is not without conflict. Sexual expression itself carries with it multiple and contradictory identities and experiences: loving and violence, pride and humiliation, empowerment and oppression, and pleasure and shame. Stanley Aronowitz notes that sex is connected to autonomy and the "chief mechanism for instituting bourgeois morality" and circumscribing that autonomy is guilt (1981, 293). Given the historical and present-day connection of sexuality and immorality, and the centrality of the body and sexuality on the dance floor, it is no wonder women experience their bodies in dance with contradictory emotions of guilt and a sense of freedom.

As well, female desire in general has been "restricted to zones protected and privileged in the culture: traditional marriage and the nuclear family" (Vance 1984, 3). Inscription into femininity and family, part of the ideological hegemony, is challenged where desire is present outside of the sanctioned home and relations. Popular culture, then, and particularly "going out dancing," becomes a site of intense conflict for women in the way it allows for a certain freedom of expression of desire and sexuality, if not exactly condoning it, in the public sphere.

This is related to the cultural imperative to be a good girl, that is, one who keeps her sexuality private, and certainly does not express her erotic powers. Audre Lourde, in *The Uses of The Erotic: The Erotic as Power*, writes that the suppression of women's eroticism is an effective way to control women's sense of empowerment.[8] It is a way to reproduce relations of domination and subordination through controlling women's sexuality and its inherent power.

> The erotic is a resource within each of us that lies in a deeply female and spiritual plane, firmly rooted in the power of our unexpressed or unrecognized feeling. In order to perpetuate itself, every oppression must corrupt or distort those various sources of power within the culture of the oppressed that can provide energy for change. For women, this has meant a suppression of the erotic as a considered source of power and information in our lives. We have been taught to suspect this resource, vilified, abused, and devalued within Western society. On the one hand, the superficially erotic has been encouraged as a sign of female inferiority; on the other hand, women have been made to suffer and to feel both contemptible and suspect by virtue of its existence. (Lourde 1984, 53)

Women are not supposed to realize this power, to "flaunt" their sexuality or to express pleasure in it, but only to feel ashamed or, at best, ambivalent about it. Rowbotham gives the example of how the historical denouncement of unwed mothers and prostitutes had more to do with the control of women's sexuality, and thus women, through the enforcement of shame, than with issues of morality (1972, 21). It is the suppression of female power in order to guarantee individual and collective male privilege.

Beyond the fears imagined and the shame projected there is always the possibility of real danger in disruption. Men's control of women's sexuality is grounded materially as well as ideologically. The physical expression of desire and sexuality in a public space, may have possibly perilous, concrete consequences. Those consequences—insofar as unknown others are involved—range from felling bothered by intrusive men to fearing potential violence to actually experiencing violence, shame, or guilt. The dance floor illustrates why feminists debate sexuality as "simultaneously a domain of restriction, repression, and danger as well as a domain of exploration, pleasure, and agency" (Vance 1984, 1). The way sexual freedom and safety are in tension implies that the positive, energizing, sensual pleasures of going out dancing are often outweighed by the fear of danger. Exploitation, rape, harassment, brutality, guilt, and shame lurk as shadowy threats.[9]

There is another source of contradiction and guilt for some women—what Dimien calls the "special cultural tension between feminism and sexuality" (1984, 14). The "political correctness" of not engaging in stereotypical feminine behavior can mean that dancing in certain ways, or even at all, is bending to dominant expectations, since sexual expressiveness in a male-defined space is seen as intrinsically degrading to women. The way the space is defined by men was apparent in, for example, the language at the Big Bop. We were there on "Girls Night Out" when the cover charge is waived for women, an explicit construction of the space as male. Participating in a dominant cultural practice, one where a prime site of women's oppression—her body—is the focus of activity, may be viewed as consent and even collaboration, not refusal.

CONCLUDING QUESTIONS: PARADOXES OF RESISTANCE

It is the contradiction of contesting hegemonic forms and practices on the very ground which contributes to their production and reproduction that the root of the paradoxical nature of resistance lies. Ultimately there are a multitude of positions, politically correct or not, that a woman can take up dancing in a club. As I have argued, dancing as popular cultural form is not entirely aligned with dominant definitions of femininity and female sexuality. However, the degree of opposition within a space that potentially subordinates women can range from merely theoretical resistance to embodied challenge, from unconscious and thus unintentional to deliberate and collective. In the first case, by virtue of being there in public, taking up space and enjoying the sensuality and sexuality of herself dancing, a women (regardless of consciousness) is in some ways contesting the dominant notions of femininity. In the second instance, women can overtly disrupt and challenge the status quo by ignoring social conventions and imperatives like coupled heterosexuality and politely restrained dancing.

Yet there are paradoxes of resistance at work here. Haug reminds us of the limits and possibilities of challenging the dominant culture's meanings, of the way claims are made on our subjectivities by the available forms and practices, and of the necessity for compromise—that is, the paradox of opposition's embeddedness in dominant culture.

> In an effort to make their lives meaningful, individuals attempt to resist the encumbrances of the dominant culture. It is however virtually impossible for them entirely to abandon traditional norms and expectations. On the other hand they can—and indeed do—find compromise solutions that extend the limits of their capacity for action. Thus we witness individuals searching for a meaning to life within pre-existing structures, yet at the same time negating them. (1987, 44)

Our after-the-fact criticisms of many of the practices and relations of power (both overtly visible and subtly sensed) at the club did not prevent us from having a pleasurable evening. We circumvented the contradictions partly because we are not without contradictions and splits within ourselves. Socialized within the dominant culture, there are parts of ourselves that are comfortable with the scene: we have not escaped internalization of certain oppressive practices as natural.

A parallel can be drawn to Erica Carter's (1984) analysis of postwar West German female commodity consumption patterns. She describes how nylon stockings, when purchased by working-class girls, represent hard-earned cash spent on a pleasure that had been orchestrated by the market, as "one of the more visible manifestations of American cultural hegemony" (191). Alternately, in the case of 15-year-old Annette, the fragile stockings become a mode of escape and an indulgence in a legitimate sphere of pleasure, a "moment of disorder and disruption [that] marks the displacement of potentially more grandiose demands for self-determination onto the only site where they may be realistically met" (212). "Artificial silk" stockings become the symbol that begs the question of consumption as "passive manipulation or active appropriation?" as well as the question of the limits of framing activity as resistance. The paradox of this refusal is in its restriction to a private and individual moment of empowerment, and ultimately in its powerlessness.

This kind of reversal which produces a paradox in individual resistance was evident at the Big Bop. Dancing alone on the club floor, one woman violates another dominant practice: I have the sense that men cannot bear seeing a woman dance alone and they feel that "boy, if she dances like that she must be sending out invitation vibes." Her indifference to "cruising" men and the prevalent social relations on the floor, coupled with sensuality of her dancing, resulted in her being framed as sexually inviting, a dangerous, contradictory, and uncomfortable position. She dampened her energetic movements, and consequently her pleasure. She tells me she no longer goes out dancing, preferring the privacy of her room. Thus the act of personal rebellion worked here mostly as a form of self-control, and partial reinsertion of self back into the dominant order.

Equally paradoxical is the ability of resistance to feed indirectly into dominant social expectations while apparently subverting authority, thereby canceling out the power of the refusal. One now classic example is Paul Willis's often cited research, *Learning to Labour*, where he examined how working-class kids took their respective places in the social order. It was not entirely by learning their subordinated roles in school. Rather, in the process of rejecting hegemonic education they eliminated the possibilities of moving outside their particular circumstances. This is the resistance that leads to social reproduction, not change, even in its rebelliousness (Aronowitz 1981).[10]

There is a dilemma around deliberate refusal that is posed by being in a space such as the Big Bop as feminists. Since one traditional way of defining women is to consider them as sex objects, it is important for women to resist this positioning entirely. This means denying ourselves the pleasure of dancing in a public space that is predominantly heterosexual—a large percentage of Toronto's clubs. Yet, demanding sexual freedom that has not been women's is also important and political; by doing so we render sexual exploration and expression as legitimate, feminist, activities.

Another dilemma in dancing as oppositional is raised when claiming creative rights on the dance floor and disrupting dominant practices becomes a form of "dance terrorism." Dance terrorism might be viewed as the underside of taking space for one's own pleasure; going too far, it makes rebellion an infringement on others' pleasure and expectations of a night out dancing. Contestation of the available and dominant practices by an individual can be viewed as resistance or as inflicting havoc. Dance terrorism may be very different from women making space for themselves or enjoying their bodies in dance publicly; it violates the liberal notion of freedom to be or do whatever one likes as long as it is consensual. However, making sure no one else notices a woman's resistance on the dance floor seriously limits the emancipatory power of disruption while destroying any political possibility, and contributes to the self-regulation in which women engage off the dance floor.

These contradictions of resistance—the way it necessitates compromise, its role in social reproduction, and the way rebellion itself leads to reproduction—leave unresolved the perplexing and contradictory nature of resistance. When are nylon stockings or taking up space on a club dance floor forms of resistance and when are they social reproduction, the inscription of self into the social order? Our positive appropriation of the practices of the dance floor did not change the power relations of the scene, although we felt temporarily, and joyfully, empowered. In engaging in this particular form of popular culture we were both contesting certain hegemonic constructions of femininity and contributing to the reproduction of this kind of scene with it attendant social relations. Did we represent a genuine challenge to the dominant social relations and practices or were we merely indulging desires that had been orchestrated through forms of popular culture? Must moments of resistance always be as Grossberg writes, "local, fragile, hesitant, and temporary, waging a kind of guerrilla warfare with little or no organizational support" (1986, 187)? The dilemma is articulated differently in Hebdige's *Subculture: The Meaning of Style:*

> I would like to think this Refusal is worth making, that these gestures have a meaning, that the smiles and the sneers have some subversive value, even if, in the final analysis, they are, like Genet's gangster pin-ups, just the darker side of sets of regulations, just so much graffiti on a prison wall. (1979, 3)

I believe, as McDonough does, that dance does have something to offer in the way of resistance:

> The doing of dance has the potential to direct our passionate and rightful anger at injustice outward. When we embody our feelings by facing them, owning them and giving shape to them through movement, along with others, we validate our righteous indignation against oppression and foster our innate strength (1987, 5)

This is not to romanticize the potential for popular dance as a basis for social transformation but to locate the impact of women dancing back in the articulation of a broader project and larger collective action. Feminists have increasingly been claiming dance as a legitimate social activity and creating the alternate spaces within which to engage in it. But equally important is to not be isolating ourselves from other women nor to be decreasing the visibility of women who are, intentionally or not, contesting dominant practices in public spheres. Rather than be on the margins, we should be both organizing and disorganizing spaces in which to dance, to engage our rightful desires and pleasures.

PHILIP R. D. CORRIGAN

Chapter Seven

The Making of the Boy: Meditations on What Grammar School Did With, To, and For My Body

For Philip, Arthur, George, and myself; we lived there 1952–1960.

Officers and gentlemen...Officers and gentle-
men...(shouted at the class by Antony Harding,
English Master, Haberdashers' Aske's Hatchman
Boys' School, 1958)

Whatever the Weaknesses of the school, there
can be little doubt that in a real sense most of
the boys, especially if they stayed into the
sixths, were better people for having been with
us for five, six, or seven years.[1] (E. H. Goddard,
Head Master of Haberdashers' Aske's Hatchman
Boys' School, 1932–1961).

    1. *Scramble/Hysteria (for Jacques Lacan)*: There can be little
doubt? Officers? Whatever the weaknesses? Gentlemen? That in a

real sense. Gentlemen? Most of the boys. Officers? WERE BETTER PEOPLE (Officers and Gentlemen). For having been with us, been with us, been with us, for five, six, or seven years. For FIVE, SIX, or SEVEN years. (15,000 hours, isn't it?) Officers and Gentlemen. Little doubt. Officers. That in a real sense, and a REAL sense. Gentlemen. Better People, better people. Officers and Gentlemen. SERVE AND OBEY. SERVE AND OBEY. SERVE. SERVE. (I do not apologize for this, this was what The Terror was/is like! P.R.D.C.).

2. *Discourse, Of Course (for Michel Foucault)*: In the medium level (some messy place between the micro and the macro) it is unusual to have access to indefinitive accounts concerning authority over our lives. Of course, we often have those terse and tense (dense) documents produced within their rhetorics, half-held by their reasons, from their repertoires, from such, such were and are their resources; but rarely a clear grammar of their rules, that are no games.[2] A school report; a marriage (or any other) license; a social (security/insurance?) number; a certificate to preach, to teach, to doctor, to drill into mouths, to dispense or to dispel, does not show and tell us much; although they are all radically in/forming. This rendering that follows is "fortunate" in being assisted by a discourse of one of Them; one of the authorized men, who ruled and regulated my life from 1952 to 1960.[3]

3. *Getting There (for Stanley George Corrigan)*: I was born on June 9, 1942, in Paddock Wood, Kent, England, U.K., Europe at 2 p.m. (my mother, Norah, said, to the nurse, "Oh, that's when I normally clock in"[4]; the nurse replied (prophetically?), "Well, you're clocking in within this one, certainly!"). We, Mum and I, then lived for a while with her sister, Edith Richards (but by then, Galt), at 76 Duncroft, Plumstead, London S.E. 18., and there was a war on, don't you know? My father, Stan, and my uncle, Bob (Edith's husband), were away at the War, soldiering somewhere. The connections, for these men, to (their) wives and the lives of (their) children, were accomplished by aerographs-photographs and letters, micro-reduced and sent at a special rate for the wives of servicemen—avalanched to them in unknown places "over-seas." Mum, Edith, Nicolette (Edith's daughter), and I survived the War despite some bombing, including a V2 Rocket that landed on the top of the hill that partly comprises Duncroft; I was shitting at the time, on the pot; the pot (and its contents?) were never found. I too survived this; thin, gawky, blond curls and a tense smile, with my hands in tension too.

Dad came home. (Uncle Bob, Edith's husband, did, also, but

with cancer. He died soon. I recall him only as the man others visited whilst I was given a glass of milk and a pear, a seeming exotic fruit after the ravages of warfare). I hit Dad and said (and here may be the first discourse use of my life?) "Why is this man eating my butter" (there being butter rationing, along with so much else, at the time).

Thus family life began: first at Villas Road, Plumstead (but lower Plumstead), and then, around the time of the birth of my brother Paul (1948), we moved to Coldharbour Estate, a new council (i.e. public) housing estate in Eltham, London. Infant School, Primary School. Thence we moved to 166 Swingate Lane, a "prefab" (a special sort of bungalow, built to replace housing "lost" in the bombing) back in Plumstead (upper) within a few yards of Duncroft, Edith, and former reality. My home, 1950–1960. Two bedrooms only, so Paul and I slept in the same room for all my years there, and Primary School continued ("You're so strange, Philip Corrigan, you must be an only child," Miss Bennett, Teacher, Timbercroft Primary School, 1950).

In London, as most of England and Wales at that time (the 1950s, remember them?) children at state schools "sat" (a lovely word) their 11-plus Examination. The percentile thus accomplished gave entry to four different kinds of high/secondary schools: private (normally fee-paying); grammar; central/technical; and secondary modern. This, essentially a tripartite division (the very able, the able/average, and the less than able, corresponding to a somewhat unequal law of thirds), was a secondary structuration that corresponds to the deep primary structure[5] of English (and Welsh) schooling as indicated by the three "Great Commissions" of the 1860s: Clarendon for the elite/ruling class schools; Taunton for the middling sort; and Newcastle for ordinary folks. Its rhetorical legislative moment was provided by the 1944 Education Act with is slogan "Secondary Education for All." We have to recall that until then, most people left school at 10, 11, 12, or 13 (as the school leaving age was raised), with "an elementary education."

I "passed" (a word redolent with meaning for the rest of my life; when will I be found out?) but in the second grouping within the "top" London percentile. The top top grouping were "offered" the "chance" to be scholarship students at essentially elite fee paying schools, usually for boys, notably Christ's Hospital.[6] The middle grouping of the "top," like me, had "access" to 10 or so state grammar schools across London. The third grouping (still within the top 10–15% or so) had only the choice of London or local central/technical schools, or local secondary moderns. This set of social relations was clouded but not really changed by the comprehensivization of the 1960s and 1970s, since streaming within much larger secondary schools represented tripartism in miniature. But Corrigan's "Law of Thirds" applies almost exactly in England and Wales as in the U.S.A., as in Canada: a "small" third go to significant post-secondary schooling; a large third obtain a school learning certificate of some kind or other; a "third" (of varying sizes) drop out or leave without any "useful" certification at all. But then what social structure could "cope with" 100% "A" students, all ready for university? How would schooling then "sort," "mark," "park," and "store" relevant labor power/social identities?

Of course, largely outside and beyond all of this were the private schools of England that have successfully been reproducing the male ruling class for several centuries: Eton, Harrow, Winchester, Marlborough, Westminster, and so on, the schools that produced some of my anti-heroes including Guy Burgess, Kim Philby, Anthony Blunt, and Donald MacLean and, in a constrasting but connected register, Eric Blair, and George Orwell.[7] I can still, with an accuracy of 80%, tell a "public" (i.e. private) school "boy" at 100 paces: they will never touch their lips, they will always speak as if they know, as if they are right....they will bray. They are effortlessly there, not "grubby little pushers."

My father's elder brother, Bert, had obtained a scholarship in the much more difficult times of the 1910s, to go precisely to Haberdashers' Aske's Hatcham Boys' School. His doing so had blocked my father's chances since scholarships then, as later, never really covered all the costs of trying to be upwardly mobile; so, generally, working-class families sent the first "successful" boy onwards and upwards and blocked all girls and any subsequent boy. In my mother's family, the same "rule" applied; Charley, the only boy, was sent to Woolwich Polytechnic to learn to be a draughtsman, which did him good as the "wild colonial boy" with the groundnut scheme, and two "spells" in Rhodesia/Zambia with Consolidated Trust (on the latter, he commented that the servants were not the same; hooray, for that!). It is not without its enduring moment to see how masculinity-as-primogeniture worked for those without property. So, I was interviewed, with Dad, at Aske's, as I shall henceforth call it (although the full name is distinctive as being the longest name for any grammar school in England[9]). And "they" accepted me (and Dad, by then a Civil Servant, no less!). It turns out they had to accept both (a) a proportion of all boys in the top and middle 10% and (b) some proportion of "local" boys (from Deptford) in the top 25%; hence a double entry of a (differentiated) working class.

4. *The Object, Itself (for E. H. Goddard)*: The school. In fact, for me, from 1952 to 1960, simply School. Six hundred or so boys, in five buildings on top of Telegraph Hill, New Cross, London S.E. 14. At the entrance, a statue of Robert Aske, the "founder," Master of the Haberdashers' Company, one of the London Guilds, in between the two glorious revolutions (i.e. bourgeois victories) of 1666 and 1688; he died in 1684. In the middle of the five-junction road system, a sandbin (for the winter ice and, rarely, snow), source of the school "song," The Sandbin, and an irregular satirical magazine, *Sandbin*, posing itself against the august and proper *Askean*. I have never "gone back," so this and any subsequent description relies on a memory of upwards of 28 years ago, although some sketches I have attempted previously.[10] I was "accepted" (oh, the yearn-yawn of that now, but then....) which is like "passing" for the second time.

So I "start" in September 1952. The school is about an hour bus ride from my home, which was on the outskirts on London (I discover, to my horror, in 1986, that it is really The Suburbs!). My parents discover, in 1960, that they have to pay out enormous sums (relative to their incomes) for "extras" which are nonetheless essential (e.g. "No son of Mine is not going to have....") for at least three (later four) kinds of uniform. For summer, blue blazer, grey flannels, white shirts; for winter, black jacket, black trousers, white shirts; for sports, rugby clothes for winter and cricket gear for summer. Plus socks, caps, proper raincoats, ties, gym clothes, badges, and so on....

So someday in September 1952, I travel to the school for the second (but, really, the first) time by 126 and then 53 London Transport Bus (my travel paid for by the London County Council/LCC Education Committee—the former, as the Greater London Council, abolished; and the latter, as the ILEA, about to be abolished, by the Conservative Government). This first day is imprinted with horror for the rest of my life. Although a State School, the rules of Aske's allow—for the better making of the boy—forms of legitimated violence by some boys (senior or bigger, in some respects) on "new" boys. Three kinds can hurt me, I learn: just for these days, all boys in forms II through VI (they take their clean white handkerchiefs, soak them in water, and turn them into "coshes" to beat me (and the others) around the head; laughing, laughing). E. H. Goddard, then Head Master, lamented the use of coshes and bicycle chains by *les autres*—working-class boys not admitted to the school—but was oblivious to this mass, legitimated brutality which was, for him I presume, all good, clean fun! Secondly, for ever, Prefects—boys in the VIth form (lower or upper) who have been given the accolade of officership no doubt a part of their gentlemanhood, with the right to hit, punish, hurt, and hurt again. Thirdly, quite differently, to use the terms of Paul Willis,[11] the lads, those "allowed" into the school, but never really accepted, who formed the bullies of the playground as well as the major constituents of the C stream (in a three-stream, cohort-year, system). But to keep everything neat and confusing, the upper forms within such a cohort were not called A and B, but "GF" or "LF" (for German-and-French, or Latin-and-French), whereas, the C stream were signified by a simple "F." For the rest of my days, I'll never forget the bodily terror I lived those first few weeks and months. Since then, by chance(?), I've often lived opposite, overlooking, or near school "play" grounds and I've watched the violencing and pain and hurt that these "free" spaces engender. Deep lessons are learned there about the danger of "play," about the risks involved in not paying attention to who is around.

The fearfulness has never left me; by then (as now) the skinny kid from South London. Of course, this random (and that was the terror of it) violence was never all that there was to fear; there were The Masters. (Oh yes, the teachers were called Masters and wore gowns all the time.) They used a variety of forms of violence over the years: from the dark sarcasm and pointed humor which pinioned me among giggling, derision, denial; through the forms of punishment that entailed time, as detention after school and the grand slam: "Saturday Morning Detention," or the writing out "lines" (e.g. "I must not chew gum in school" 50, 100, or 150 times—Foucault must have suffered some of this!); to the hurting of the body the random violence of the cuff against the ear, the slap around the face, the book thrown hard into the face, the twisting of the arm, the enforced placing of growing, gangly body in a desk far too small, the slipper/plimsoll applied to the bum, multiply; and there, at the end of the chamber of horrors, the cane. But, in modes which I now recognize as North American, the fear of being sent to your "House Master," your "Head of Junior School," or the Head Master. Alongside, around, all of this was the permitted violence of the compulsory periods of gym(nastics) and sport, let alone music and art (not normally thought to be occasions for brutality, but they were, oh yes!).

So, I lived my years there, certainly the early ones, say from 1952 to 1956, '57, '58 (I cannot now be certain) in a state of terror, of fear, of bodily turmoil. The numerous rules (and the consequences of their infraction) encouraged a certain mentality, a definite masculinity. The Making Of The Boy was a comprehensive project. It also involved, somewhere along the line, learning that I couldn't speak of this, above all complain of this, at home. I learned tactics to cope. I became good at evacuating my body (I can still do this; and, as then, time against a clock, like meat cooking in a regulated oven); I became good at being a clown—all elbows and knees—to get a laugh, to generate anything other than the violence; I became good at being good, performing expressively in reading and writing and (less so) speaking "it" right, so I got patted on the head by the very hands that, before and after, would hit me so hard in the face that my lips bled and my head rang. I learned to internalize anger, hatred, refusal, so greatly, that I tend now to weep when I see films like *If* (my brother wept every day before going to his grammar school, Colfe's, for the first few terrifying years).

But I know now, coldly, what I learned then, there is no (for me) saving of this system: "Geordie," Alan Price sang in his Jarrow Song, of the English Parliament, "burn it down, burn it down...." Exactly. My dream for many years, somewhat abated now, was the cool cleansing fire of the flame-thrower applied first to the statue of Robert Aske. Many good friends disagree, seeing (as in that violent monument to vicious feudalism, Durham Cathedral something worth preserving). "Geordie, burn it down, burn it down...."[12]

5. *The Subject, Himself (for Norah Rebecca Frances Corrigan)*: Each day, during school term, I traveled by bus between these two worlds, located in their different parts of London. I had walked to the last of my primary schools (Timbercroft). The Aske's School day was from 9 a.m. until 4 p.m., with about 90 minutes for lunch-time break. To open the day there was School Assembly (except for boys of parents who indicated their dissent, in writing), constructed around Church of England Christianity, with a dosage of Royalism/Imperialism thrown in, mostly boring though. The Masters would go up onto a platform (also used as the stage for the school dramatic productions), the boys would stand in rows,

graded upwards and backwards from the stage by age/form-level in school, except Prefects would wander the ends of rows. There was a hymn, some reading from the Bible, a prayer, and then—from time to time—announcements, usually from the Head Master (but once from the Chairman of the Board of Governors, who gave us a homily about the "tone" of the School). You know, what is peculiar is that I find this hard to write, 28 years later. As I write (paralleling Freud's talking cure?), I feel some of the bodily memories so strongly and affectively (even affectionately) that I want to have some of "that" back. Despite (because of, even) the anger which is certainly there, this remembering is sentimental, sorrowful, at times marked by tears. And, what, then, is all of that about, if not, in part, all I am trying to show and convey here (as with my other recent work?). The Masters would then file out and then, by year (i.e., age) we too would disassemble to go to our classes.

As I have said, the school was structured by forms (e.g., 1LF, 1GF, 1F comprised the First Year) with a Form Master. But school also had other modes of structuration. To explain, I must provide a little more history. Although dating from the 1684 will of Robert Aske, the Haberdashers' Company only became big in education in the later 19th century,[13] ending up with four substantial grammar schools, two for boys and two for girls. Although in receipt of various State funds, it was not until the 1920s that a major restructuring took place, resulting in two essentially private schools (for boys in Hampstead, later moved to Elstree, and for girls in Acton) in relation of "direct grant" from the then Board of Education; and two in New Cross both "aided" by the Local Eduction Authority (here the LCC). These, in 1946, were transformed into "voluntary controlled" schools under the terms of the 1944 Act. I mention this only because it is from the "imaginary" of the longer tradition (in fact, between the 1680s and the 1870s, the Aske's School had educated very small numbers, mostly "sons of decayed liverymen or freemen of the Company"), which was that older, "grammar" school tradition of private schooling with filiations to the Great Public (i.e. private) Schools, that frames "The Tradition" of *this* School. Thus, one mode of organization was "Houses"—named after individual Masters—into which a boy was enrolled (no choices) before he arrived at school. Alongside a Form Master, I had a House Master; my House was Prince's. Houses, residually copying the notion of residential location in boarding schools, provided a structure within the school that encouraged differentiated *esprit de corps* (e.g., Prince's versus

Harris's) for sport, for debates, but, also, at a different level, for indication of the "worthiness" of the House and all the members within it, e.g. if a Prince's boy became School Captain. School Captains were boys in the Upper Sixth, already Prefects, selected to be the Head Boy in the whole school.

A third mode of structuration—not of major significance to those in the "Junior" forms—were the school societies and clubs, e.g. the Literary and Debating Society, the Chess Club, or the one formed coincidental with my arrival in "Senior" school, the "21 Club" (a group who shared their writings and published anthologies of their poems and short stories). A fourth form of structuration was much more significant, for me: the School Cadet Forces (CCF), again only of relevance to boys over 15. I will return to that later. But in the main, for those first years, the organization that mattered was, and is, fairly standard across many educational experiences: courses and classes: how else are schooled subjects made?

From the very beginning, our academic work was oriented to a series of public examinations, "set" by University Examining Boards (ours was London, the General Certificate of Education), the "Ordinary" level of which was "sat" at the age of 16 or so (although in many such grammar/private schools there was a "Remove" system which—for an elite group—entailed sitting such examinations at the age of 15). This is a broad-based curriculum organized around established, "traditional" academic subjects (English Language, English Literature, Mathematics, Biology, Physics, Chemistry, Geography, History, Latin, French, German are the ones I can recall; the LF/GF alternation already explained meant that from a very early point, some streaming resulted in taking *either* Latin *or* German.

In the early forms, classes tended to be together, to stay in a room to which the specialized subject Master came, or to move to specialized rooms (laboratories, art rooms, geography rooms, etc.). Later, there were ability groupings, called "sets" (alpha, beta, gamma). In addition, as I have indicated, there were compulsory periods of music, gymnastics/physical education, art, religious instruction, and organized sports (rugby in winter, cricket in summer, with long distance running in between). There were, finally, some 15 minutes of "play" time in the "play"ground during the morning and afternoon sessions, as well as "free" time on either side of the lunches provided at the school. A ritual in themselves.

After the "Ordinary" levels, those who passed "well" in a

sufficient number stayed on into the Sixth Form (divided into Lower and Upper Sixths) to study for GCE "Advanced" Level; much smaller groups, with a more leisurely (yet concentrated) pace. Some, as was *intended* for me, would then stay on for a further term or year to prepare for the Oxford University Entrance Examination; to do "Scholarship" or "Special" Level GCEs; *or*, to re-sit their "A" levels to pass them or gain a better grade. I "passed" sufficiently "well" (not being entered at all for Mathematics or any science subject, failing English Literature very badly) "my" "O" levels to stay on into "the Sixth," where I was also being "prepared" for entry into Oxford; except I left, twice in fact, once during 1959–60.[14] Persuaded back to stay, I "sat" "my" "A" levels (passed "well" in three subjects, English Literature, Geography, and History) *and then left.*

It was only years later that I learned that the place of my first full-time employment, Shoreditch Public Library, now part of the London Borough of Hackney, was within sight of the first ever school, called "hospital," established consequent upon the will of Robert Aske, the Founder, in the 17th century. Another related "quirk" of fate was the chance of my entering, but as a shop servant, the Haberdashery "world"—clothing and accessories. I had worked, as a Saturday job, for two clothing stores for many years. I had two interviews on the same day: at the first, to work in a shop, the employment manager said I was "overqualified" (*had* I obtained this job, I would have worked in a shop opposite The Houses of Parliament). At the second, the committee thought me suitable because I was over six feet tall, and could, therefore reach the top shelves in the public library! Overqualifications in and of the body seem to help sometimes.

Yes, *the* Founder. Each year, there was a special ritual that connected the Great Tradition of elite schooling, Englishness, Christianity, and capitalist masculinity with the little world of this School: Founder's Day/Speech Day. We'd gather in Hall,[15] like for Assembly, but I think with chairs provided, the front rows with guests and parents, and on the stage not just Masters plus the Head, but Governors[16] and then representatives of the Worshipful Company of Haberdashers, including the Master (oh yes, long before *le Maitre*, J. Lacan or the subtle studies of Michel Foucault, I knew there were Masters beyond Masters!). A huge figure, draped in furs (I suspect beaver), floppy hat, preceded by bearers of standards, moving slowly down the side aisle. A speech from the School Captain (in Latin? then in English? I forget), prizes awarded, a speech from this or that Old Boy, the Chairman of the Governors, The Master of the Worshipful Company....Terroristic tedium.[17]

6. *The Body, Myself (for Roland Barthes, who showed me how)*: People grow between the ages of 11 and 18. These "tweenage" years are distinctive in the making of masculinities and femininities,[18] since not only does the body change, but bodymeanings and the image-repertoire of bodies become, in contradictory ways, "available." I've hinted, no more, at some of the body-images I carried within myself (it is *very* important not to pretend that I *could* know then what I *may* know now, so all of this writing is subject to distortion). From photographic evidence, it is possible to see a plump blond-haired baby grow suddenly gawky, thin, "shoot-up," hair turned black, legs like sticks, all elbows and knees, and glasses (from age 10). "Skinny" sums it up quite well (not that there is any joy in the *other* of that, "fat"). There had been some "rough and tumble" in the Primary School, but little to mark me—*at school*—with regard to violence (home is another story, one I am not telling here). But there was fear and, that special term that haunts me to this day, "awkwardness," plus its correlate, always with me, "nervousness": a worrier, not a warrior.

The entry into Aske's was marked first by the need for the uniform (i.e., this was known in advance and was how I *had* to represent my body on Day 1). Centering the uniform was the badge on the left breast pocket of blue blazers (in spring/summer) and black jackets (in autumn and winter) *and* its motto "Serve and Obey." OK! But the cap should never be forgotten (not to wear a cap—from home to school, from school *all the way* home—was to be punished, by prefects, a beating, a detention. The same with the tie. One "devilish prank" was for the lads to take my cap and refuse to give it back! Now, uniforms have been argued for along egalitarian lines (thus nobody can "stand out" through the money of their parents) but this is *almost* nonsense (it could be true *if* there was a standard supplier *and* the clothes were reasonably priced) for there are a range of differential markers that allow money to speak. So, within a few weeks, the subtle differences in uniform began to make themselves clear. Moreover, although I did not have the language then, such distinctions were related to those whose class culture fitted them more easily for Aske's and those who found it hard, or were soon "told" they they did not fit in.

Which brings me to voice, that trace of the body, of the "I" with which we are *engrained* ("Who's that?" on the phone, "Oh, it's you...."; "You ok?" earing someone, "You don't sound too good"). Ways of speaking convey much more than what is "said." The Head Master did two kinds of extra teaching: elocution and the "Sixth Form 'gas' periods." (By "gas" is meant neither methane nor petroleum, but "talk" (or better, *discourse* about "subjects of the day"; Goddard was especially concerned to teach us "vocabulary."). The elocution involved the memorizing of Literature (usually Poetry) and its pronouncement as performance, as "public speaking," indeed, as a kind of acting.[19] So there were two "terrors" here, the memorizing ("Will I remember, will I get it right?") and the required way of speaking ("Will I speak it right?"). If I add that this entailed "being summoned" (interpolating in academic forms) insofar as nobody knew who would be *asked* to speak the Word, we can add another dimension. To be "called upon" thus was to have to stand up, repeat, *and* yet pronounce properly. Outside of the Junior Forms, modern technology entered: the performances were tape-recorded. To this day, I'll never forget the Head Master trying to find a voice on the tape, finding mine, and saying, "Oh No! That's Corrigan, that's a terrible example." This form of naming, "Corrigan," is also not without its significance for understanding one's self. Just that, "Corrigan." So, adaptive and taught, among ourselves, as fellow schoolboys ("students," to this day, means those *not* at school but at university or college), we thought and spoke to/of each other in a like manner: "Ware," "Fox," "Grey," "Corrigan."

Now I can understand School as a theater of regulated performances; then I made sharper distinctions between "academic" and "non-academic" than I can now see to be true. That memorizing, speaking forth, being summoned of the elocutionary period was really the same as doing Physical Education, Geography, Art, Biology, Sports, English...Especially if I tell you that when written work was returned, it was done with comments, publicly;[20] some other forms of written work had to be read out loud. Which reminds me of one felt bodily linkage between these two worlds, Home & School: Homework. Homework was set (fair enough, it is in many high schools, you may think) but was regulated by a *Home Work Diary* which had to be signed every week by a parent or guardian thereby ensuring the enrollment of the home into parental pedagogy!

More mundanely, and thus one of those regulative features which goes without saying, I now think of the hours sitting in uncomfortable desks, usually two by two (even when I was not subject to the publishment of a small sized desk, at the very front, under the Master's eye, hand, stick, book...) 45 minutes of discomfort, being held in place, by the rule and the gaze: registered in the morning after Assembly, and in the afternoon before lessons started. Ticked in tedium. But, at least, I could learn rules for performance (and evasion, sitting very still, putting my hand up third or fourth, not drawing any attention to myself) for the "academic" subjects; the others comprised different dangers. In woodwork, it was the awkwardness (although when I made a string-covered stool, somewhat wobbly, it was a triumph); in music, both being tone deaf and watching too much tv (when played the *William Tell Overture* I was somewhat too loud in my whisper "It's the Lone Ranger"), plus not having the money that playing an instrument implies; in gymnastics, a lack of muscle power and a hatred of the organized (sanctioned) violence plus a pathology against being made to compete (in those games, anyway). Sports, though they were the worst: the sheer madness of rugby—running with/trying to stop someone running with a ball! Tackling them, or being tackled. Why? Cricket was tedium, although (like so many I have heard of since) you can hide in the outfield until some fool swings a potential catch/boundary toward you. Long distance running was "the best," since the route was round the streets beyond the sports field and involved a cafe; 50 or so boys running round and round and round *and* round the streets, so the few of us in the cafe drinking tea and eating bacon sandwiches could be missed (or so we thought, until one day, the Sports Master turned up and came storming in).

In my 15th year, without any consultation, I was conscripted in a Cadet branch of the Royal Army (that it was affiliated with the Irish Guards is the opposite of pleasing to me!) The School had a Combined Cadet Force (CCF)—this was the fourth kind of uniform my parents had to contribute toward the cost of. Every Thursday, I had to dress in a private's uniform and travel from home on buses, dressed like that! The school uniform was bad enough, attracting not simply the possibility of being beaten up, but surveillance of another kind: ("Dear Headmaster, I was on a 53 bus on the evening of XYZ and observed a boy from your school *not* wearing his cap/tie/jacket; smoking; behaving improperly, etc. etc."). Sit through "normal" lessons and then, in the afternoon engage in this military madness: marching, parades, learning how to use rifles, machine guns, climbing ropes, crawling through mud.

If that was not bad enough, we had "real" soldiers (as opposed to the History Master (a Colonel), the Chemistry Master (a Captain), and the Religious Instructor (a Flight-Lieutenant), dressing up for the day). The real military murderer was only revealed when Suez happened in 1956, and he disappeared into the Commando for a term; that he normally taught math, largely through applying a thick plimsoll to the bum, only confirmed my worst prejudices!

So these huge Sergeants, and especially Regimental Sergeant-Majors, from the Irish Guards tried to make us REAL men. Perhaps the only distinction—in measurable social change—I shall ever be able to change in my life, is Arthur's and my refusal to "do it": "Oh, Sergeant-Major, I've loaded this Bren-gun and how do I fire it?" Shrieking with fear, "Point that gun away from me boy, NOW!" But that was later, that was after the compulsory attendance at a *real* army barracks in Norfolk (sleeping under canvas, in straw, all the best for making the boy!) but my first introduction to homosexual joy, so one should not complain too loudly! (Later), after some sustained antics ("Now, sergeant-major, let me get this clear, if I pull this pin out, this grenade goes off...in how many seconds..." "Don't touch that pin, boy, DO NOT TOUCH THAT PIN"). The other technique was exact obedience[21] —marching into walls, into each other.

Before any quick reader of this smiles and moves on, I want to talk of some of the negativities in this resistance, even refusal. It produces an obstinacy, compounded of fear and anger—once punished in gym, and told to hang on the Wall-bars, I did, to the point where I had to have my hands pried off and be given resuscitation. So the anti-making of the boy, within these regulated regulations, through these social forms, does not produce a liberated, or a progressive, man. It produces a survivor mentality and one which speaks to "Getting them [back]," a mentalite not unlike youth and adult gang warfare. Notice how I spoke of burning down the statue, not killing the Head Master. It's a dumb anger (in all the multiple senses intended there); it is also very masculine. It is connected with a discovery, only after his death, that I was (considered to be) very like my father: stubborn, obstinate, angry, tearful—faintly ridiculous, in fact. But, as Roland Barthes was the best to expose for men, *all* these fixatives are partial, so many coins from the ideal ego; and the Ego Ideal hovers all the time, judging, silently; who, then, is now the proper man? So, all these momentary flashes, kaleidos*cop* again, have attempted to portray, is the tightening of the body, the way that the gaze works within this authority structure. In School, as in any total institution, the crucial ecology to understand is that of the ruling relations or, more bluntly: What matters and to whom, when, how? Put— falsely, in my view—from the other side, this becomes: What can I/we get away with? I say "falsely" because I think this is true of "the lads" but not true of me (and you, most of you reading this); for us the body is tightened, shaped, spaced, timed, and worded to *their* tunes and we carry the wounds for a long, long time. Forever? One feature of it, for me (for men?), is being smart, being clever: trying to read and write around their lines, their borders, their limits of variation. But doing this (which I am doing here, as I have been for over 28 years) is to write with language and forms which are remarkably *theirs*! Reading the Goddard book made me both angry and depressed; a depression close to suicidal, in fact. There is the assurance, confidence, call it what you will—certainty, certainly; and the flashes (which do connect with my memories) of, yes, the word I would use is *dedication*, perhaps also Dick Hebdige's concept of *convocation*. He celebrates Labour's triumphant election in 1945, his book ends with the three words "humanity, justice and freedom." But then the bile rises, the squirming starts. It *was* hateful. It *did* twist me around. I *did* "leave" (even if I returned, caught up by the one Master who could have reached me then...).

I did not go to Oxford, but who won in that refusal? Two friends went: Arthur, who tried to commit suicide twice; Michael, who "obtained" a fourth class degree and entered management ("personnel manager") and was soon strike-breaking. Others I have met who might have been like me found it very hard, to put it mildly. But? It displaced me, not going; it certainly did not lessen the elbows and knees.

Coda: The 1980s/Reflexions (for Derek Sayer who shares "it"): All I am trying to say is that bodies matter schooling. They/we are the subjects who are taught, disciplined, measured, evaluated, examined, passed (or not), assessed, graded, hurt, harmed, twisted, re-worked, applauded, praised, encouraged, enforced, coerced, consensed....To have around volumes of educational theory (however radical) that never mentions bodies, and their differentiation, seems to me now, slightly stupid.[22] In a more extended emphasis, bodies may be what (who) is being schooled because by now—I hope—we cannot so easily separate minds, psyches, emotions *off* from bodies. The making of the boy, an ongoing project in English elite and mimicry-elite schools, entails (part of) the making of masculinities: the voice, dress, hands (cut your nails, boy), hair ("Corrigan, you are so *farouche!*"), shoes, socks, trousers/pants, shirts, jackets, ties, caps...I mean, come on, *caps!* But, I was beaten through and through for not wearing my cap; I was beaten for talking when I should not, and not talking when I should. Likewise, I was denigrated for reading what I should not, and not reading what I should. Punished for being "too clever" (a very exact designation in English upper-class rhetoric; usually implied is "too clever by half"), and punished for not being clever enough. No wonder in my first-ever sociological writings I attacked either/or dualisms and all dichotomies as traps and delusions and later came to appreciate Bateson's work on double-binds. Now, also, I can situate what took place (part, and only part, of what "happened" to me, for I also "happened to," "accomplished," and "composed" my "self" too) in terms of social semiotics in which the ideal body operates (whether actually, really, present or not) as the classification device. This figure in dominance is not part of what is being arranged, divided, sorted, compared, and contrasted, but is the *medium* (and, thus, mediation; in a word, grammar) through which all of that is accomplished. The ideal is never actually accomplished, the making of the boy is never finished, perfection is always postponed. The school motto is exact: Serve *and* Obey, since there are always higher orders, masters beyond masters, standards beyond standards. Very English. The whole system works to arrange and echo back a series of rewards and punishments in which, of course, punishments can be or become rewards—the class clown, the one who dared—and some rewards can be or become punishments, e.g., the teacher's pet, the favored boy...in which there is a retreating horizon of perfection, staked out with minefields and pats-on-the-head.

None of what I am saying is particularly novel *except* that I want to insist that this pedagogy works on the mind and emotions, on the unconscious, and, yes, on the soul, the spirit, *through the work done on, to, by, with, and from the body.* Of all the regulated expressive forms, the most central is that of the bodily, and a particular series of embodiments: in writing, in speaking, in walking ("Don't slouch, Corrigan!"), in activity ("Well done/run/played/ shot...boy!"), as/in *performance.* Subjection is thus the simultaneous bending of the knee/bowing of the head (metaphors and realities at the same time) and performing of the act in ways that make the bodily subject feel good and also Good ("Good boy..."). I'll say it again, the contrastive couplet, Good/Bad, is the most powerful in the English language, the fulcrum from which a fountain of accumulating descriptors firework forth, sparks from the wheel, sparks from the hammer and anvil, that go into the making of the boy, *the iron in the soul*. And, of course, and immediately, it was not *that bad*. It is the mundane, tedious ordinariness of this set of regulated relations and social forms that needs the closest possible attention (along with the complex uncovering that this form of social re-membering entails) if we are to make sense, different senses, of how schooling works to produce subjectivities. It is, thus, no triumphalist sense that I seek to convey, more like that of an Unhappy Consciousness (which is the center of Paul Willis's often misread *Learning to Labour*) because this work on, with, by, and from the body is not a matter of a surface-effect, but a structuring deep grammar. The dialectic of this grammar turns on the double-bind of uniformity (the making of the boy; "most of the boys...were better people") *and* being good/doing well. The latter, literally, "breaks ranks," but those different "steps forward" simultaneously set up the ideal standards where we should *all* be, whom we should *all* become, *take one pace forward*!

Some postcards from the front line: one day, consequent to "the lads" grabbing me in the playground, beating me up and so tearing my jacket that it was unwearable, I turned up to school with a *grey* jacket—600 boys in blue or black jackets, one (me) in grey—then I felt it. As I also felt, against my tearful protests, the visit of the parents to the school to complain to *the* Head Master that this had happened, my subsequent summons to "see the Head" and my refusal to name names (my reason being that I feared greater punishment if I did so). Constant, from day 1 of gymnastics/sport, comments on my thin body and my physical, muscular inadequacies: some norm to which I/it was being compared (and yet, nakedly under the showers, we were all different) culminating in the showing of a film about The Camps (now we would say The Holocaust), Belsen, Buchenwald, Auschwitz, I forget, and in the darkened dinning hall, when the *victims* came on screen, a voice, "There's Corrigan," and ribald laughter. Fear, for my safety, in the school, fear around the school (a danger zone where "Boys-from-the-other-school" could jeer and heckle and beat us up), fear on the bus journeys, whether in school or army uniforms: an alternation, in other words, of desire—wanting to have everything in place when under school surveillance, wanting to have nothing in place when outside the gaze, in both places to be ordinary (years later, having a different understanding when Lacan said, "I am always never where I speak"). And then the gang-pseudo-rape I have discussed elsewhere which connected for me, by then almost 17 years old and in the Lower Sixth, a lot of "things." I began to see the connection between male group violence *and* masculine (I will *not* say only heterosexual) sexuality *and* the violence of my father at home—the awful words yelled at me by "the mob" who symbolically raped me were "Let's Get Corrigan." I further connected this with the Catch-22s of School (described earlier as the uniformity/doing well dialexis, dire logic), about the dangers of stepping out of line.

The incident is one which had its pedagogic side—later, when I could recollect in tranquility—because I was then the stage manager for one of those dramatic productions the Head Master liked so much, in this case, *King Lear*. Now stage managers are lowly, but essential staff, serving (and obeying) the Great Officers of the Stage—Directors of various sorts, Authors (if alive and present), and so on, but with some power (interestingly that of exact repetition: *what* they say and *how* they say it, lighting, sounds, curtain rises and falls, scenery shifts and so on...) A few short years later (if that was 1959, I am thinking I already was connected, since I brought *Gemini* magazine with the first (?) English translation of Brecht on the "E-Effect" in the same year) I would understand what I had understood through Brecht and later through Marx. I would know what I had known. I would valorize myself, I would recognize that I had been *trying to define myself* (which may be now, in the late 20th century, an oxymoron, certainly for the discourse theorists!). But here is *The Catch* and here is why I feel we have to attend to the bodily traces, the emotional sentiments, to recover them as part of an archeology not simply of the social self but of that which is objectively subjective (the social as the self) and that which is subjectively objective (the self as the social). The cognitive is useless, a (re)sounding board, a relay, an amplifier which is fixed, there is no play there, no give (and take).

Resistance to the regime I have been describing does not evade the grammar because what is at work in the making of the boy is a repertoire (multivariate complex classificatory schema) which is best thought (as it is lived, by me, now as then) as a maze, a labyrinth.

A tiny digression. Long before Foucault, a friend of Antony Harding's established the theory of "The Breathing Act"; this was the ur-legislation with which They could get you if all else failed them, i.e. by breathing you were breaking that law! Antony was a sign of The Other. Having been himself to Aske's, then to "Teddy Hall" (St. Edmund's Hall, Oxford University) to "read" English, *he went to America.* He had all the ethos that the former would provide (it was he, after all, with his bellowing "Officers and Gentlemen," but then telling us it was from D. H. Lawrence), but had this Otherness, from the YOU/ESS/EH. Not of course entirely because or from him, but from that "place" (quite mythic, as unreal *as* the ideal making of the boy) that we—Arthur, George, Philip, and myself—could sustain ourselves. But through what means, with what mediations? Books, music (rock and roll *and* bebop), films (of course) but then, and here is the repertoire in play, through the origins of modernism (not a word I think I knew then), the Americans in Paris (and sometimes in London), symbolism, surrealism, *imagisme*, a false and falsifying (except for bebop, perhaps!) set of roots and routes, no more "me" than the school ethos. A counter-culture, certainly, but as alternative, as supple-mentation, as different ways of being clever, being smart; it was as alienating (without distanciation) as entering into the normalizing discourse of the school. Later sustained by me—oh I was so much younger then—by days of respectable public librarianship (with *its* uniform appearance) and nights of poetry, jazz, drugs, *night-life.* Until nervous breakdown number one, or number thirteen? But only in slight ways could this countering of Their culture picture their ethos and hardly dent the eidos of their School. Besides which, here the worm turns harder and deeper, all of this flowered during the years of the Sixth Form when They permitted a certain differentiation, a certain independence, a certain *eccentricity* (a word which stills me as I write it, as it immobilizes me when I live it). Character, in England, has that triple play: normalizing (a boy of good character...), role-selection (as in drama), and ironic humor ("He's a real character, that one..."). But the limits of varia-tion were no different. There was still the staged management of the body with that curiously wounding contradiction implying exact replication with difference, with sparkle: all the signs of making an effort ("Could try harder...).

The *serving* and the *obeying* were still there. What I have found, and I speak of myself here *emphatically*, is that the regime I have been exploring here leads to a strategy of *being smart*. This is only one of its alternations (another is the amassing of money, but I do not think Aske's produces entrepreneurialism in excess) but one which I think copes with, tames rebellion; or, better, re-takes revolution (which would be refusing to play!) and restages it as, precisely, rebellion, that which can be indulged by the young. From my extensive reading of and about Philby, Burgess, MacLean, Blunt, and the others, it is clear that *a lot of the time* they continued to play this game, to indulge themselves to revenge on their schools, their fathers, the bloody bosses.

The Great Game indeed! This multiplex and multiform resistance-as-rebellion (entailing, quite centrally, getting back at Them) produces a scribbling, verbalizing, succeeding *critique* which engages in a constant, highly masculine, (re)presentation of self as speaking against the Father, the Master which in *no way at all* evades the grammar or the repertoire of the body. In fact, this mode of resisting rebelliousness sustains an evasion of the bodily and the emotional which is highly functional for the masculine economy. So, as I finally came to realize, somewhere about 1980, i.e. 20 years after leaving school, the procedures I have described— which do not, of course, operate alone—render most men who fall on Their side of the mental/manual division of labor, *bodyless* (hence, and of course, the whole industry of the 1970s and beyond about "The Body," like a second or third schooling). The slim, wiry, "fit" boyish yuppies can face the ugly, fat, obese, "unfit" male working class (baseball hats and beer guts) in a shared division of labor within patriarchy; mentalized or manualized into (as) power. Neither division of this monstrous regiment can speak their fear, remember their affective loss, sense the differential repressions and (yes, in that forgotten Freudian sense) resistances of their tweenage schooling. Of course they/we can, but as heroism (including *its* supplementation, anti-heroism)!

I do not think any of this personal, idiosyncratic, peculiar: it is intimately connected with the dominating political currents of the 1980s—militarism, monetarism, nostalgia, violence. In general (being crude to be clear), only three refusals stand out as the grounds for a possible socialism: all and any politics of liberation which centers bodies as those who need *differently* to define themselves (a constellation which includes all anti-racist, anti-imperialist, and feminist struggles); second, a politics which examines the *grammars* of domination which lead to a denial of the bodily and emotional, especially when done in the name of progress (as much by the left as the right), almost uniquely feminisms; third, residually and scattered, an anarchist politics which sees no great progress in Thingification taking the place of Statolatory, of Administration replacing Politics, that centers the peculiar, the particular, the specific and the lived, and is intensely suspicious of all Great Truths and Big Pictures and Totalizations, almost always partly *there* in communitarian, single-issue and many feminisms, and in situationism.

Insofar as—and of course they do—such refusals exist within schooling, then schools are sites where such significant struggles (struggles over the meaning of the sign) continue, but they are rarely recognized, let alone valorized for this; nor is the work of teachers who mainly "mark time" and convey the axiom: "If In Doubt, Speak your Uncertainty." Usually, as The Who sang it ("Won't Be Fooled Again"): the parting on the right is now the parting on the left. More of the same, equally unacknowledged morality posing as the only and unproblematic Way To Be Good. Way To Go. Being Smart. Being Clever.

As I have argued already elsewhere[23] we (teacherly persons) have to start by being careful, and *then* start within that by taking care of ourselves. Caring involving as it does repairing, entails remembering, catching up the lost threads, the funny, awkward, difficult, silly moments when we felt this, or sensed that. Telling stories, but neither as self-effacing (even if "hiding in the light") evasions, nor as pointed jokes, but more as digressions, lightening, a little, turning, a little, baffling, for a while, the powers of the grammar. Not much? True. Enough? Certainly! The last certainty, *here is where I have to start*, with me, unmaking the making of the boy. Thank you.

HENRY A. GIROUX

Chapter Eight

Postmodernism as Border Pedagogy: Redefining the Boundaries of Race and Ethnicity

Within the current historical conjuncture, the political and cultural boundaries that haves long constituted the meaning of race and cultural politics are beginning to shift. The question of race figures much differently at the beginning of the 1990s than it did a decade ago for a number of reasons. First, the population of America's subordinate groups are changing the cultural landscapes of our urban centers. According to recent demographic projections, Blacks and Hispanics will "constitute a decided majority in nearly one-third of the nation's fifty largest cities....and blacks alone will be the major racial group in at least nine major cities, notably Detroit, Baltimore, Memphis, Washington D. C., New Orleans, and Atlanta."[1] In this case, populations traditionally defined as the Other are moving from the margin to the center and challenging the ethnocentric view that people of color can be relegated to the periphery of everyday life.

Second, while people of color are redrawing the cultural

demographic boundaries of the urban centers, the boundaries of power appear to be solidifying in favor of rich, white, middle and upper classes. The consequences will have a dramatic effect on race relations in the next decade. For example, escalating unemployment among black teenage youth poses a serious threat to an entire generation of future adults; in many urban cities the dropout rate for non-white children exceeds 60 percent (with New York City at 70 percent);[2] the civil rights gains of the 1960s are slowly being eroded by the policy makers and judicial heirs of the Reagan Era and the tide of racism is aggressively rising in the streets, schools, workplaces, and campuses of the United States.[3] In the Age of Reagan and Bush, equity and social justice are given low priority next to the "virtues" of collective greed and individual success. As class divisions grow deeper, intra-class and racial tensions mask the need for collective struggles for social and political justice. As the white working class sees its dream of moving up the social and economic ladder imperiled, it is increasingly coming to view affirmative action, social policy programs, and the changing nature of national and cultural identity as a threat to its own sense of security and possibility. Instead of embracing blacks and other ethnic groups as allies in the struggle to dismantle the master narratives of Eurocentric domination with the discourse of democratic struggle and solidarity, the legacy of institutional and ideological racism appears to have once again reached a dangerous threshold that impedes rather than extends such a goal. As we move into a postmodern world that is progressively redrawing the boundaries established by nationalism, ethnocentrism, and Eurocentric culture, the United States appears to be refiguring its political, social, and cultural geography in a manner that denies rather than maintains a democratic community. Instead of engaging a politics of difference, community, and democracy with respect to the principles of justice, equality, and freedom, the current neo-conservative government appears more eager to sever "the links between democracy and political equality.[4]

The smell of totalitarianism is in the air. Its primary expression is found in the resurgence of racism in this country. Racial slurs are now regularly incorporated into the acts of some rock stars and stand-up comedians;[5] the dominant culture seems indifferent or even hostile to the deepening poverty and despair affecting a growing population of blacks in the underclass in our nation's cities; the growing dropout rate among black students is met with insulting diatribes and the refusal to engage the racism prevelant in our nation's schools;[6] the black family is not high-lighted for its resiliency amidst the most degrading economic and social conditions but is condemned as a cause of its own misery.[7] Increasingly, racial hatred is erupting into racist terror. Growing racial tensions have resulted in outbreaks of violence in Chicago's Marquette Park, Baltimore's Hampden section, Philadelphia's Fishtown and Feltonville, and a number of other cities. Two black youths, Michael Griffith and Yusuf Hawkins, were killed recently by racist-inspired mobs in Howard Beach and Bensonhurst. Civil rights demonstrations have been met by overt white hostility and racist attacks. What needs to be stressed is not only that minorities are increasingly open to ideological and physical assaults, but that the very fate of our society as a democratic nation is at risk. Central to the effort to reconstruct this nation as a democratic society is the need to rethink the project of race, and cultural and economic justice. Moreover, this is not merely a political issue; it is eminently a pedagogical one as well. Racism is an ideological poison that is learned, it is a social historical and social construction that seeps into social practices, needs, the unconscious, and rationality itself. If it is to be challenged at the institutional level, at the very centers of authority, it must first be addressed as an ideological concern for the ways in which it is produced, sustained, and taken up within a cultural politics secured within wider dominant relations of power.

This is not a new insight and generations of black leaders have raised its banner in elegant and courageous ways. The fight against racism has always been seen as an important political objective by those committed to democratic struggle. But in most cases, this concern has been framed within a discourse of modernism that has failed to place race and ethnicity at the center of a radical politics of democracy, difference, and cultural struggle. In what follows, I want to argue for a postmodern discourse of resistance as a basis for developing a cultural politics and anti-racist pedagogy as part of a larger theory of difference and democratic struggle. In developing this perspective, I will first address in general terms the failings of various versions of modernist discourse; next I will argue that the foundations for an anti-racist pedagogy can be taken up by drawing selectively upon the discourses of a critical postmodernism, the discourse of narrative and difference that has largely emerged in the work of black feminist writers, and a neo-Gramscian discourse that articulates difference with a notion of a democratic public philosophy. I will conclude by

suggesting how these discourses provide some important elements
for developing specific pedagogical practices.

REFIGURING THE BOUNDARIES OF MODERNISM

The dominant discourses of modernity have rarely been able
to address race and ethnicity as an ethical, political, and cultural
marker in order to understand or selfconsciously examine the
notions of justice inscribed in the modernist belief in change and
the progressive unfolding of history.[8] In fact, race and ethnicity
have been generally reduced to a discourse of the Other, a discourse that regardless of its emancipatory or reactionary intent,
often essentialized and reproduced the distance between the
centers and margins of power. Within the discourse of modernity,
the Other not only sometimes ceases to be a historical agent, but
is often defined within totalizing and universalistic theories that
create a transcendental rational white, male, Eurocentric subject
that both occupies the centers of power while simultaneously
appearing to exist outside time and space. Read against this
Eurocentric transcendental subject, the Other is shown to lack any
redeeming community traditions, collective voice, or historical
weight—and is reduced to the imagery of the colonizer. By separating the discourse of the Other from the epistemic and material
violence that most postmodernist critics have identified as central
to the character and definition of Western notions of progress,
modernist discourses were never able to develop an adequate
understanding of racism that could serve as a form of cultural criticism capable of redefining the boundaries and articulations
between itself and the subordinate groups it continually oppressed.
In this sense, modernism in its various forms served to repress the
possibility of linking the construction of its own master narratives
and relations of power with the simultaneous creation of alternative narratives woven out of the pain, misery, and struggle of subordinate groups.[9] Modernist discourses, in part, have served to
solidify the boundaries of race and ethnicity either by creating biological and scientific theories that "proved" the inferiority of
blacks and other subordinate groups, or in its more liberal forms
created the self-delusion that the boundaries of racial inequality
and ethnicity were always exclusively about the language, experiences, and histories of the Other and had little to do with power
relations at the core of its own cultural and political identity as

the discourse of white authority. In the first instance, the ideology of racism and degraded Otherness can be found, as Cornel West points out, in the logics of three central European traditions: the Judeo-Christian, scientific, and psychosexual. He is worth quoting at length on this issue:

> The Judeo-Christian racist logic emanates from the biblical account of Ham looking upon and failing to cover his father Noah's nakedness and thereby receiving divine punishment in the form of blackening his progeny. Within this logic, black skin is a divine curse owing to disrespect for and rejection of paternal authority. The scientific racist logic rests upon a modern philosophical discourse guided by Greek ocular metaphors, undergirded by Cartesian notions of the primacy of the subject and the preeminence of representation and buttressed by Baconian ideas of observation, evidence, and confirmation that promote and encourage the activities of observing, comparing, measuring, and ordering physical characteristics of human bodies. Given the renewed appreciation and appropriation of classical antiquity, these activities were regulated by classical aesthetic and cultural norms. Within this logic, the notions of black ugliness, cultural deficiency, and intellectual inferiority are legitimated by the value laden, yet prestigious, authority of science. The psychosexual racist logic arises from the phallic obsessions, Oedipal projections, and anal-sadistic orientations in European culture that endow African men and women with sexual prowess; view Africans as either cruel, revengeful fathers, frivolous, carefree children, or passive, long-suffering mothers; and identity Africans with dirt, odious smell, and feces. In short, Africans are associated with acts of bodily defecation, violation, and subordination. Within this logic, Africans are walking abstractions, inanimate things or invisible creatures. For all three white supremacist logics, which operate simultaneously in the modern West, Africans personify degraded otherness, exemplify radical alterity, and embody alien difference.[10]

It is important to emphasize that modernity's drive to systematize the world by mastering the conditions of nature and human life represents a form of social modernism that must not be confused with the more emancipatory elements of political modernism. On the one hand, the project of social modernity has been carried out under the increasing domination of relations of capitalist production characterized by a growing commodification, bureaucraticization, homogenization, and standardization of everyday life. Such a project has been legitimized, in part, through an appeal to the Enlightenment project of rationality, progress, and humanism. On the other hand, the legacy of political modernism provides a discourse that inaugurates the possibility of developing social relations in which the principles of liberty, justice, and equality provide the basis for democratic struggles. If the ravages of modernism have led to overt forms of racism and colonialization, their victories have provided a discourse of rights, universal education, and social justice.

As I mentioned in the introduction to this book, modernity is not a unified discourse, and its networks of meanings and social practices have included a Western-style counterdiscourse that also offered liberals and radicals spaces for challenging racist practices and ideologies.[11] This challenge can be seen, of course, in the traditions of rupture and dissent in this country that extend from the abolitionist movement to the the civil rights legislation of the 1960s and to the more recent efforts by contemporary activists and artists to counter the increasing racism of the 1980s. As noble as these responses have been, at least in intent, few of them have adquately theorized racism as part of a wider discourse of ethics, politics, and difference.[12] Unable to step beyond the modernist celebration of the unified self, totalizing notions of history, and universalistic models of reason, liberal and radical discourses have been unable to explore the limits of the absolutist character of their own narratives regarding race and difference. Within these discourses, ethics and politics were removed from any serious attempt to engage contingency, particularity, partiality and community within a notion of difference free from binary oppositions, hierarchical relations, and narratives of mastery and control. But modernity has also failed to challenge with any great force the white supremicist logics embedded in the ideological traditions cited by Cornell West. Similarly, it has failed to account for the power of its own authority as a central component in structuring the very notion of Otherness as site for objectification and marginalization.

The emancipatory promise of plurality and heterogeneity as the basis for new forms of conversation, solidarity, and public culture never fully materialized within the more liberal and radical discourses of Western modernity. Caught within the limiting narratives of European culture as the model of civilization and progress, liberal and radical theorists have never been able to break away from Western models of authority that placed either the individual white male at the center of history and rationality or viewed history as the unproblematic progressive unfolding of science, reason, and technology.

For example, dominant strains of liberal ideology have fashioned their anti-racist discourses on a Eurocentric notion of society that subordinates the discourse of ethics and politics to the rule of the market, an unproblematic acceptance of European culture as the basis of civilization, and a notion of the individual subject as a unified, rational self which is the source of all cultural and social meaning. The central modernist political ideology at work here, as Stanley Aronowitz has pointed out is "that a free market and a democratic state go hand in hand."[13] Unfortunately for liberals, it is precisely this assumption that prevents them from questioning how they, as a dominant group, actually benefit from racist ideologies and social relations, even as they allegedly contest such practices. By assuming that the middle class, which bears the values of individualism and free market rationality, is the only agent of history, liberals are blind to the corruptions implicated in the exercise of their own authority and historical actions.[14]

Within this multilayered liberal discourse, the attack on racism is often reduced to policy measures aimed at eliminating racist institutional barriers in the marketplace, providing compensatory programs to enhance the cultural capital and skills of blacks (as in various remedial programs in education or the workplace such as Headstart or the now defunct Job Corps project), or is relegated to patronizing calls for blacks to muster up the courage and fortitude to compete in a manner consistent with the drive and struggle of other ethnic groups who have succeeded in American society.

Though the theoretical sweep is broad and oversimplified here, the basic issue is that modernist discourse in its various forms rarely engages how white authority is inscribed and implicated in the creation and reproduction of a society in which the voices of the center appear either invisible or unimplicated in the historical and social construction of racism as an integral part of their own collective identity. Rather than recognizing how differences are historically and socially constructed within ideologies and material practices that connect race, class, and gender within webbed connections of domination, liberals consign the struggle of subordinate groups to master narratives that suggest that the oppressed need to be remade in the image of a dominant white culture in order to be integrated into the heavenly city of Enlightment rationality.

Eurocentric radical discourses of modernity have also failed to develop a complex and adequate theory of racism as part of a wider theory of difference and democratic struggle. The classic instance in this case is represented by those versions of Marxism which have reduced struggle and difference to a reductionist logo-centricism which universalizes the working class as the collective agent of history. Marxism buys the productivist discourse of modernity but rejects the liberal notion of the middle class as the agent of history. Economism in its Marxist form rejects the rule of the market as the end of ideology and inserts in its place the rule of the working class as the projected end of history. In this view, racism is historically tied to the rise of capitalism and is afforded no independent status as an irreducible source of either exploitation or struggle. In this instance, the notion of historical agency loses its pluralist character. As a consequence, racism is subsumed within the modernist logic of essentialism in which reason and history seem to move according to some inner logic outside of the play of difference and plurality. In effect, class struggle becomes the all embracing category that relegates all other struggles, voices, and conflicts to simply a distraction in the march of history.[15]

Radical social theorists have long offered a challenge to the classical Marxist theory of race, but it is only within the last few decades that such work has advanced the category of difference beyond the essentialism of black nationalism, cultural separatism, staged pluralism, and the discourse of avant-garde exoticism.[16] The failure of modernism around race can be seen in the ways in which it has structured the discourse of educational reform on this issue.

Educational Theory and the Discourse of Race and Ethnicity

Within the discourse of modernism, dominant educational approaches to race and ethnicity imitate many of the worst dimensions of liberal ideology and radical essentialism.[17] Questions of Otherness are generally fashioned in the discourse of multicultural education, which in its varied forms and approaches generally fails to conceptualize issues of race and ethnicity as part of the wider discourse of power and powerlessness. Questions of representation and inclusion suppress any attempts to call into question the norm of whiteness as an ethnic category that secures its dominance by appearing to be invisible. Modernism's emancipatory potential within multicultural education finds expression in the call to reverse negative images of blacks and other ethnic groups as they appear in various forms of texts and images. Missing here is any attempt either to critique forms of European and American culture that situate difference in structures of domination or to reconstruct a discourse of race and ethnicity in a theory of difference that highlights questions of equality, justice, and liberty as part of an ongoing democratic struggle. Multiculturalism is generally about Otherness, but is written in ways in which the dominating aspects of white culture are not called into question and the oppositional potential of difference as a site of struggle is muted.[18] Modernism and dominant forms of multicultural education merge in their refusal to locate cultural differences in a broader examination of how the boundaries of ethnicity, race, and power make visible how "whiteness" functions as a historical and social construction, "an unrecognized and unspoken racial category" that secures its power by refusing to identify culture as a problem of politics, power, *and* pedagogy.[19] As a critical discourse of race and pedagogy, multiculturalism needs to break out of its silence regarding the role it plays in masking how white domination colonizes definitions of the normal.[20] In effect, critical educators need to move their analyses and pedagogical practices away from an exotic or allegedly objective encounter with marginal groups, and raise more questions with respect to how the dominant self is always present in the construction of the margins. As Toni Morrison points out, the very issue of race requires that the bases of Western civilization will require rethinking.[21] It means that the central question may not be why Afro-Americans are absent from dominant narratives, but "What intellectual feats had to be performed by the author or his critic to erase [blacks] from a society seething with [their] presence, and what effect has that performance had on the work? What are the strategies of escape from knowledge?"[22] This means refiguring the map of ethnicity and difference outside of the binary oppositions of modernism. What is at stake here is more than the politics of representation. Issac Julien and Kobena Mercer state the issue clearly:

One issue at stake, we suggest, is the potential break-up or deconstruction of structures that determine what is regarded as culturally central and what is regarded as cultural marginal.... Rather than attempt to compensate the, "structured absences" of previous paradigms, it would be useful to identify the relations of power/knowledge that determine which cultural issues are intellectually prioritized in the first place. The initial stage in any deconstructive project must be to examine and undermine the force of the binary relation that produces, the marginal as a consequence of the authority invested in the centre.[23]

Implicit in this perspective are a number of political and pedagogical challenges that can be taken up by radical educators as part of a broader theoretical attempt to deconstruct and displace some of the more powerful ideological expressions of a hegemonic theory of multicultural education. First, critical educators need to reveal the political interests at work in those forms of multicultural education that translate cultural differences into merely learning styles; the ideological task here is to challenge those mystifying ideologies that separate culture from power and struggle while simultaneously treating difference as a technical rather than a political category. Second, critical educators need to challenge those educational discourses that view schooling as a decontextualized site free from social, political, and racial tensions. What has to be stressed here is the primacy of the political and the contextual in analyzing issues of culture, language, and voice. Third, critical educators must ideologically engage theories of multicultural education that attempt to smother the relationship between difference and power/empowerment under the call for harmony and joyful learning. At the same time, they must further the development of a theory of difference that takes as its starting point issues of power, domination, and struggle.[24] But an anti-racist pedagogy must do more than reconceptualize the political and pedagogical struggle over race, ethnicity, and difference as merely part of the language of critique, it must also retrieve and reconstruct possibilities for establishing the basis for a progressive vision that makes schooling for democracy and critical citizenship an unrealized yet possible reality. In doing so, it is necessary to provide some central theoretical principles for developing the foundation for an anti-racist pedagogy. In what follows, at the risk of repeating some of my comments on postmodernism in the Introduction, I will argue that there are elements of a postmodern discourse that offer valuable insights for engaging in such a task.

POSTMODERNISM AND THE SHIFTING
BOUNDARIES OF OTHERNESS

Postmodernism is a culture and politics of transgression, it is a challenge to the boundaries in which modernism has developed it discourses of mastery, totalization, representation, subjectivity, and history.[25] Whereas modernism builds its dream of social engineering on the foundations of universal reason and the unified subject, postmodernism questions the very notion of meaning and representation. Postmodernism not only opens up a new political front within discourse and representation, it also criticizes the notion of the unified subject as a Eurocentric construct designed to provide white, male, Christian bosses and workers with a legitimating ideology for colonizing and marginalizing those Others who do not measure up to the standards of an "I" or "We" wielding power from the center of the world.[26]

Postmodernism also rejects the modernist distinction between art and life. In doing so, it rejects the modernist distinctions between elite culture and the culture of everyday life. As a discourse of disruption and subversion, postmodernism does not argue that all referents for meaning and representation have disappeared; rather, it seeks to make them problematic, and in doing so reinscribes and rewrites the boundaries for establishing the conditions for the production of meaning and subjectivity.[27] For example, in treating cultural forms as texts, postmodernism multiplies both the possibilities of constructing meaning and the status of meaning itself. In this sense, postmodernism redraws and retheorizes the objects and experiences of politics by extending the reach of power and meaning to spheres of the everyday that are often excluded from the realm of political analysis and pedagogical legitimation. In this case, the field of political contestation is not restricted to the state and the workplace, but also includes the family, mass and popular culture, the sphere of sexuality, and the terrain of the refused and forgotten. In the discourse of modernism, there is a world held together by the metanarrative of universal reason and social engineering.[28] Therefore, the central question for modernists has been "How can I interpret and master this world? How do I constitute myself within it?" Postmodernism does not begin from such a comfortable sense of place and history. It subordinates reason to uncertainty and pushes its sense of distrust into transgressions that open up entirely different lines of inquiry. Sygmunt Bauman captures the political and epistemological shifts between modernism and postmodernism in the different questions and lines of inquiry they each pursue. He writes:

> [Postmodernists] have hardly any axioms they may use as a confident start, nor do they have a clear address. Before they turn to exploring the world, they must find out what world(s) there is (are) to be explored. Hence: "Which world is it? What is to be done in it? Which of my selves is to do it?"—in this order....the typically modern questions are, among others: "What is there to be known? Who knows it? How do they know it, and with what degree of certainty?" The typically postmodern questions do not reach that far. Instead of locating the task for the knower, they attempt to locate the knower himself [sic]. "What is a world? What kinds of worlds are there? How are they constituted, and how do they differ?" Even when sharing concern about knowledge, the two types of inquiry articulate their problems differently: "How is knowledge transmitted from one knower to another, and with what degree of reliability?" as against "What happens when different worlds are placed in confrontation, or when boundaries between worlds are violated?" Not that postmodern questions have no use for "certainty"; not even reliability." The one-upmanship of modernist epistemology looks hopelessly out of place in that pluralist reality to which the postmodern ontological inquiry is first reconciled and then addressed. Here that overwhelming desire of power which animated the search for the ultimate (and which alone could animate it) raises little passion. Only eyebrows are raised by the self-confidence which once made the pursuit of the absolute look as a plausible project.[29]

In the above quote, Bauman articulates an antagonism that has become a central feature of postmodernist discourse. That is, postmodernism rejects those aspects of the Enlightenment and Western philosophical tradition that rely on master-narratives "which set out to address a transcendental Subject, to define an essential human nature, to prescribe a global human destiny or to proscribe collective human goals."[30] Within this perspective all claims to universal reason and impartial competence are rejected in favor of the partiality and specificity of discourse. General abstractions that deny the specificity and particularity of everyday life, that generalize out of existence the particular and the local, that smother difference under the banner of universalizing categories are rejected as totalitarian and terroristic.

But there is more at stake here than simply an argument against master-narratives or the claims of universal reason, there is also an attack on those intellectuals who would designate themselves as the emancipatory vanguard, an intellectual elite who have deemed themselves to be above history only to attempt to shape it through their pretentions to what Dick Hebdige (1986) calls an "illusory Faustian omnipotence."[31] In some versions of the postmodern, not only does totality and foundationalism not lead to the truth or emancipation, but in actuality to periods of great suffering and violence. The postmodernist attack on master-narratives is simultaneously a criticism of an inflated teleological self-confidence, a dangerous transcendentalism, and a rejection of the omniscient narrator.[32] Read in more positive terms, critical postmodernists are arguing for a plurality of voices and narratives, that is, for narratives of difference that recognize their own partiality and present the unrepresentable, those submerged and dangerous memories that provide a challenge to white supremacist logics and recover the legacies of historically specific struggles against racism. Similarly, postmodern discourse is attempting with its emphasis on the specific and the normative to situate reason and knowledge within rather than outside particular configurations of space, place, time, and power. Partiality in this case becomes a political necessity as part of the discourse of locating oneself within rather than outside of history and ideology.

Related to the critique of master-narratives and theories of totality is another major concern of critical postmodernism: the development of a politics that addresses popular culture as a serious object of aesthetic and cultural criticism, on the one hand, and one that signals and affirms the importance of minority cultures as historically specific forms of cultural production on the other.[33] Postmodernism's attack on universalism, in part, has translated into a refusal of modernism's relentless hostility to mass culture, and its reproduction of the elitist division between high and low culture.[34] Not only has postmodernism's reaffirmation of popular culture challenged the aesthetic and epistemological divisions supportive of academic disciplines and the countours of what has been considered "serious" taste, it has also resulted in new forms of art, writing, filmmaking, and types of aesthetic and social criticism.[35] Similarly, postmodernism has provided the conditions necessary for exploring and recuperating traditions of various forms of Otherness as a fundamental dimension of both the cultural and the sociopolitical sphere. In other words, postmodernism's stress on the problematic of Otherness has included: a focus on the importance of history as a form of counter-memory;[36] an emphasis on the value of the everyday as a source of agency and empowerment;[37] a renewed understanding of gender as an irreducible historical and social practice constituted in a plurality of self and social representations;[38] and an insertion of the contingent, the discontinuous, and the unrepresentable as coordinates for remapping and rethinking the borders that define one's existence and place in the world.

Another important aspect of postmodernism is that it provides a series of referents for both interrogating the notion of history as tradition and for redrawing and rewriting how individual and collective experience might be struggled over, understood, felt, and shaped. For example, postmodernism points to a world in which the production of meaning has become as important as the production of labor in shaping the boundaries of human existence. Three issues are at stake here. First, the notion that ideological and political structures are determined and governed by a single economic logic is rejected. Cultural and social forms contain a range of discursive and ideological possibilities that can only be grasped within the contextual and contradictory positions in which they are taken up; moreover, while such forms are reproduced under the conditions of capitalist production, they influence and are influenced by such relations. This is not a rejection of materialist analyses of culture as much as a rejection of the vulgar reductionism that often accompanies its classical interpretations. Second, labor does not provide the exclusive basis for either meaning or for understanding the multiple and complex ensemble of social relations that constitute the wider society. In this case, social antagonisms grounded in religious, gender, racial, and ethnic conflicts, among others, possess their own dynamism and cannot be reduced to the logic of capitalist relations. More specific, the various discourses of historical materialism no longer describe the social order. Third, how subjects are constituted in language is no less important than how they are constructed as subjects within relations of production. The world of the discursive, with its ensemble of signifying terms and practices, is essential to how people relate to themselves, others, and the world around them. It is the textual world through which people develop a sense of self and collective identity and relate to one another; this is not a world that can be explained merely in terms of causal events that follow the rule-bound determinations of physical and economic laws.[39] The political economy of the sign does not displace political economy, it simply assumes its rightful place as a primary category for understanding how identities are forged within particular relations of privilege, oppression, and struggle. In pursuing this line of inquiry, postmodernism serves to deterritorialize the map of dominant cultural understanding. That is, it rejects European tradition as the exclusive referent for judging what constitutes historical, cultural, and political truth. There is no tradition or story that can speak with authority and certainty for all of humanity. In effect, critical postmodernism argues that traditions should be valued for their attempts to name the partial, the particular, and the specific; in this view, traditions demonstrate the importance of constituting history as a dialogue among a variety of voices as they struggle within asymmetrical relations of power. Traditions are not valued for their claims to truth or authority, but for the ways in which they serve to liberate and enlarge human possibilities. In other words, tradition does not represent the voice of an all-embracing view of life; instead, it serves to place people self-consciously in their histories by making them aware of the memories constituted in difference, struggle, and hope. Tradition in postmodern terms is a form of counter-memory that recovers complex, yet submerged identities that constitute the social and political construction of public life.[40]

Postmodernism rejects the modernist discourse on history which views it as uniform, chronological, and teleological. In contrast, it argues for a view of history that is decentered, discontinuous, fragmented, and plural. Jim Collins rightly argues that postmodernism challenges this view of historiography by problematizing "histories that seek to minimize heterogeneity in pursuit of a dominant style, collective spirit, or any other such unitary conception."[41] He elaborates on this by arguing:

> The common denominator of all such histories, from Oswald Spengler's *The Decline of the West* to Will Wright's *Six Guns in Society*, has been the privileging of homogeneous structures that allow historians to draw rather neat generaliza-

tions that support far more grandiose claims about culture
"as a whole." Emphasis has been placed repeatedly on the
diachronic changes between periods, movements, moods, etc.
instead of on synchronic tensions within those subdivi-
sions—which would naturally undermine any unitary formulations concerning a particular period's representation of
itself in a specific time....The chief way to break this spell is
to begin with a different set of priorities—specifically that
most periods are a "mixture of inconsistent elements," and
that different art forms, discourses, etc., all have their own
history as well as a societal history....To account for these
differences, histories that have been predicated on theories of
evolution, mass consciousness, or Zeitgeist, must be replaced
by histories that emphasize synchronic tensions, the frag-
mentation of mass consciousness, and the possibility of more
than one Zeitgeist per culture.[42]

It is worth emphasizing here that postmodernism raises
central questions about not simply how to rethink the meaning of
history and traditions, but it also forces us in the absence of a discourse of essences and foundationalism to raise new and different
questions. In this case, as Chantal Mouffe has pointed out, postmodernism provides us with the possibility of understanding the
limits of traditions so we can enter into dialogue with them, particularly with respect to how we may think about the construction of political subjects and the possibility of democratic life.[43]
Finally, and at the risk of great simplification, a postmodernism of resistance challenges the liberal, humanist notion of the
unified, rational subject as the bearer of history.[44] In this instance,
the subject is neither unified nor can such a subject's action be
guaranteed in metaphysical or transhistorical terms. Postmodernism not only views the subject as contradictory and multilayered, it rejects the notion that individual consciousness and
reason are the most important determinants in shaping human
history. It posits instead a faith in forms of social transformation
that are attentive to the historical, structural, and ideological
limits which shape the possibility for self-reflection and action. It
points to solidarity, community, and compassion as essential
aspects of how we develop and understand the capacities we have
for how we experience the world and ourselves in a meaningful
way.[45] But it does so by stressing that in the absence of a unified
subject, we can rethink the meaning of solidarity through a recog-

nition of the multiple antagonisms and struggles that characterize both the notion of the self and the wider social reality. By recognizing the multiplicity of subject positions which mediate and are produced by and through contradictory meanings and social practices it becomes possible to create a discourse of democratic values that requires a "multiplication of democratic practices, institutionalizing them into ever more diverse social relations...[so that] we are able not only to defend democracy but also to deepen it."[46] In different terms, postmodernism offers a series of referents for rethinking how we are constituted as subjects within a rapidly changing set of political, social, and cultural conditions.

What does this suggest for the way we look at the issue of race and ethnicity? Postmodern discourse provides a theoretical foundation for deconstructing the master-narratives of white supremacist logics and for redrawing the boundaries between the construction of experience and power. In the first instance, by challenging the concept of master-narratives, critical postmodernism has opened up the possibility for launching a renewed attack on the underlying assumptions that have allowed the dominant culture to enforce its own authority and racist practices through an unproblematic appeal to the virtues of Western civilization. In challenging the notions of universal reason, the construction of a white, humanist subject, and the selective legitimation of high culture as the standard for cultural practice, postmodern criticism has illuminated how Eurocentric-American discourses of identity suppress difference, heterogeneity, and multiplicity in its efforts to maintain hegemonic relations of power. Not only does postmodernism provide new ways to understand how power works in constructing racist identities and subjectivities, it redefines culture and experience within multiple relations of difference that offer a range of subject positions from which people can struggle against racist ideologies and practices. By calling into question the themes of "degraded Otherness and subaltern marginality" postmodernism offers new theoretical tools for attacking "notions of exclusionary identity, dominating heterogeneity, and universality—or in more blunt language, white supremacy."[47] Postmodern engagements with foundationalism, culture, difference, and subjectivity provide the basis for questioning the modernist ideal of what constitutes a decent, humane, and good life. Rather than celebrate the narratives of the "masters," postmodernism raises important questions about how narratives get constructed, what they mean, how they regulate particular forms of moral and social experience, and how they presuppose and embody particular epistemological and political views of the world. Similarly, postmodernism attempts to delineate how borders are named; in fact, it attempts to redraw the very maps of meaning, desire, and difference, inscribing the social and individual body with new intellectual and emotional investments, and calling into question traditional forms of power and their accompanying modes of legitimation. All these developments redefine theory by moving it far beyond—and in opposition to—the concerns embodied in the ideologies and questions that have defined the underlying racist principles which have remained unchallenged as a central aspect of modernist discourse.

For educators interested in developing an anti-racist pedagogy, postmodernism offers new epistemologies for rethinking the broader and specific contexts in which democratic authority is defined; it offers what Richard Bernstein calls a healthy "suspiciousness of all boundary-fixing and the hidden ways in which we subordinate, exclude, and marginalize.[48] Postmodernism also offers educators a variety of discourses for interrogating modernism's reliance on totalizing theories based on a desire for certainty and absolutes.

In order for postmodernism to make a valuable contribution to the development of a critical pedagogy of race, educators must combine its most important theoretical insights with those stories and narratives that illuminate how difference and resistance are concretely expressed within communities of struggle organized around specific anti-racist practices. In this way, the project of an anti-racist pedagogy can be deepened by expanding its discourse to increasingly wider spheres of social relations and practices. Postmodern discourse must also do more than redefine difference as an integral aspect of the construction of educational life. Similarly, postmodernism must do more than reconstruct the theoretical discourse of resistance by recovering knowledge, histories, and experiences that have traditionally been left out of dominant accounts of schooling, everyday life, and history. Most important, there is a vital need for postmodernism to open up and establish public spheres among non-academic audiences and to work with such audiences as part of the struggle to fight racism and other forms of domination while simultaneously struggling to revitalize democratic public life. What is important to stress is the recognition that a critical postmodernism needs to provide educators with a more complex and insightful view of the relationship between culture, power, and knowledge. When linked with the language of democratic public life, the notions of difference, power, and specificity can be understood as part of a public discourse that broadens and deepens individual liberties and rights *through rather than against* a radical notion of democracy.

In what follows, I want to further develop how a postmodern discourse of resistance might be elaborated and advanced through the discourse of black feminists, and writers whose work serves to rewrite and reinscribe the relations between power and issues of difference, struggle, identity politics, and narrative.

AFRO-AMERICAN FEMINIST WRITERS AND THE DISCOURSE OF POSSIBILITY

Black women feminists have been writing against the grain for a long time in this country.[49] Most important, they have given the politics of resistance and solidarity a new meaning in the diverse ways in which they have struggled, as Barbara Christian puts it, "to define and express our totality rather than being defined by others."[50] Within the diverse body of material that makes up this work, there is a language both of critique and possibility. It is woven out of forms of testifying, narratives, and theorizing that reconstruct the meaning of difference while simultaneously rewriting the meaning of history as a basis for sustaining community memories and developing viable forms of collective struggle. The tensions that permeate this work range from suffering and resistance to a sense of healing and transcendence. For example, in the work of the novelist Paule Marshall we encounter the attempts to reconstruct "the past and the need to reverse the present social order."[51] In the work of political writers such as June Jordan, Audre Lorde, Bell Hooks, and Hazel Carby there is an ongoing attempt to re-theorize the notion of voice as part of the shifting construction of identities forged in differences, especially those constituted out of class, race, and gender.[52] There is also an attempt to theorize voice as a historically specific cultural site from which one learns to create an oppositional consciousness and identity, a standpoint that exists not only as that which also opposes domination, but also enables and extends individual and social capacities and possibilities for making human connections and compassionate communities of resistance and liberation.[53]

Within this work, a discourse of difference and solidarity

emerges which is multilayered and dialectical. First, all these black women offer, in different ways, a critique of difference as it is constructed through the codes and relations of the dominant culture. Second, black feminist writers have criticized the emancipatory notion of difference put forward by white feminists in the last decade while at the same time developing a more radical notion of the politics of difference and identity politics. Third, there is a brilliant reconstruction of difference in these works through the development of narratives as forms of dangerous memory that provide the foundation for communities of resistance and a radical ethics of accountability. In the next section, I will analyze each of these elements of difference before addressing their pedagogical implications for developing what I call a border pedagogy of resistance.

Unlike many radical and postmodern theories, the work of black feminists is deeply concerned with developing a politics of difference that locates the dynamics of domination in the center rather than on the margins of power. In effect, black feminists have attempted to uncover how complex modes of inequality are structured through racial, class, and gender divisions that lie at the heart of the dominant culture and by definition serve to shape its most basic institutional and ideological forms. A number of issues are at work here. First, there is the need to establish that racial identities are also white, and must be seen as specific historical and social constructions. In this way, questions of ethnicity must be seen as part of a broader discussion of racism. This is imperative in order to understand how whiteness serves as a norm to privilege its own definitions of power while also concealing the political and social distinctions embedded in its essentialist constructions of difference through the categories of race, gender, and class.

Within this perspective, difference cannot be understood outside the dynamics of silencing, subjugation, and infantilization. By focusing on the ways in which white ethnicity exercises power, designates Otherness in terms that degrade and cheapen human life, and hides its own partiality in narratives of universality and common sense, black feminists have been able to redefine what it means for people of color to come to voice and to speak in their own terms. To struggle within a politics of voice, within these practices, means that blacks have to reject a politics of the center in which the Other is reduced to an object whose experiences and traditions are either deemed alien by whites or whose identity has to bear exclusively the historical weight of Otherness and racialization. Hazel Carby illuminates this point well:

> ...one way to rethink the relationship between the social, political and cultural construction of blackness and marginality, on the one hand, and assumptions of a normative whiteness within the dominant culture, on the other, is to examine the ways in which that dominant culture has been shaped and transformed by the presence of the marginalized. This means a public recognition that the process of marginalization itself is central to the formation of the dominant culture. The first and very important stage is...to recognize the cultural and political category of whiteness. It seem obvious to say it but in practice the racialization of our social order is only recognized in relation to racialized "others."[54]

What Carby points to is part of a broader theoretical attempt by black feminists to reject narrow notions of black identity while also calling into question the structured absences that historically and socially locate white ethnicity within subject positions that blind many whites to the mechanisms of cultural apartheid and relations of power that are constitutive of what it means to be part of a dominant Eurocentric culture in America. As Coco Fusco puts it, "Endemic to this history are structured absences that function to maintain relations of power. To put it bluntly, no one has yet spoken of the 'self' implicit in the 'Other' or of the ones who are designating the 'Others.' Power, veiled and silent, remains in place."[55] Black feminists have provided an enormous service by shifting the discussion of difference away from an exclusive concern with the margins and in doing so have made it clear that any analysis of racial identity must include an analysis of how the "dominant other" functions to actively and systematically conceal its own historical and cultural identity while devaluing the identity of other racial groups. By challenging how boundaries of difference have been constructed through dominant Eurocentric codes and binarisms, it becomes possible to deepen our understanding of how white ethnicity is constructed in its attempts to position others. It also becomes possible to rethink the issue of subjectivity and resistance outside the crippling essentialisms that have characterized dominant humanist theory. Identity is no longer something that is fixed but fluid, shifting, and multiple. At the same time, oppression can now be seen in its multiple antagonisms and social relations. Once dominant culture is racialized within the discourse of ethnicity and existing power relations, it becomes possible to write history from the perspective of those engaged in the struggle against cultural genocide. Voices now begin to emerge from different locations and are no longer authorized to speak through a Eurocentric perspective that defines them in its own interests. Bell Hooks links this emergence of multiple voices as part of a wider struggle for a politics and identity that is crucial to the reconstruction of black subjectivity. She writes:

> We return to "identity" and "culture" for relocation, linked to political practice—identity that is not informed by a narrow cultural nationalism masking continued fascination with the power of the white Hegemonic Other. Instead identity is evoked as a stage in a process wherein one constructs radical black subjectivity. Recent critical reflections on static notion of black identity urge transformation of our sense of who can we be and still be black. Assimilation, imitation, or assuming the role of rebellious exotic other are not the only available options and never have been. This is why it is crucial to radically revise notions of identity politics, to explore marginal locations as spaces where we can best become whatever we want to be while remaining committed to liberatory black liberation struggle.[56]

Central to the notion of difference put forth by many black feminists is a notion of anti-racism that refigures the meaning of ethnicity as a social and historical construct. Such a view signals the end of the essentialist black subject as well as the structured absence of whiteness as a racial category. The strategic importance of this issue has been theoretically developed in the writing of a number of black feminists who have criticized the ways in which the notion of difference has been taken up by many white middle class feminists in the struggle over sexuality and gender.

> Those of use who have been forged in the crucibles of difference—those of us who are poor, who are lesbians, who are black, who are older—know that survival is not an academic skill. It is learning how to stand alone, unpopular and sometimes reviled, and how to make common cause with those others identified as outside the structures in order to define and seek a world in which we can all flourish. It is learning

how to take our differences and make them strengths. For the master's tools will never dismantle the master's house. They may allow us temporarily to beat him at his own game, but they will never enable us to bring about change.[57]

In this quote Audre Lorde uses the notion of difference as a referent for critique and as a basis for advancing the emancipatory possibilities in a radicalized notion of difference. In the first instance, she argues against various versions of contemporary feminism which limit domination to the sphere of sexual relations and, in doing so, develops a discourse of difference that excludes questions of racism, class domination, and homophobia. Under the banner of feminist struggle and liberation, many contemporary feminists have unconsciously reconstructed the Eurocentric logocentrism they claimed they were attacking. In effect, while the center was being reconstructed as an affirmation of feminism in the service of an attack on patriarchy, it functioned to re-create existing margins of power while denying the voices of working class women, lesbians, and women of color. As Lorde points out, "The absence of these considerations weakens any feminist discussion of the personal and the political. It is a particular academic arrogance to assume any discussion of feminist theory without examining our many differences, and without a significant input from poor women, black and Third World women, and lesbians."[58] Lorde is not merely criticizing a feminist perspective that refuses to examine differences as they are constructed outside the worlds of white, middle class women, she is also arguing that in this refusal of difference lie the seeds of racism and homophobia. She recognizes that whites have a heavy cultural, political, and affective investment in ignoring differences. For to recognize such differences is to immediately call into play the asymmetrical relations of power that structure the lives of white and black women differently. For white middle class women, this often invokes guilt and forces them to "allow women of Color to step out of stereotypes...[-and] it threatens the complacency of these women who view oppression only in terms of sex."[59] Lorde is eloquent on this issue.

Poor women and women of Color know there is a difference between the daily manifestations of marital slavery and prostitution because it is our daughters who line 42nd Street. If white American feminist theory need not deal with the differences between us, and the resulting difference in our oppressions, then how do you deal with the fact that the women who clean your houses and tend your children while you attend conferences on feminist theory, are for the most part, poor women and women of Color? What is the theory behind racist feminism? In a world of possibility for us all, our personal visions help lay the groundwork for political action. The failure of academic feminists to recognize difference as a crucial strength is a failure to reach beyond the first patriarchal lesson. In our world, divide and conquer must become define and empower.[60]

But Lorde, like a number of black writers, is not content either to limit her analysis to the racism inherent in narrowly defined feminist theories of difference or to deconstructing forms of cultural separatism which argue that blacks only need to bear witness to the positive moments in their own stories. These are important political and strategic issues, but Lorde is also concerned about developing a politics of solidarity and identity that views difference as a dynamic human force that is "enriching rather than threatening to the defined self when there are shared goals."[61] In this case, black women writers have attempted to develop a politics of difference that celebrates its creative function while at the same time arguing for new forms of community rooted in definitions of power and patterns of relating that allow diverse groups of people to reach out beyond their own interests in order to forge living connections with a multitude of differences for the purpose of developing a democratic culture and society.

At issue here is a politics of resistance in which difference is explored through the category of voice and solidarity. It is important to stress, even at the expense of overstating the issue, that black feminists have attempted to develop a notion of black subjectivity and voice that portrays black women outside the narrow confines of an essentialist and stereotypical reading. In this case, there is an attempt to develop a notion of self and identity that links difference to the insistence of speaking in many voices, to fasten a notion of identity that is shifting and multiple rather than static and singular. Central here is the need to engage voice as an act of resistance and self-transformation, to recognize that as one comes to voice one establishes the precondition for becoming a subject in history rather than an object.[62] In analyzing a portion of her own experience in attending all-black segregated schools, Bell

Hooks comments on how she learned to recognize the value of an education that allowed her to speak in many voices. She writes:

> In part, attending all-black segregated schools with black teachers meant that I had come to understand black poets as being capable of speaking in many voices....The black poet, as exemplified by Gwendolyn Brooks and later Amiri Baraka, had many voices—with no single voice being identified as more or less authentic. The insistence on finding one voice, one definitive style of writing and reading one's poetry, fit all too neatly with a static notion of self and identity that was pervasive in university settings. It seemed that many black students found our situations problematic precisely because our sense of self, and by definition our voice, was not unilateral, monologist, or static but rather multi-dimensional. We were at home in dialect as we were in standard English. Individuals who speak languages other than English, who speak patois as well as standard English, find it a necessary aspect of self-affirmation not to feel compelled to choose one voice over another, not to claim one as more authentic, but rather to construct social realities that celebrate, acknowledge, and affirm differences, variety....To claim all the tongues in which we speak, to make speech of the many languages that give expression to the unique cultural reality of a people.[63]

As part of a politics of difference, an anti-racist pedagogy would have to investigate the relationship between language and voice as part of a wider concern with democratic struggles and antagonisms. Instead of talking about literacy, radical educational theory would have to educate teachers and administrators to speak and listen to many languages and understandings of the world. Not only would this open up the possibility for many people to speak from the decided advantage of their own experiences, it would also multiply and decidely transform the discursive and nondiscursive sites from which administrators, teachers, students, parents, and neighborhood people could engage in dialogue and communities of solidarity. A radical educational discourse would also educate people to the tyranny that lies beneath logocentric narratives, truths that appear to exist beyond criticism, and language that undermines the force of democratic encounters. In this

context, June Jordan is illuminating in sharply contrasting the
implications of a language of difference with the reality that most
people find themselves in at the current historical juncture in the
United States.

> I am talking about majority problems of language in a demo-
> cratic state, problems of a currency that someone has stolen
> and hidden away and then homogenized into an official
> "English" language that can only express non-events involv-
> ing nobody responsible, or lies. If we lived in a democratic
> state our language would have to hurtle, fly, curse, and sing,
> in all the common American names, all the undeniable and
> representative and participating voices of everybody here. We
> would not tolerate the language of the powerful and, thereby,
> lose all respect for words, per se. We would make our lan-
> guage conform to the truth of our many selves and we make
> our language lead us into the equality of power that a demo-
> cratic state must represent....This is not a democratic state.
> And we put up with that. We have the language of the power-
> ful that perpetuates that power through the censorship of dis-
> senting views.[64]

Another important element in the theory and politics of difference that has emerged in the writings of black feminists is the
importance of stories, of narrative forms that keep alive communities of resistance while also indicting the collective destruction
that mobilizes racism, sexism, and other forms of domination.
Barbara Christian argues that black people have always theorized
in narrative forms, "in the stories we create, in riddles and
proverbs, in the play with language, since dynamic rather than
fixed ideas seem more to our liking."[65] The narratives that are at
work here are grounded in the discourse of everyday life, they are
polyphonic, partial, and vibrant. And yet such narrative forms are
produced amid relations of struggle. Toni Cade Bambara claims
such stories are grounded in relations of survival, struggle, and
wide-awake resistance. She writes:

> Stories are important. They keep us alive. In the ships, in the
> camps, in the quarters, field, prisons, on the road, on the run,
> underground, under siege, in the throes, on the verge—the
> storyteller snatches us back from the edge to hear the next
> chapter. In which we are the subjects. We, the hero of the

tales. Our lives preserved. How it was, how it be. Passing it along in the relay. That is what I work to do: to produce stories that save our lives.[66]

The development of narrative forms and stories in the work of writers like Zora Neale Hurston, Paule Marshall, Toni Morrison, Alice Walker, and Toni Cade Bambara challenge the ways in which knowledge is constructed, illuminate the relationship between knowledge and power, and reinscribe the personal and the political so as to rewrite the dialectical connection between what we learn and how we come to learn given our specific location in history, experience, and language.[67] The literature of black feminist writers extends and challenges postmodernism's view of narratives. These writings link the form and substance of narrative storytelling to issues of survival and resistance and, in doing so, add a more progressive political character to narrative structure and substance than is developed in postmodern analyses. The development of stories in this literature becomes a medium for developing forms of historical consciousness that provide the basis for new relations of solidarity, community, and self-love. For example, Michelle Gibbs Russell links the political and the pedagogical in the use of storytelling and so demonstrates the radical potential it assumes as a form of self and social empowerment,

> The oldest form of building historical consciousness in community is storytelling. The transfer of knowledge, skill, and value from one generation to the next, the deliberate accumulation of a people's collective memory, has particular significance in diaspora culture....Political education for black women in America begins with the memory of four hundred years of enslavement, diaspora, forced labor, beating, bombings, lynchings, and rape. It takes on inspirational dimensions when we begin cataloguing the heroic individuals and organizations in our history who have battled against those atrocities, and triumphed over them. It becomes practical when we are confronted with the problem of how to organize food cooperatives for women on food-stamp budgets or how to prove one's fitness as a mother in court. It becomes radical when, as teachers, we develop a methodology that places daily life at the center of history and enables black women to struggle for survival with the knowledge that they are making history. One setting where such connections can be

made is the classroom. In the absence of any land, or turf, which we actually control, the classroom serves as a temporary space where we can evoke and evaluate our collective memory of what is done to us, and what we do in turn.[68]

As a pedagogical practice, the recovery and affirmation of stories that emanate from the experience of marginal groups can also serve in an emancipatory way to re-center the presence of white authority. Such stories cannot be used exclusively as a basis for whites to examine their own complicity in the construction of racism; they can also help privileged groups listen seriously to the multiple narratives that constitute the complexity of Others historically defined through reifications and stereotypes that smother difference within and between diverse subordinate groups. Of course, such stories also need to provide the opportunity to raise questions about what kinds of common claims regarding a discourse of ethics, accountability, and identity politics can be developed between whites and people of color around such narrative forms. I believe that by foregrounding and interrogating the variety of textual forms and voices that inform such narratives, students can deconstruct the master-narratives of racism, sexism, and class domination while simultaneously questioning how these narratives contribute to forms of self hatred and contempt that surround the identities of blacks, women, and other subordinate groups.[69] Similarly, the stories of marginal groups provide counternarratives that call into question the role that whites and other dominant groups have and continue to play in the perpetuating oppression and human suffering. Sharon Welch is instructive on this issue. She argues that listening to and engaging the stories of the Other can educate members of white, Eurocentric culture to a redefinition of responsibility through what she calls an ethic of risk and resistance. She writes:

> Particular stories call us to accountability. As dangerous memories of conflict, oppression and exclusion, they call those of us who are, often unknowingly, complict in structures of control to join in resistance and transformation. For those of us who are members of the Western elite, by reason of race, gender, education, or economic status, we are challenged by the stories of the marginalized and oppressed to grasp the limits of our ethical and political wisdom—the

limited appeal of our capitalist economic system, our limited appreciation of the vitality and determination of other peoples to shape their own identities....We in the first World are not responsible for others; we are responsible for ourselves—for seeing the limits of our own vision and for rectifying the damages caused by the arrogant violation of those limits.[70]

Welch is arguing for a dialectical notion of narrative. She rightly argues that the narratives of subordinate groups need to be recovered as "dangerous memories" that rewrite and reinscribe the historical threads of community forged in resistance and struggle. She also argues that such stories are needed to construct an ethical discourse that indicts Eurocentric-American master-narratives so they can be critically interrogated and discarded when necessary in the interests of constructing social relations and communities of struggle that provide healing, salvation, and justice.

BORDER PEDAGOGY AS POSTMODERN RESISTANCE

If the construction of anti-racist pedagogy is to escape from a notion of difference that is silent about other social antagonisms and forms of struggle, it must be developed as part of a wider public discourse that is simultaneously about the discourse of an engaged plurality and the formation of critical citizenship. This must be a discourse that breathes life into the notion of democracy by stressing a notion of lived community that is *not* at odds with the principles of justice, liberty, and equality.[71] Such a discourse must be informed by a postmodern concern with establishing the material and ideological conditions that allow multiple, specific, and heterogeneous ways of life to come into play as part of a border pedagogy of postmodern resistance.[72] This points to the need for educators to prepare students for a type of citizenship that does not separate abstract rights from the realm of the everyday, and does not define community as the legitimating and unifying practice of a one-dimensional historical and cultural narrative. Postmodernism radicalizes the emancipatory possibilities of teaching and learning as part of a wider struggle for democratic public life and critical citizenship. It does this by refusing forms of knowledge and pedagogy wrapped in the legitimizing discourse of the sacred and the priestly; its rejecting universal reason as a foundation for human affairs; claiming that all narratives are partial; and performing a critical reading on all scientific, cultural, and social texts as historical and political constructions.

In this view, the broader parameters of an anti-racist pedagogy are informed by a political project that links the creation of critical citizens to the development of a radical democracy; that is, a political project that ties education to the broader struggle for a public life in which dialogue, vision, and compassion remain critically attentive to the rights and conditions that organize public space as a democratic social form rather than as a regime of terror and oppression. It is important to emphasize that difference and pluralism in this view do not mean reducing democracy to the equivalency of diverse interests; on the contrary, what is being argued for is a language in which different voices and traditions exist and flourish to the degree that they listen to the voices of others, engage in an ongoing attempt to eliminate forms of subjective and objective suffering, and maintain those conditions in which the act of communicating and living extends rather than restricts the creation of democratic public spheres. This is as much a political as it is a pedagogical project, one that demands that anti-racist pedagogical practices be developed within a discourse that combines a democratic public philosophy with a postmodern theory of resistance. Within this perspective, the issue of border pedagogy is located within those broader cultural and political considerations that are beginning to redefine our traditional view of community, language, space, and possibility. It is a pedagogy that is attentive to developing a democratic public philosophy that respects the notion of difference as part of a common struggle to extend and transform the quality of public life. In short, the notion of border pedagogy presupposes not merely an acknowledgment of the shifting borders that both undermine and reterritorialize dominant configurations of power and knowledge, it also links the notion of pedagogy to the creation of a society in which there is available a multiplicity of democratic practices, values, and social relations for students to take up within different learning situations. At stake here is a view of democracy and learning in which multiplicity, plurality, and struggle become the raison d'etre of democratic public life. Chantal Mouffe has elaborated this position in neo-Gramscian terms better than anyone else. She writes:

> If the task of radical democracy is indeed to deepen the democratic revolution and to link together diverse democratic

struggles, such a task requires the creation of new subject-positions that would allow the common articulation, for example of antiracism, antisexism, and anticapitalism. These struggles do not spontaneously converge, and in order to establish democratic equivalences, a new "common sense" is necessary which would transform the identity of different groups so that the demands of each group could be articulated with those of others according to the principle of democratic equivalence. For it is not a matter of establishing a mere alliance between given interests but of actually modifying the very identity of those forces. In order that the defense of workers' interests is not pursued at the cost of the rights of women, immigrants, or consumers, it is necessary to establish an equivalence between these different struggles. It is only under these circumstances that struggles against power become truly democratic.[73]

Mouffe's position should not suggest that this is merely a political task to be established and carried out by an elite, a party, or a specific group of intellectuals. More important, it is a pedagogical task that has to be taken up and argued for by educators who take a particular political stand on the meaning and importance of radical democracy as a way of life. Such a position not only rejects the one-sided and undemocratic interests that inform the conservative argument which collapses democracy into the logic of the market or butresses the ideology of cultural uniformity, but also rejects leftist versions of an identity politics that excludes the other as part of reductive discourse of assertion and separatism.

What is being called for here is a notion of border pedagogy that provides educators with the opportunity to rethink the relations between the centers and the margins of power. That is, such a pedagogy must address the issue of racism as one that calls into question not only forms of subordination that create inequities among different groups as they live out their lives but, as I have mentioned previously, also challenges those institutional and ideological boundaries that have historically masked their own relations of power behind complex forms of distinction and privilege. What does this suggest for the way we develop the basic elements of an anti-racist pedagogy?

First, the notion of border pedagogy offers students the opportunity to engage the multiple references that constitute different cultural codes, experiences, and languages. This means providing the learning opportunities for students to become media literate in a world of changing representations. It means offering students the knowledge and social relations that enable them to read critically not only how cultural texts are regulated by various discursive codes but also how such texts express and represent different ideological interests. In this case, border pedagogy establishes conditions of learning that define literacy inside the categories of power and authority. This suggests developing pedagogical practices that address texts as social and historical constructions; it also suggests developing pedagogical practices that allow students to analyze texts in terms of their presences and absences; and most important, such practices should provide students with the opportunity to read texts dialogically through a configuration of many voices, some of which offer up resistance, some of which provide support.

Border pedagogy also stresses the necessity for providing students with the opportunity to engage critically the strengths and limitations of the cultural and social codes that define their own histories and narratives. Partiality becomes, in this case, the basis for recognizing the limits built into all discourses. At issue here is not merely the need for students to develop a healthy skepticism towards all discourses of authority, but also to recognize how authority and power can be transformed in the interest of creating a democratic society.

Within this discourse, students engage knowledge as a border-crosser, as a person moving in and out of borders constructed around coordinates of difference and power.[74] These are not only physical borders, they are cultural borders historically constructed and socially organized within maps of rules and regulations that serve to either limit or enable particular identities, individual capacities, and social forms. In this case, students cross over into borders of meaning, maps of knowledge, social relations, and values that are increasingly being negotiated and rewritten as the codes and regulations which organize them become destabilized and reshaped. Border pedagogy decenters as it remaps. The terrain of learning becomes inextricably linked to the shifting parameters of place, identity, history, and power. By reconstructing the traditional radical emphasis of the knowledge/power relationship away from the limited emphasis of mapping domination to the politically strategic issue of engaging the ways in which knowledge can be remapped, reterritorialized, and decentered, in the wider interests of rewriting the borders and coordinates of an oppositional cultural politics, educators can redefine the teacher student relationship in ways that allow students to draw upon their own personal experience as real knowledge.

At one level this means giving students the opportunity to speak, to locate themselves in history, and to become subjects in the construction of their identities and the wider society. It also means defining voice not merely as an opportunity to speak, but to engage critically with the ideology and substance of speech, writing, and other forms of cultural production. In this case, "coming to voice" for students from both dominant and subordinate cultures means engaging in rigorous discussions of various cultural texts, drawing upon one's personal experience, and confronting the process through which ethnicity and power can be rethought as a political narrative that challenges racism as part of broader struggle to democratize social, political, and economic life.[75] In part, this means looking at the various ways in which race implicates relations of domination, resistance, suffering, and power within various social practices and how these are taken up in multiple ways by students who occupy different ethnic, social, and gender locations. In this way, race is never discussed outside broader articulations, nor is it merely about people of color.

Second, a border pedagogy of postmodern resistance needs to do more than educate students to perform ideological surgery on master-narratives based on white, patriarchal, and class-specific interests. If the master-narratives of domination are to be effectively deterritorialized, it is important for educators to understand how such narratives are taken up as part of an investment of feeling, pleasure, and desire. There is a need to rethink the syntax of learning and behavior outside the geography of rationality and reason. For example, this means that racism cannot be dealt with in a purely limited, analytical way. An anti-racist pedagogy must engage how and why students make particular ideological and affective investments and occupy particular subject positions in regard to issues concerning race and racism. This means attempting to understand the historical context and substance of the social and cultural forms that produce in diverse and multiple ways the often contradictory subject positions that give students a sense of meaning, purpose, and delight. As Stuart Hall argues, this means uncovering both for ourselves as teachers as well as for the students we are teaching "the deep structural factors which have a tendency persistently not only to generate racial practices and structures but to reproduce them through time and which therefore account for their extraordinarily immovable character."[76] In addition to engaging racism within a politics of representation, ideology, and pleasure, it is also important to stress that any serious analyses of racism also has to be historical and structural. It has to chart out how racist practices develop, where they come from, how they are sustained, how they affect dominant and subordinate groups, and how they can be challenged. This is not a discourse about personal preferences or dominant tastes but a discourse about economics, culture, politics, and power.[77]

Third, a border pedagogy offers the opportunity for students to air their feelings about race from the perspective of the subject positions they experience as constitutive of their own identities. Ideology in this sense is treated not merely as an abstraction but as part of the student's lived experience. This does not mean that teachers reduce their role to that of an intellectual voyeur or collapse his or her authority into a shabby form of relativism. Nor does it suggest that students merely express or assess their own experiences. Rather, it points to a particular form of teacher authority grounded in a respect for a radically decentered notion of democratic public life. This is a view of authority that rejects the notion that all forms of authority are expressions of unwarranted power and oppression. Instead, it argues for forms of authority that are rooted in democratic interests and emancipatory social relations, forms of authority that, in this case, begins from a standpoint from which to develop an educational project that rejects politics as aesthetics, that retains instead the significance of the knowledge/power relationship as a discourse of criticism and politics necessary for the achievement of equality, freedom, and struggle. This is not a form of authority based on an appeal to universal truths, it is a form of authority that recognizes its own partiality while simultaneously asserting a standpoint from which to engage the discourses and practices of democracy, freedom, and domination. Put another way, this is a notion of authority rooted in a political project that ties education to the broader struggle for public life in which dialogue, vision, and compassion remain critically attentive to the liberating and dominating relations that organize various aspects of everyday life.

This suggests that teachers use their authority to establish classroom conditions in which different views about race can be aired but not treated as simply an expression of individual views or feelings.[78] Andrew Hannan rightly points out that educators must refuse to treat racism as a matter of individual prejudice and counter such a position by addressing the "structural foundations of [the] culture of racism."[79] An anti-racist pedagogy must demonstrate that the views we hold about race have different historical and ideological weight, forged in asymmetrical relations of power, and that they always embody interests that shape social practices in particular ways. In other words, an anti-racist pedagogy cannot treat ideologies as simply individual expressions of feeling, but as historical, cultural, and social practices that serve to either undermine or reconstruct democratic public life. These views must be engaged without silencing students, but they must also be interrogated next to a public philosophy that names racism for what it is and calls racist ideologies and practices into account on political and ethical terms.

Fourth, educators need to understand how the experience of marginality at the level of everyday life lends itself to forms of oppositional and transformative consciousness. For those designated as Others need to both reclaim and remake their histories, voices, and visions as part of a wider struggle to change those material and social relations that deny radical pluralism as the basis of democratic political community. It is only through such an understanding that teachers can develop a border pedagogy which opens up the possibility for students to reclaim their voices as part of a process of empowerment and not merely what some have called an initiation into the culture of power.[80] It is not enough for students to learn how the dominant culture works to exercise power, they must also understand how to resist power which is oppressive, which names them in a way that undermines their ability to govern rather than serve, and prevents them from struggling against forms of power that subjugate and exploit. For example, Lisa Delpit's call for educators to integrate black students into what she unproblematically addresses as "the culture of power" appears to be blind to how such power is constructed in opposition to democratic values and used as a force for domination.[81] This is not to suggest that the authority of white dominant culture is all of one piece, nor is this meant to imply that it should not be the object of study. What is at stake here is forging a notion of power that does not collapse into a form of domination, but is critical and emancipatory, that allows students to both locate themselves in history and to critically, not slavishly, appropriate the cultural and political codes of their own and other traditions. Moreover, students who have to disavow their own racial heritage in order to succeed are not becoming "raceless" as Signithia Fordham has argued, they are being positioned to accept subject positions that are the source of power for a white, dominant culture.[82] The ability of white, male, Eurocentric culture to normalize and universalize its own interests works so well, in this case, that Fordham underemphasizes how whiteness as a cultural and historical construction, as a site of dominant narratives, exercises the form of authority which prevented black students from speaking through their own memories, histories, and experiences. Delpit and Fordham are right in attempting to focus on issues of powerlessness as they relate to pedagogy and race, but they both obscure this relation by not illuminating more clearly how power works in this society within the schools to secure and conceal various forms of racism and subjugation. Power is multifaceted and we need a better understanding of how it works not simply as a force for oppression but also as a basis for resistance and self and social empowerment. Educators need to fashion a critical postmodern notion of authority, one that decenters essentialist claims to power while at the same time fighting for relations of authority and power that allow many voices to speak so as to initiate students into a culture that multiplies rather than restricts democratic practices and social relations as part of a wider struggle for democratic public life.

Fifth, educators need to analyze racism not only as a structural and ideological force, but also in the diverse and historically specific ways in which it emerges. This is particularly true of the most recent and newest expressions of racism developing in the United States and abroad among youth in popular culture, and in its resurgence in the highest reaches of the American government.[83] This also suggests that any notion of an anti-racist pedagogy must arise out of specific settings and contexts. Such a pedagogy must allow its own character to be defined, in part, by the historically specific and contextual boundaries in which it emerges. At the same time, such a pedagogy must disavow all claims to scientific method or for that matter to any objective or transhistorical claims. As a political practice, an anti-racist pedagogy has to be constructed not on the basis of essentialist or universal claims but on the concreteness of its specific encounters, struggles, and engagements. Roger Simon outlines some of the issues involved here in his discussion of critical pedagogy.

Such a form of educational work is at root contextual and conditional. A critical pedagogy can only be concretely discussed from within a particular "point of practice"; from within a specific time and place and within a particular theme. This means doing critical pedagogy is a strategic, practical task not a scientific one. It arises not against a background of psychological, sociological, or anthropological universals—as does much educational theory related to pedagogy—but from such questions as: "How is human possibility being diminished here?"[84]

Sixth, an anti-racist border pedagogy must redefine how the circuits of power move in a dialectical fashion among various sites of cultural production.[85] We need a clearer understanding of how ideologies and other social practices which bear down on classroom relations emerge from and articulate with other spheres of social life. As educators, we need a clearer understanding of how the grounds for the production and organization of knowledge is related to forms of authority situated in political economy, the state, and other material practices. We also need to understand how circuits of power produce forms of textual authority that offer readers particular subject positions, that is, ideological references that provide but do not rigidly determine particular views of the world.[86] In addition, educators need to explore how the reading of texts are linked to the forms of knowledge and social relations that students bring to the classroom. In other words, we need to understand in terms of function and substance those social and cultural forms outside the classroom that produce the multiple and often contradictory subject positions that students learn and express in their interaction with the dominant cultural capital of American schools.

Finally, central to the notion of border pedagogy are a number of important pedagogical issues regarding the role that teachers might take up in making a commitment to fighting racism in their classrooms, schools, communities, and the wider society. The concept of border pedagogy also helps to locate teachers within social, political, and cultural boundaries that define and mediate in complex ways how they function as intellectuals who exercise particular forms of moral and social regulation. Border pedagogy calls attention to both the ideological and the partial as central elements in the construction of teacher discourse and practice. In part, this suggests that to the degree that teachers make the construction of their own voices, histories, and ideologies problematic they become more attentive to Otherness as a deeply political and pedagogical issue. In other words, by deconstructing the underlying principles which inform their own lives and pedagogy, educators can begin to recognize the limits underlying the partiality of their own views. Such a recognition offers the promise of allowing teachers to restructure their pedagogical relations in order to engage in open and critical dialogue questions regarding the knowledge taught, how it relates to students lives, how students can engage with such knowledge, and how such practices actually relate to empowering both teachers and students. Within dominant models of pedagogy, teachers are often silenced through a refusal or inability to make problematic with students the values that inform how they teach and engage the multifaceted relationship between knowledge and power. Without the benefit of dialogue, an understanding of the partiality of their own beliefs, they are cut off from any understanding of the effects their pedagogies have on students. In effect, their infatuation with certainty and control serves to limit the possibilities inherent in their own voices and visions. In this case, dominant pedagogy serves not only to disempower students, but teachers as well. In short, teachers need to take up a pedagogy that provides a more dialectical understanding of their own politics and values; they need to break down pedagogical boundaries that silence them in the name of methodological rigor or pedagogical absolutes; more important, they need to develop a power-sensitive discourse that allows them to open up their interactions with the discourses of various Others so that their classrooms can engage rather than block out the multiple positions and experiences that allow teachers and students to speak in and with many complex and different voices.[87]

What border pedagogy makes undeniable is the relational nature of one's own politics and personal investments. But at the same time, border pedagogy emphasizes the primacy of a politics in which teachers assert rather than retreat from the pedagogies they utilize in dealing with the various differences represented by the students who come into their classes. For example, it is not enough for teachers to merely affirm uncritically their students' histories, experiences, and stories. To take student voices at face value is to run the risk of idealizing and romanticizing them. It is crucial that critical educators do more than allow such stories to be heard. It is equally important for teachers to help students find a language for critically examining the historically and socially constructed forms by which they live. Such a process involves more than allowing students to speak from their own histories and social formations, it also raises questions about how teachers use power to cross over borders that are culturally strange and alien to them.

At issue here is not a patronizing notion of understanding the Other, but a sense of how the self is implicated in the construction of Otherness, how exercising critical attention to such a relationship might allow educators to move out of the center of the dominant culture to its margins in order to analyze critically the political, social, and cultural lineaments of their own values and voices as viewed from different ideological and cultural spaces. It is important for teachers to understand both how they wield power and authority and how particular forms of authority are sedimented in the construction of their own needs along with the limited subject positions offered them in schools. Border pedagogy is not about engaging just the positionality of our students but the nature of our own identities as they have and are emerging within and between various circuits of power. If students are going to learn how to take risks, to develop a healthy skepticisms towards all master-narratives, to recognize the power relations that offer them the opportunity to speak in particular ways, and be willing to address their role as critical citizens who can animate a democratic culture, they need to see such behavior demonstrated in the social practices and subject positions that teachers live out and not merely propose.

If an anti-racist pedagogy is to have any meaning as a force for creating a democratic society, teachers and students must be given the opportunity to put into effect what they learn outside the school. In other words, they must be given the opportunity to engage in anti-racist struggles in their effort to link schooling to real life, ethical discourse to political action, and classroom relations to a broader notion of cultural politics. School curriculum should make anti-racist pedagogies central to the task of educating students to animate a wider and more critically engaged public culture, it should not merely allow them to take risks but also to push against the boundaries of an oppressive social order. Such projects can be used to address the relevance of the school curriculum and its role as a significant public force for linking learning and social justice to the daily institutional and cultural traditions of society and reshaping them in the process. All schools should have teachers and students participate in anti-racist curriculum that in some way link up with projects in the wider society. This approach redefines not only teacher authority and student responsibility, but places the school as a major force in the struggle for social, economic, and cultural justice. In this case, a critical postmodern pedagogy of resistance points to challenging not only the oppressive boundaries of racism, but all those barriers which undermine and subvert the construction of a democratic society.

Notes and Reference

INTRODUCTION

Notes

1. Representative analyses of the range of disciplines and writers who inhabit this slippery landscape known as postmodernism can be found in Foster (1983); Huyssen (1986); Kroker and Cook (1986); Hebdige (1989); Hutcheon (1989); Aronowitz and Giroux (1991).

2. The debate over the periodization and meaning of modernism has a long history and is taken up quite brilliantly in Anderson (1984). Of course, this also points to the unstable ground on which definitions of postmodernism have been developed. Dick Hebdige (1986) provides a sense of the range of meanings, contexts and objects that can be associated with the postmodern:

> the decor of a room, the design of a building, the diegesis of a film, the construction of a record, or a "scratch" video, a TV commercial, or an arts documentary, or the "intertextual" relations between them, the layout of a page in a fashion magazine or critical journal, an anti-teleologial tendency within epistemology, the attack on the "metaphysics of presence," a general attenuation of feeling, the collective chagrin and morbid projections of a post-War generation of Baby Boomers confronting disillusioned middle age, the "predicament" of reflexivity, a group of rhetorical tropes, a proliferation of surfaces, a new phase in commodity fetishism, a fascination for "images," codes and styles, a process of cultural, political or existential fragmentation and/or crisis, the "de-centering" of the subject, an "incredulity towards metanarratives," the replacement of unitary power axes by a pluralism of power/discourse formations, the "implosion," the collapse of Cultural hierarchies, the dread engendered by the threat of nuclear self-destruction, the decline of the University, the functioning and effects of the new miniaturized technologies, broad societal and economic shifts into a "media, consumer" or "multinational" phase, a sense (depending on whom you

read) of "placelessness" or the abandonment of placelessness ("critical regionalism") or (even) a generalized substitution of spatial for temporal coordinates. (78)

3. The now classic defense of modernity in the postmodern debate can found in Jurgen Habermas (1983, 1987). For more extensive analyses of modernity, see: Marshall Berman (1982); Eugene Lunn (1982); Bernstein (1985); David Frisby (1986); David Kolb (1986); William Connolly (1988); Larsen, N. (1990). An interesting comparison of two very different views on modernity can be found in Berman (1988) and Nelly Richard (1987/1988).

4. A representative sample of postmodern feminist works include: Behnabib and Cornell (1987); Kaplan (1988); Morris (1988); Hutcheon (1989); Flax (1989); Diamond and Quinby, (1988); Nicholson (1990)

References

Alcoff, L. (1988). Cultural feminism vs. poststructuralism: The identity crisis in feminist theory. *Signs, 13*(3), 405-436.

Anderson, P. (1984). Modernity and revolution. *New Left Review*, No. 144, 96-113.

Appignanensi, L. and G. Bennington, (eds.). (1986). *Postmodernism: ICA Documents 4*. London: Institute of Contemporary Arts 32-51.

Aronowitz, S. (1987/1988). Postmodernism and politics. *Social Text*, No. 18, 94-114.

Aronowitz, S. and H.. A. Giroux, (1988). Schooling, culture, and literacy in the age of broken dreams. *Harvard Educational Review, 58*(2), 172-194.

Aronowitz, S. and H. A. Giroux, (1991). *Postmodern Education: Politics Culture and Social Criticism*. Minneapolis: University of Minnesota Press.

Barthes, R. (1972). *Critical essays*. New York: Hill and Wang.

Bartkey, S. L. (1988). Foucault, femininity, and the modernization of patriarchal power. In I. Diamond and L. Quinby (eds.). *Feminism and foucault: reflections on resistance* 61-86.

Baudrillard, J. (1987). Modernity. *Canadian Journal of Political and Social Theory, 11*(3), 63-72.

———— (1988). *Selected writings* (M. Poster, Ed.). Stanford: Stanford University Press.

Bell, D. (1976). *The cultural contradictions of capitalism.* New York: Basic Books.

Benhabib, S. and D. Cornell, (1987). *Feminism as Critique.* Minneapolis University of Minnesota Press.

Berman, M. (1982). *All that is solid melts into air: The experience of modernity.* New York: Simon & Schuster.

———— (1988). Why Modernism Still Matters. *Tikkun,* 4(1), 11–14, 81-86.

Bernstein, R. (ed.). (1985). *Habermas and modernity.* Cambridge: MIT Press.

Birke, L. (1986). *Women, feminism, and biology: the feminist challenge.* New York: Metheun.

Bookchin, M. (1990). *Remaking Society.* Boston: South End Press

Calinescu, M. (1987). *Five faces of modernity: modernism, avant-garde, decadence, kitsch, postmodernism.* Durham, N.C.: Duke University Press.

Cherryholmes, C. (1988). *Power and criticism: Poststructural investigations in education.* New York: Teachers College Press

Christian, B. (1987). The Race for Theory. *Cultural Critique* 6: 51-64.

Clifford, J. and G. Marcus, (ed.). (1986). *Writing culture: the poetics and politics of ethnography.* Berkeley: University of California Press.

Clifford, J. (1988). *The predicament of culture: twentieth century ethnography, literature, and art* Cambridge: Harvard University Press.

Collins, J. (1989). *Uncommon cultures: popular culture and post-modernism.* New York: Routledge.

Connolly, W. (1988). *Political theory and modernity.* New York: Basil Blackwell.

Connor. S. (1989). *Postmodernist culture: an introduction to theories of the contemporary.* New York: Basil Blackwell.

Curthoys, A. (1988). Culture and politics, or the shibboleths of the left. In L. Grossberg, *It's a Sin: Essays on Postmodernism, politics, and culture.* Australia: Power Publications 82-87.

De Lauretis, T. (1984). *Alice doesn't: feminism, semiotics, cinema.* Bloomington: Indiana University Press.

———— (ed.).(1986). Feminist studies/critical studies: issues, terms, contexts. In T. De Lauretis (1986). *Feminist Studies/Critical Studies.* Bloomington: Indiana University Press.

———— (1987). *Technologies of gender.* Bloomington: Indiana University Press.

Derrida, J. (1976). *Of grammatology.* G. Spivak, trans. Baltimore: Johns Hopkins University Pess.

Dewey, J. (1916). *Democracy and education.* New York: Macmillan.

Diamond, I. and L. Quinby, (1988). *Feminism & foucault: reflections on resistance.* Boston: Northeastern University Press.

Eagleton, T. (1985/1986). The Subject of Literature. *Cultural Critique,* No. 2, 95-104.

Ebert, T. (1988). The romance of patriarchy: ideology, subjectivity, and postmodern feminist cultural theory. *Cultural Critique.* 10 (fall), 19-57.

Epstein, B. (1990). Rethinking social movement theory. *Socialist Review, 20* (1), 35-65.

Featherstone, M. (1988). In Pursuit of the postmodern: An introduction. *Theory, Culture and Society,* 5(2-3) 195-215.

Feher, F. (1988). The status of postmodernity. *Philosophy and Social Criticism, 13*(2), 195-206.

Flax, J. (1988). Reply to Tress. *Signs,* 14(1), 201-203.

———— (1989). Postmodernism and gender relations in feminist theory. In Malson, M., O'Barr, J., Westphal-Wihl, S., and Wyer, M. (eds.). (1989). *Feminist theory in practice and process.* Chicago: University of Chicago Press 51-73.

Foster, H. (Ed.), (1983). *The anti-aesthetic: Essays on postmodern culture.* Washington. Bay Press.

Foucault, M (1977a). *Language, counter-memory, practice: Selected essays and interviews.* D. Bouchard (Ed.). Ithaca: Cornll University Press.

———— (1977b). *Power and knowledge: Selected interviews and other writings* G. Gordon (Ed.). New York: Pantheon

———— (1979). *Discipline and punish: the birth of the prison.* New York: Vintage Books.

———— (1980). *The history of sexuality, volume 1: an introduction.* New York: Vintage Books.

Fox-Genovese, E. (1986). The claims of a common culture: Gender, race, class and the canon. *Salmagundi,* 72(fall), 131-143.

Frisby, D. (1986). *Fragments of Modernity*. Cambridge: M.I.T. Press.

Fraser, N. (1985). What is critical about critical theory? The case of Habermas and gender. *New German Critique*, 12 (2), 97-131.

———— (1989). *Unruly practices*. Minneapolis: University of Minnesota Press.

Fraser, N. and L. Nicholson, (1988). Social criticism without philosophy: an encounter between feminism and postmodernism. In. A. Ross. (ed). *Universal abandon? the politics of postmodernism*. Minneapolis: University of Minnesota Press 83-104.

Giroux, H. and R. Simon, (1988). Critical pedagogy and the politics of popular culture. Cultural Studies, 2(3), 294-320.

———— (1989). Popular culture, schooling, and everyday life. Massachusetts: Bergin & Garvey Press.

Giroux, H. (1988a). *Schooling and the struggle for public life*. Minneapolis: University of Minnesota Press.

———— (1988b). *Teachers as intellectuals*. Massachusetts: Bergin & Garvey Press.

Giroux, H. and P. McLaren, (1989). Introduction in H. Giroux and McLaren, P. (eds.) *Critical pedagogy, the state, and cultural struggle*. New York: The State University New York Press.

Gramsci, A. (1971). *Selections From Prison Notebooks*, ed. and Trans. Q. Honre and G. Smith. New York: International Press.

Grossberg, L. (1988). Putting the Pop back into postmodernism. In A: Ross, ed., *Universal abandon*. Minneapolis, Minnesota: University of Minnesota Press, 167-190

Groz, E. A., D. Threadgold, D. Kelly, A.Cholodenki, (eds.). (1986). *Futur*fall: excursions into postmodernity*. Australia: Power Institute of-Fine Arts

Grumet, M. (1988). *Bitter milk: women and teaching*. Massachusetts: University of Massachusetts Press.

Habermas, J. (1979). *Communication and the evolution of society*. Boston: Beacon Press.

———— (1981). Modernity versus postmodernity. *New German Critique*, 8(1), 3-18.

———— (1982). The entwinement of myth and enlightenment. *New German Critique*, 9(3), 13-30.

—————— (1983). Modernity-An incomplete project. In H. Foster (Ed.). *The anti-aesthetic: Essays on postmodern culture*. Washington: Bay Press 3-16.

—————— (1987). *The philosophical discourse of modernity*, trans by F. Lawrence. Cambridge: MIT Press.

Hannam, M. (1990). The dream of democracy. Arena, no. 90, 109-116.

Haraway, D. (1989). Situated knowledges: the science question in feminism and the privilege of partial perspective. *Feminist Studies* 14 (3), 575-599.

Harding, S. (1986). *The science question in Feminism*. Ithaca: Cornell University Press.

Hartsock, N. (1987). Rethinking modernism: Minority vs. majority theories. *Cultural Critique*, No. 7, 187-206.

Hassan, I. (1987). *The postmodern turn: essays in postmodern theory and culture*. Ohio: Ohio State University Press.

Haug, F. et al (1987). *Female sexualization: A collective work of memory*. London: Verso Press.

Hebdige, D. (1986). Postmodernism and; 'the other side.' *Journal of Communication Inquiry*, 10(2), 78-99.

—————— (1989). *Hiding in the light*. New York: Routledge.

Hooks, B. (1989). *Talking back*. Boston: South End Press.

Hicks, E. (1988). Deterritorialization and border writing. In R. Merrill (Ed.), *Ethics/Aesthetics: Post-Modern Positions*. Washington, D. C.: Maisonneuve Press 47-58.

Hirsch Jr., E. D. (1987). *Cultural literacy: what every American needs to know*. Boston: Houghton Mifflin company.

Hutcheon, L. (1988). Postmodern problematic. In R. Merrill (Ed.), *Ethics/aesthetics: Post-modern positions*. Washington, D. C.: Maisonneuve Press 1-10.

—————— (1989). *The politics of postmodernism*. New York: Routledge.

Huyssen, A. (1986). *After the great divide*. Bloomington: Indiana University Press.

Institute of Contemporary Art, Boston. (1988). *Utopia post utopia: configurations of nature in recent sculpture and photography*. Boston: Institute of contemporary Art.

Jagger, A. M. (1983). *Feminist politics and humanist nature.* New Jersey: Rowman & Allanheld.

Jameson, F. (1984). Postmodernism or the Cultural Logic of Late Capitalism. *New Left Review* No. 146: 53-93.

—— (1988). Regarding postmodernism-a conversation with Fredric Jameson, in A. Ross, ed., *Universal abandon.* Minneapolis: University of Minnesota Press 3-30

Kaplan, C. (1987). Deterritorializations: the rewriting of home and exile in western feminist discourse. *Cultural Critique,* No. 6, 187-198.

Kaplan, E. (1988). Introduction. In Kaplan, E. (ed.). *Postmodernism and its discontents, theories practices.* London: Verso.

Kearney, R. (1988). *The wake of imagination.* Minneapolis: University of Minnesota Press.

Keller, E. F. (1985). *Gender and science.* New Haven: Yale University Press.

Kellner, D. (1988). Postmodernism as social theory: Some challenges and problems." *Theory, Culture and Society,* 5(2 & 3), 239-269.

Kolb, D. (1986). *The critique of pure modernity: Hegel, Heidigger, and after Chicago*: Uniersity of Chicago Press.

Kristeva, J. (1981). Oscillation between power and denial. In E. Marks and I. de Courtivron (eds). *New french feminisms.* New York: Schocken Books, 165-167.

Kroker, A. and D. Cook, (1986).. *The postmodern scene: execremental culture and hypera-esthetics.* Montreal: New World Perspectives.

Lacan, J. (1968). *Speech and Language in Psychoanalysis,* trans. by A. Wilden. Baltimore: The Johns Hopkins University Press.

Laclau, E. and C. Mouffe, (1985). *Hegemony and socialist strategy.* London: Verso Books.

Laclau, E. (1988a). Politics and the limits of modernity. In A. Ross (ed.). *Universal abandon? The politics of postmodernism.* Minneapolis: University of Min nesota Press 63-82.

—— (1988b). Building a new left: an interview with Ernesto Laclau. *Strategies,* 1 (1), 10-28.

Larsen, N. (1990). *Modernism and hegemony: a materialist critique of aesthetic agencies.* Minneapolis. University of Minnesota Press.

Lash, S. and J. Urry, (1987). *The end of organized capitalism*. Madison: University of Wisconsin Press.

Lather, P. (1989). Postmodernism and the politics of enlightenment. *Educational Foundations* 3(3), 7-28.

Lipsitz, G. (1990). *Time passages: collective memory and american popular culture*. Minneapolis: University of Minnesota Press.

Lunn, E. (1982). *Marxism and modernism*. Berkeley: University of California Press.

Lyotard, J. (1984). *The postmodern condition*. Minneapolis: University of Minnesota Press.

Malson, M., J. O'Barr, S. Westphal-Wihl, and M. Wyer, (1989a). Introduction. In M. Malson, J. O'Barr, S. Westphal-Wihl , and M. Wyer, (eds.). *Feminist theory in practice and process*. Chicago: University of Chicago Press, 1-13.

———— (eds.).(1989b). *Feminist theory in practice and process*. Chicago: University of Chicago Press.

McCarthy, T. (1987). Introduction. In Habermas, J. *The philosophical discourse of modernity*. Cambridge: MIT Press, vii-xvii.

McLaren, P. (1986). Postmodernism and the death of politics: A Brazilian reprieve. *Educational Theory*, 36(4), 389-401.

McLaren, P. and R. Hammer, (1989). Critical pedagogy and the postmodern challenge: toward a critical postmodernist pedagogy of liberation. *Educational Foundations*, 3(3), 29-62.

McRobbie, A. (1986). Postmodernism and Popular Culture. In *Postmodernism: ICA Documents 4*. London: Institute of Contemporary Art, 54-58.

Merrill, R. (1988). Foward-ethics/aesthetics: a Post-modern position. In R. Merrill (ed.). *Ethics/aesthetics: post-modern positions*. Washington, D. C.: Maisonneuve Press.

Michnik, A. (March 11, 1990). *Notes on the revolution*. The New York Times Magazine.

Minh-ha, T. (1989). *Women, native, other: writing postcoloniality and feminism*. Bloomington: Indiana University Press.

Morris, M. (1988). *The pirate's fiancee: Feminism, reading, postmodernism*. London: Verso Press.

Mouffe, C. (1988). Radical democracy: Modern or postmodern? In A. Ross (ed.). *Universal abandon? The politics of postmodernism*. Minneapolis: University of Minnesota Press, 31-45.

———— (1989). Toward a radical democratic citizenship, *Democratic Left* 17(2), 6-7.

Newman, C. (1985). *The post-modern aura*: The age of fiction in an age of inflation. Evanston, Illinois: North Western University Press.

———— (1986). Revising modernism, representing postmodernism. In L. Appignanensi and G. Bennington (eds.). *Postmodernism: ICA Documents 4*. London: Institute of Contemporary Arts 32-51.

Nicholson, L. (1990). *Feminism/Postmodernism*. New York: Routledge.

Oreskes, M. (March 18, 1990). America's politics loses way as its vision changes world. *The New York Times* Vol. CXXXIX, No. 48, 178 (Sunday), 1, 16].

Owens, C. (1983). The discourse of others: feminists and postmodernism. In Foster, H. (Ed.). *The anti-aesthetic: essays on postmodern culture*. Washington: Bay Press, 57-82.

Peller, G. (1987). Reason and the mob: the politics of representation. *Tikkun*, 2(3), 28-31, 92-95.

Penley, C. (1989). *The Future of an Illusion: Film, Feminism and Psychoanalysis*. Minneapolis: University of Minnesota

Popkewitz, T. (1988). Culture, pedagogy, and power: issues in the production of values and colonialization. *Journal of Education*. 170(2), 77-90.

Poster, M. (1989). *Critical theory and poststructuralism*. Ithaca: Cornell University Press.

Rosaldo, R. (1989). *Culture & truth: the remaking of social analysis*. Boston: Beacon Press.

Richard, N. (1987/1988). Postmodernism and periphery. *Third Text*, 2, 5-12.

Rorty, R. (1979). *Philosophy and the mirror of nature*. Princeton: Princeton University Press.

———— (1985). Habermas and Lyotard on postmodernity. In Richard Bernstein (Ed.), *Habermas and modernity*. Cambridge: MIT Press 161-176.

Ross, A. (ed.), (1988). *Universal abandon? The politics of postmodernism*. Minneapolis: University of Minnesota Press.

Roth, R. (1988). The colonial experience and its postmodern fate. *Salmagundi* 84 (Fall), 248-265.

Ryan, K. (1989). *Politics and culture: working hypotheses for a post-revolutionary society*. Baltimore: The Johns Hopkins University Press.

Said, E. (1983). Opponents, audiences, constituencies, and community. In H. Foster (Ed.). *The anti-aesthetic: Essays on postmodern culture,* Washington: Bay Press, 135-159.

Scott, J. W. (1988). *Gender and the politics of history.* New York: Columbia University Press.

Sculley, J. (1988). *Line break: poetry as social practice.* Seattle: Bay Press.

Smith, P. (1988). *Discerning the subject.* Minneapolis: University of Minnesota Press.

Shapiro, S. (1990). *Between capitalism and democracy.* Westport: Bergin and Garvey Press.

Showalter, E. (1989). Introduction: the rise of gender. In Showalter, E (ed.). (1989). *Speaking of Gender.* New York: Routledge, pp. 1-13.

Simon, R. (forthcoming). *Teaching against the grain.* Westport: Bergin and Garvey.

Spanos, W. (1987). *Repetitions: The postmodern occasion in literature and culture.* Baton Rouge: Louisiana State University Press.

Spivak, G. (1987). *In other worlds: essays in cultural politics.* New York: Metheun.

Thompson, E. P. (January 29, 1990). History turns on a new hinge. *The Nation.* 117-122.

Tyler, S. (1987). *The unspeakable: discourse, dialogue, and rhetoric in the postmodern world.* Madison: University of Wisconsin Press.

Walzer, M. (1987). *Interpretation and Criticism.* Cambridge: Harvard University Press.

Warren, M. (1988). *Neitzche and Political Thought.* Cambridge: MIT Press.

Weeden, C. (1987). *Feminist practice and poststructuralist theory.* London: Blackwell.

Welch, S. D. (1985). *Communities of resistance and solidarity: a feminist theology of liberation.* New York: Orbis Books.

CHAPTER 1

Notes

*For Henry Giroux with respect and affection

1. Bibliographical citations to the key texts are found in the references which also refer to previous articles where I discuss postmodern theory in more detail; here I am supposing familiarity with postmodern

positions and will concentrate on application rather than explication of postmodern theory.

2. While Postman's critique of television (1985) is often provocative and incisive, his categorical framework invites the sort of deconstruction of binary oppositions which is a central part of many postmodern epistemologies. For his book is structured around an opposition between rational, logical, discursive, and coherent print discourse ("The Age of Exposition") and an irrational, incoherent, and fragmented electronic media discourse ("The Age of Entertainment"). Print media are serious, important, contextual, and conducive to democracy and other fine values, while electronic media and the culture of the image is trivial, frivolous, and subversive of everything valuable in life (religion, education, politics, etc.). This binary absolutism covers over the more negative aspects of print culture and presents a purely negative view of image and electronic culture. I shall offer a competing view of media culture in my forthcoming book on television (in press).

3. For a further critique of postmodern cultural theory and the explication of a political hermeneutics which builds an yet goes beyond postmodern theory, see Best and Kellner, 1987.

4. For attempts to link deconstructive analyses with ideology critique, see Ryan 1982 and Spivak 1987. In the following discussion, I assume the saliency of the poststructuralist and postmodernist critiques of much "modern" epistemology and metaphysics—that is, of theoretical positions embedded in the philosophical discourses of modernity. Whether these critiques are properly "postmodern," or merely a self-reflexive version of "modern" critique is difficult to clearly answer. That is, in a sense, deconstruction is very modernist precisely in its criticisms of the discourses of modernity. In any case, it is clear that critiques of modern epistemology and the attempts to develop new methods of reading, writing, and textuality that are sometimes described as "postmodern" is a fruitful contribution to a new radical pedagogy which we might choose to call postmodern—or one may well be perfectly and legitimately happy to interpret such a pedagogy as a variant of modern pedagogy. Indeed, in this essay, I shall argue that a new radical pedagogy should combine positions that are deemed modern and postmodern, or are claimed by both discourses.

5. The method of reading ads and interpretation of advertising which follows is indebted to the work of Robert Goldman (1987, 1988). See also John Berger (1973) and Judith Williamson (1978) for excellent pedagogical introductions to reading advertisements critically.

6. The tobacco leaf is (for insects) one of the most sweet and tasty of all plants—and therefore it requires a large amount of pesticides to keep

insects from devouring it. Cigarette makers use chemicals to give a distinctive smell and taste to the product and use preservatives to keep it from spoiling. Other chemicals are used to regulate the burning process and to filter out tars and nicotine. While these latter ingredients are the most publicized dangers in cigarette smoking, actually the pesticides, chemicals, and preservatives may well be more deadly. Scandalously, cigarettes are one of the most unregulated products in the U.S. consumer economy (European countries, for example, carefully regulate the pesticides used in tobacco growing and the synthetics used in cigarette production). Government-sponsored experiments on the effects of cigarette smoking also use generic cigarettes, which may not have the chemicals and preservatives of name brands; thus no really scientifically accurate major survey on the dangers of cigarette smoking has ever been done by the U.S. government. The major media, many of which are part of conglomerates with heavy interests in the tobacco industry, or which depend on cigarette advertising for revenue, have never really undertaken to expose to the public the real dangers concerned with cigarette smoking and the scandalous neglect of this issue by government and media in the United States. Cigarette addiction is thus a useful object lesson in the unperceived dangers and destructive elements of the consumer society and the ways these dangers are covered over. (My own information on the cigarette industry derives from an *Alernative Views* television interview which Frank Morrow and I did with Bill Drake on the research which will constitute his forthcoming book.

7. For an interesting revelation of how the advertising world itself is worried about forthcoming taxes on their product, see "What's Ahead? Read My Lips: Taxes," *Advertising Age*, Nov. 7, 1988, p. 1.

8. Further explorations of what can be done about advertising can be found in Harms and Kellner, in press and in my forthcoming book *Television, Politics, and Society: Toward a Critical Theory of Television*.

References

Aronowitz, S. and H. A. Giroux, (1985). *Education under siege: The conservative, liberal, and radical debate over schooling*. South Hadley, Massachuetts: Bergin and Garvey.

Association of National Advertisers (1988). *The Role of Advertising in America*. USA.

Barthes, R. (1972). *Mythologies*. New York: Hill and Wang.

Baudrillard, J. (1981). *Toward a Critique of the Political Economy of the Sign*. St. Louis: Telos Press.

——— (1983a). *Simulations*. New York: Semiotext(e).

———— (1983b). *In the shadow of the silent majorities*. New York: Semiotext(e).

Berger, J. (1973). *Ways of seeing*. New York: Viking Press.

Berman, Marshall (1982). *All that is solid melts into air*. New York: Simon and Schuster.

Best, S. and Kellner, D. (1987). (Re)watching television: Notes toward a political criticism. *Diacritics*. Summer: 97-113.

Britton, Andrew (1988). The Myth of Postmodernism. *Cineaction* 13/14: 3-17.

Cahoone, L. E. (1988). *The dilemma of modernity*. Albany, New York: State University of New York Press.

Derrida, J. (1976). *Of grammatology*. Baltimore: Johns Hopkins University Press.

Giroux, H. A. (1983). *Theory and resistance in education*. South Hadley, Massachuetts: Bergin & Garvey.

———— (1988). *Schooling and the struggle for public life*. Minneapolis: University of Minnesota Press.

Gitlin, T. (1987). (ed.) *Watching television*. New York: Pantheon.

Goldman, R. (1987). Marketing fragrances: Advertising and the production of commodity signs. *Theory, Culture & Society*. Vol. 4. 691-725.

———— The mortise and the frame. Critical Studies in Mass Communication. forthcoming 1988.

Habermas, J. (1987). *The philosophical discourse of modernity*. Cambridge, Massachuetts: MIT Press.

———— (1989). *On the structural transformation of the public sphere*. Cambridge, Massachuetts: MIT Press.

Harms, J. and D. Kellner (1989). New theoretical perspectives on advertising. forthcoming.

Henry, J. (1963). *Culture against man*. New York: Random House.

Hirsch, E. D. (1987). *Cultural literacy*. Boston: Houghton Mifflin.

Jameson, F. (1983). Postmodernism and the consumer society. In Hal Foster, (ed.) *The Anti-Aesthetic*. Port Washington, New York: Bay Press.

———— (1984). Postmodernism, or the cultural logic of late capitalismi. *New Left Review*. 146: 53-93

270 Notes and References

Kellner, D. (1987). Baudrillard, semiurgy and death. *Theory, Culture & Society*. 4:1: 125-146.

—— (1988). Postmodernism as social theory: Some challenges and problems. *Theory, Culture & Society*. Vol. 5, Nos. 2-3: 239-270.

—— (1989a). *Critical theory, marxism, and modernity*. Cambridge and Baltimore: Polity Press and Johns Hopkins University Press.

—— (1989b). *Jean Baudrillard: From Marxism to postmodernism and beyond*. Cambridge and Palo Alto: Polity Press and Stanford University Press.

—— (1989c). Fashion, advertising, and the consumer society. *In Radical Perspectives on Mass Commmunications and Culture, Forthcoming. Sage*.

—— (1989d). *Television, politics, and society: Toward a critical theory of television*. Forthcoming Westview Press.

Kolb, D. (1986). *The Critique of Pure Modernity*. Chicago: University of Chicago Press.

Kroker, A., and D. Cook, (1986). *The Postmodern Scene*. New York: St. Martin's Press.

Lyotard, J. F. (1984). *The Postmodern Condition*. Minneapolis: University of Minnesota Press.

McLuhan, M. (1964). *Understanding Media*. New York: Signet.

Postman, N. (1985). *Amusing Ourselves to Death*. New York: Viking.

Ryan, M. (1982). *Marxism and Deconstruction*. Baltimore: Johns Hopkins University Press.

Sontag, S. (1969). *Against Interpretation*. New York: Dell.

Spivak, G. (1987). *In other worlds*. New York: Metheun.

Ulmer, G. L. (1985). *Applied Grammatology*. Baltimore: Johns Hopkins University Press.

Williamson, J. (1978). *Decoding Advertisements*. London: Marion Boyers.

CHAPTER 2

Notes

1. Iris Marian Young, "Impartiality and the Civic Public: Some Implications of Feminist Critiques of Moral and Political Theory," Seyla

Benhabib and Drucilla Cornell, eds., *Feminism as Critique: On the Politics of Gender* (Minneapolis: University of Minnesota Press, 1987), p. 76.

2. Ibid.

3. Henry A. Giroux, "Crisis and Possibilities in Public Education," *Teachers as Intellectuals: Toward A Critical Pedagogy of Learning* (Granby, Massachusetts: Bergin and Garvey, 1988, p. 177.

4. Daryl McGowan Tress, "Comment on Flax's 'Postmodernism and Gender Relations in Feminist Theory,'" *Signs: Journal of Women in Culture and Society* (Volume 14, no. 1, 1988) p. 197.

5. Ibid.

6. Michel Foucault, *The Order of Things* (New York: Vintage Books, 1973); Gilles Deleuze and Felix Guattari, *Anti-Oedipus: Capitalism and Schizophrenia* (New York: The Viking Press, 1977)

7 . Luce Irigary, *This Sex which is not one*, Trans. Catherine Porter (Ithaca, New York: Cornell University Press, 1985).

8. Barbara Christian, "The Race for Theory," *Feminist Studies (14/1* Spring 1988) 75-76.

9. Luce Irigaray, *Speculum of the Other Woman*, trans. Gitlian C. Gill (Ithaca, New York: Cornell University Press, 1985), p. 129.

10. Luce Irigaray, *This Sex Which Is Not One*, trans. Catherine Porter (Ithaca, New York: Cornell University Press, 1985), pp. 166-167

11. Irigaray, *This Sex Which is Not One*, p.112. See the contrasting affirmations of collective and individual identity in Alice Walker, *In Search of Our Mother's Gardens: Womenist Prose* (New York: Harcourt Brace Jovanovich, 1983); Audre Lorde, *Sister Outsider: Essays and Speeches* (Trumansberg, NY: The Crossing Press, 1984); Paula Gunn Allan, *The Sacred Hoop: Recovering the Feminine in American Indian Traditions* (Boston: Beacon Press, 1986); Gloria Anzaldera, *Borderlands/La-Frontera: The New Mestiza* (San Francisco: Spinsters/Aunt Lute, 1987); Gloria Anzaldera and Cherrie Moraga, eds., *This Bridge Called My Back: Writings by Radical Women of Color* (Watertown, MA: Persephone Press, 1981); Mary Daly, *Pure Lust Elemental Feminist Philosophy* (Boston: Beacon Press, 1987); June Jorden, *Civil Wars* (Boston: Beacon Press, 1981); Ann Cameron, *Daughters of Copperwoman* (Vancouver: Press Gang Publishers, 1981).

12. Daryl McGowan Tress, "Comment on Flax's 'Postmodernism and Gender Relations in Feminist Theory'", p. 197.

13. Ibid.

14. Jane Flax, "Reply to Tress," *Signs: Journal of Women in Culture and Society* (1988) vol. 141 no.1, p. 202.

15. Alastair MacIntyre, *After Virtue: A Study in Moral Theory*, 2nd ed. (Notre Dame, Ind: University of Notre Dame Press, 1984), p. 14.

16. Ibid.

17. Michel Foucault, *The Use of Pleasure: The History of Sexuality Volume Two*, trans. Robert Hurley (New York: Pantheon Books, 1985).

18. MacIntyre, *After Virtue*, p. 162.

19. Ibid., p. 159.

20. Ibid., p. 148.

21. Robert Farris Thompson, *Flash of the Spirit: African and Afro-American Art and Philosophy* (New York: Random House, 1983).

22. Seyla Benhabib, "The Generalized and The Concrete Other: The Kohlberg-Gilligan Controversy and Feminist Theory" in *Feminism as Critique*, p. 57.

23. Nancy Fraser, "Toward a Discourse Ethic of Solidarity," *Praxis International*, 5:4 1986, pp. 425-29.

24. Beverly Harrison, *Making the Connections: Essays in Feminist Social Ethics*, ed. Carol S. Robb (Boston: Beacon Press, 1985), p. 250.

25. Ibid.

26. Sandra Harding, *The Science Question in Feminism* (Ithaca, N.Y.: Cornell University Press, 1986), p. 191.

27. Jürgen Habermas, "Questions and Counterquestions" in Bernstein, *Habermas and Modernity* (Cambridge, MA: MIT Press, 1985), p. 194.

28. Jürgen Habermas, "What is Universal Pragmatics?" in *Communication and the Evolution of Society* (Boston: Beacon Press, 1974), p. 3.

29. Anthony Giddens, "Reason Without Revolution? Habermas's *Theorie des Kommunikativen Handelns*" in Bernstein, ed., *Habermas and Modernity*, p. 97.

30. Ibid.

31. Ibid., p. 105.

32. Habermas, *Communication and the Evolution of Society*, p. 97.

33. Jürgen Habermas, *Knowledge and Human Interests*, (Boston: Beacon Press, 1971), pp. 43-63, 301-317.

34. Habermas, "Questions and Counterquestions," p. 214.

35. Giddens, "Reason Without Revolution?" pp. 117-119.

36. Giddens, pp. 117-118.

37. Richard Katz, *Boiling Energy: Community healing Among the Kalahari Kung* (Cambridge, MA: Harvard University Press, 1984).

38. Barbara Christian, "The Race for Theory," p. 68.

39. Giddens, "Reason Without Revolution?" pp. 126-127.

40. Paule Marshall, *The Chosen Place, The Timeless People* (New York: Random House) 1984.

41. Giddens, "Reason Without Revolution?" pp. 116-117.

CHAPTER 3

Notes

1. We take this opportunity to thank the Quad Women's Group, the undergraduate women at Penn who in the four years we met with them weekly surprised and delighted us with stories of their lives as students, daughters, lovers, and friends. This essay is infused with dreams, desires, and fears that materialized in those sessions and emerge here in our own academic dream of a story in which women stand together in their struggle to reclaim the bodies that accompany their minds.

2. The Penn Harassment Survey was sent to students, faculty, and staff in March of 1985, and the Report of the Committee to Survey Harassment at the University of Pennsylvania was published the following fall in the *Almanac*, the weekly unversity publication for staff and faculty (de Cani Fine, Sagi, and, Stern 1985). The committee reported that 1,065 of the 2,251 usable questionnaires included answers to open-ended questions. Concerning undergraduate and graduate women's responses to the open-ended question asking them to describe an experience of harassment, thirty-seven of the sixty-six undergraduate responses reported harassment by either professors or teaching assistants and forty-four of the sixty-eight graduate responses concerned professors. While we did not include their narratives in this essay, readers will be interested to learn that of the thirty-six untenured women faculty at Penn who wrote about

harassment, seventeen reported being harassed by faculty (thirteen of whom were senior) and one by her dean; that twelve of twenty responses from tenured women faculty definitely concerned another faculty member (including two department chairs); and that eighteen of the thirty-two women staff who responded reported being harassed by either their supervisors or faculty (IX-X). That any woman at Penn is potentially subject to harassment, regardless of status, reminds us that some men violate women's civil rights as a matter of course and that they do so with relative impunity inside the academy.

References

Belsey, C. (1980). *Critical practice*. New York Methuen.

Brodkey, L. (1989). On the subjects of class and gender., In *The Literacy letters College* Engish, 51(2), 125-141.

Caplan, C. (1986). *Sea changes: Essays on culture and feminism*. London: Verso.

Chodorow, N. (1978). *The reproduction of mothering: Psychoanalysis and the sociology of gender*. Berkeley: University of California Press.

de Cani, John, Michelle Fine, Philip Sagi, and Mark Stern. (1985). Report of the committee to survey harassment at the University of Pennsylvania. *Almanac, 32* (September 24), II-XII.

Fine, Michelle. (1986) Contextualizing the study of social injustice. In M. Saxe & L. Saxe (Eds.), *Advances in applied social psychology* (Vol. 3). New Jersey: Lawrence Erlbaum.

Giroux, H. (1988). Schooling and the struggle for-public life: *Critical pedagogy in the modern age*. Minneapolis: University of Minnesota Press.

Gramsci, A. (1971). *Selections from the Prison notebooks*. (New York: International Publishers.

Haraway, D. (1988) Situated knowledges: The science question in feminism and the privilege of partial perspective. *Feminist Studies, 14,* 575-599,

Harding, S. (1988) *The science question in feminism*. Ithaca: Cornell University Press.

Hartsock, N. (1985). *Money, sex, and power*. Boston: Northeastern University Press.

Kolodny, A (1988). Dancing between left and right: Feminism and the academic minefield in the 1980s. *Feminist Studies. 14,* 453-466.

Penn Harassment Survey, The. (1985). Phadelphia: Office of the Vice-Provost for Research, University of Pennsylvania.

Robertson, Claire, Constance E. Dwyer, and D'Ann Cambell. (1988). Campus harassment: Sexual harassment policies and procedures at institutions of higher learning. *Signs, 13,* 792-8 1 2.

CHAPTER 4

Acknowledgement

I would like to thank the following people for their critical readings of this paper and their valuable suggestions: Julie D'Acci, Elizabeth Ellsworth, Sally Lesher, Bonnie Trudell, and Nancy Worcester.

References

Alexander, G. M. (1987). *Scott Foresman life science.* Glenview, Illinois: Scott Foresman.

Alexander, P. (1987). *Silver Burdett & Ginn life science.* Morristown, New Jersey: Silver Burdett & Grinn.

Allen, D. G. and M. H. Whatley, (1986). Nursing and men's health: Some critical considerations. *Nursing Clinics of North-America, 21*(1), 3-13.

Bell, R., et al. (1980). *Changing bodies—changing, lives.* New York: Random House.

Bleier, R. (1984). *Science and gender. A critique of biology, and its theories on women.* New York: Pergamon.

Boston Women's Health Book Collective. (1971). *Our bodies, ourselves.* Boston: New England Free Press.

Braun, N. (1988). Sexual agreement enrages students. *The Stoutonia,* p. 1.

DeVaney, A. (1987, Dec./Jan.). The world of John Hughes. *Framework,* 16-25.

Dyer, R. (1982). Don't look now. *Screen, 23*(3-4), 61-73.

Fine, M. (1988). Sexuality, schooling, and adolescent females: The missing discourse of desire. *Harvard Educational Review, 58,* 29-53.

Fingler, L. (1981, February). Teenagers in survey condone forced sex. *Ms.,* p. 23.

Giroux, H. A. and R. I. Simon, (1988). Critical pedagogy and the politics of popular culture: Reconstructing the discourse of ideology and pleasure. *Cultural Studies, 2*(3), 294-320.

Gould, S. J. (1981). *The mismeasure of man*. New York: Norton.

Kenney, A. M. and M. T. Orr, (1984). Sex education: An overview of current programs, policies and research. *Phi Delta Kappan, 65,* 491-496.

Kuhn, A. (1985). *The power of the image: Essays on representation and sexuality*. London: Routledge and Kegan Paul.

Madaras, L. (1984). *The what's happening to my body? book for boys. a growing up guide for parents and sons*. New York: The Newmarket Press.

McCoy, K. and C. Wibbelsman, (1978). *The teenage body book*. New York: Simon and Schuster.

Myerson, M. (1986). The politics of sexual knowledge: Feminism and sexology textbooks. *Frontiers, 9,* 66-71.

Neale, S. (1983). Masculinity as spectacle: Reflections on men and mainstream cinema. *Screen, 24*(6), 2-16.

Oram, R. F. (1986). *Biology: Living systems* (5th ed.). Columbus, Ohio: Charles E. Merrill.

Pollis, C. A. (1988). An assessment of the impacts of feminism on sexual science. *The Journal of Sex Research, 25,* 85-105.

Sarrell, L. J. and P. M. Sarrell, (1981). Sexual unfolding. *Journal of Adolescent Health Care, 2,* 93-99.

Schraer, W. D. (1987). *Biology: The study of life*. Newton, Massachuettes: CEBCO. Allyn and Bacon.

Trudell, B. (1988). *Constructing the sexuality curriculum-in-use: An ethnographic study of a ninth-grade sex education class*. Unpublished doctoral dissertation, University of Wisconsin, Madison.

Whatley, M.H. (1985). Male and female hormones: Misinterpretations of biology in school health and sex education. In V. Sapiro (ed.), *Women. biology, and public policy*. Beverly Hills, California: Sage.

Whatley, M. H. (1987). Biological determinism and gender issues in sexuality education. *The Journal of Sex Education and Therapy, 13*(2), 26-29.

Whatley, M. H. & B. Trudell, (in press). School sexual abuse prevention and sexuality education: Interconnected dilemmas and dreams. *Theory Into Practice*.

Whitlock, K. and E. M. DiLapi, (1983). Friendly Fire: Homophobia in sex education literature. *Interracial Books for Children Bulletin*, 14, 20-23.

Wright, J. et al. (1988). *Prentice-Hall life science* (1st ed.). Englewood Cliffs, New Jersey: Prentice Hall.

Zilbergeld, B. (1978). *Male sexuality: A guide to sexual fulfillment.* Boston-Toronto: Little, Brown.

CHAPTER 5

Notes

*This essay has greatly profited from many conversations I have had with Henry Giroux over the last four months.

1. For a summary of some of the major themes of postmodernism, see Dick Hebdige (1988). I believe that postmodernism is a conflicting and contradictory sphere of ideological and cultural manifestations within and pronouncements about the constitution of late capitalism both with respect to the possibilities of cultural criticism and the development of an oppositional political project. It is clearly the case that there are both socially reactionary and socially emancipator strains of postmodern social theory as Henry Giroux, Hal Foster (1983), Linda Hutcheon (1988), and others have argued. There exists, I would argue, both utopian and dystopian potentialities within the current heterotopian character of post-modern society. While classical modernist dichotomies of Left.vs. Right fail to adequately characterize these strains, there is, unarguably, a subversive element in the free-play of the signifier as well as a disabling potential. The freeing of the signifier from its link to a mythic signified can certainly be used both to attack dominant signifying practices such as the notion of the transcendental self as existing outside articulation, and collapse the boundaries between high and low culture. Yet there is also a danger that postmodernism can be co-opted for commercial and ideological ends (Kaplan 1987). And while I essentially agree with Scott Lash and John Urry that "Postmodernism on one side, with its glorification of commercial vulgarity, its promotion of 'authoritarian populism,' reinforces relations of domination [and] on the other side, with its opposition to hierarchy, it is a cultural resource for resistance to such domination," (1987, 14), this essay will essentially forego an extended discussion of the enabling possibilities of the latter and will, instead, concentrate on a critique of the authoritarian servility, pronounced anti-utopianism, and incipient nihilism of the former.

2. In order to avoid a "blaming the victim" explanation of the non-contestedness within the ideological formation of today's youth, we need to acknowledge that while ideological hegemony in the United States is

irredeemably condemnable and undeniably powerful, it is not without its *contradictory* moments. A critical reading of social reality often becomes, for many students, a self-contesting exercise not because they enjoy living a yuppie narcosis but because, as Grossberg points out, "youth inserts cultural texts into its public and private lives in complex ways" (1988, 139). Grossberg rightly recognizes that in our postmodern culture, youth exists within the space between subjectification (boredom) and commodification.

3. In this context, the TV screen symbolizes a new era of recycled reality—what Baudrillard refers to as a "narcissistic and protean era of connections, contact, contiguity, feedback and generalized interface" (1983a 127)—where we witness the spectacle of meanings imploding into the flat, seamless surface of hyperreality while at the same time watch helplessly as subjectivity becomes terrorized into political inaction by the baleful dictates of commodity logic and "the constant *promise* of a plenitude forever deferred" (Kaplan 1987, 50).

4. Our consumption of signs is but itself a sign of cultural illness and is symptomatic of postmodern pathologies: narcissistic character disorders, schizophrenias, and depressions (Levin 1987). Richard Litchman (1982) has revealed to us how the very structure of capitalism condemns us from living its own moral truth by pathologizing our everyday subjectivity and provoking a deluded complicity with an often oppressive consensus reality. The "structural unconscious," which helps shape our everyday identity and disposition, is informed largely by the structural contradictions of capitalism which help to construct needs, mobilize desires, and then deny all of these (1982, 229).

5. For a similar analysis of the New Right, see McLaren & Smith (in press). Left social theorists are currently attacking a host of sacrosanct modernist themes which range from the grand myth of science as a self-correcting, self-perfecting, and apodictic universal methodology, to the transparency of the sign, to the transcendental constitutivity of the subject and its fictive stability and unitary identity across time, to the teleological myth of progress (McLaren, 1986a). Left educational theorists have been slow to respond to such an attack, but in some cases they have occupied the front ranks of the foray, since many of these myths have been responsible for fuelling the logic which has made objectivism and certainty into the new demiurge of late capitalist schooling. Yet an unintended consequence of current deconstructive assaults and attempts to construct a form of ethics outside traditional moral and political codes has been the fostering of a public climate regulated by tribunals of normalcy reflecting a brutish and often belligerent self-righteousness.

Forces on the Right, which have taken a swift and punishing advantage of the growing moral ambivalence on the Left, are not pausing to take account of which strand of postmodernism—emancipatory or reactionary—has the temporary leverage in the academy. They are smoothly injecting their ideology directly into the cultural veins of the nation through the electronic media. It's now in fashion to be "Right Wing," as George Bush made clear in his recent election campaign during which time he easily derailed the democratic platform with spectral images of Willy Horton and video clips of Mike Dukakis riding shotgun in an army tank. With the exception of Jesse Jackson and a handful of others, liberal democrats under Dukakis were unable to speak from a moral position that was able to evoke either the sympathy or the support of the American public. In this sense postmodern culture has been especially kind to the New Right, whose political effectiveness can be largely credited to its ability to use the media to mobilize consent around a normative moral vision of the future and to recontextualize difference into a consensus inequality. The often frenzied political and ideological allegiance among such a wide spectrum of individuals—which includes, among others, west coast evangelists in natty business suits, east coast private-sector executives, Midwestern service technicians, and primary labor market workers from the south—is as much a function of the way desires and needs are constituted through the body and sedimented discourses invest themselves in the flesh through what Raymond Williams called "structures of feeling" (1977) as it is a matter of making deliberate choices between conflicting discourses.

The inability of leftist social theorists to establish a politics of praxis strong enough to contest the broad and sweeping constituency of the New Right has imperiled their goal of social transformation and justice that should, ideally, provide the springboard for all social theorizing and practice. What gets unintentionally softened as a result of the relentless attack on the sovereignty of identity and the transparency of society is the very grounds of political opposition and social transformation. Without a new language of ethics and authority it is hard to construct the grounds for what Henry Giroux (1983; 1988) has called a counterpublic sphere and pedagogy for the opposition.

6. It should be pointed out that, with minor exceptions, the Left has failed to develop a critical language that is able to speak directly to the contradictions and particularities of everyday life. In other words, to maintain the requisite complexity of its concepts and formulations its language has paid a price in suggestive power. Undoubtedly, this has also been aggravated by "academic assimilation that neutralizes oppositional writing in a society that provides room for intellectual battles but little for the uses of theory as an ally of actual political resistance" (Merod 1987, 186).

Politics has now taken on a strange, hybrid meaning among Left social and political theorists within the academy, who vary enormously in their opinion and appropriation of postmodern strategies of critique. On the one hand, there are critics such as Fredric Jameson who warn against a simplistic, reductionistic view of the political (1982, 75); on the other hand, there are critics such as Jim Merod, who feel that much academic work that falls into the category of "postmodern," decidedly fails to move the reader "from the academic world of texts and interpretations to the vaster world of surveillance, technology, and material forces" (1987, 146). Harsher antagonists, such as Robert Scholes, claim that the deconstructive enterprise often operates as a form of left mandarin terrorism, both displacing "political activism into a textual world where anarchy can *become* the establishment without threatening the actual seats of political and economic power" (1988, 284) and sublimating political radicalism "into a textual radicalism that can happily theorize its own disconnection from unpleasant realities" (284). Cornell West argues that some current left allegiances satisfy "a pervasive need for Left-academic intellectuals....for the professional respectability and rigor that displace political engagement and this-worldly involvement...[while] at the same time [providing]...an innocuous badge of radicalism" (Stephanson 1988, 274).

If we take these critics of present-day Left theorizing seriously, and I believe that we should, then we should also consider the possibility that by evacuating the fallen gods of modernity and by adopting what is essentially an anti-utopian discourse, left educational theorists may have unwittingly reinstated the worst ideological dimensions of the very discourses they are attempting to renounce. In their fully-fledged frontal attack on metaphysics, a new subterranean metaphysics may have seeped into existence.

7. See Kroker and Cook (eds.) (1986).

8. For an excellent analysis of this dilemma in feminist discourse, see Alcoff (1988).

9. In confronting the vast power of the myth of identity, and in questioning the unity of the liberal, humanist subject, Left social theorists have failed to secure a stable platform from which to speak to the role of the individual as an active political agent. Their failure to situate individuals as political and ethical agents has contributed to the broader failure of constructing a public language and critical vernacular capable of speaking effectively to the daily, lived concerns of the body politic (Giroux 1988). As a result of these failures, Left social theorists have paved the way for a system grounded in absolute ethical certainty and moral closure which has turned schools into laboratories for character engineering based on a reactionary political vision. Here, subjectivities are policed, morality is dispensed, and nationalism celebrated. Here, the discursive underpinnings are provided for a national character formation which can best expedite the production and flow of capital in tough, competitive, economic times and resist the threat of the omnipresent Marxist or Third World Other. The school takes on the hybrid ethos of the local legion hall and fundamentalist revival meeting: America will prevail on the basis of

sound, unflinching, moral fibre and die-hard courage in the face of physical threat.

Translated into a curriculum directive on a national scale, the victory of the New Right has been devastating. A sweeping rearguard action to promote and bolster the simplification and infantilization of the good vs. evil morality of the mass spectacle has been accomplished with little effective resistance. School success in the postmodern era is located within the iron determinism of the capitalist will and achieved by effecting a closure of the sign to a univocal and monodimensional reading.

10. It is useful here to draw attention to the distinction Bryan Turner has made between Freud's pessimistic view of desire as its own object, and the Marxian notion of need which implies an object that can satisfy it (1984, 11). While desires are always already in the order of the signifier as protolinguistic demands (in the sense that they cannot be conceived independently of their representations) (Turner & Cartert 1986), objects of desire are never fully assimilable into desire, as desire is never wholly contained in social forms. Desire is always displaced (as in Lacan's notion that in language desire is metonymically and metaphorically displaced).

11. As cited in Turner and Carter (1986).

12. Postmodernism is very much about the noise of the body which is evident in performance art, minimalism and neo-tonality. Fred Pfeil has remarked on the "scandalously ambivalent" aspect of postmodern forms of pleasure (which he has experienced in the performances of Laurie Anderson and the production of the Wilson/Glass opera, *Einstein on the Beach*) which is "characterized both by the release of new sociopolitical forces through de-Oedipalization of middle-class American life *and* by the hegemony of this same de-Oedipalization social-sexual structure that tends to block the further development of those social forces" (1988, p. 399). What Pfeil is referring to is the "Omnipotent" return to pre-Oedipal wholeness and pleasure produced in avant-garde imagery and productions. But if we take the Oedipus complex to be more of a linguistic rather than a primarily intrafamilial phenomenon, as does Eugene Holland (following Lacan's lead), then we can make a link between such a phenomenon and certain types of social formation. Utilizing the typology of social forms developed by Gilles Deleuze and Felix Guattari (1977), Holland notices that the "name-of-the-Father" does not govern the Symbolic order in capitalist societies as it does under primitive communistic and despotic societies. Under capitalism, the Symbolic order has no fixed center, no established authority figure, and no transcendental signified since "exchange value and the market ruthlessly undermine and eliminate all traditional meanings and pre-existing social codes" (1988, 407). In other words, the "abstract calculus of capital itself" knits together the social order not by providing universal codes but by "decoding" pre-existing meanings and

codes (which "frees desire from capture and distortion by social coding") and "recoding...libidinal energy back onto factitious codes so as to extract and realize privately appropriable surplus value" (408). In other words, continuous revolution under capitalism of the means of production generates a massive decoding which liberates creative consumption and production—even revolutionizing and socializing productive forces—yet the libidinal energy which escapes the constraints of social coding nevertheless becomes recolonized through bureaucratization, the nuclear family, and consumerism.

References

Adorno, T. (1974). Culture industry reconsidered. *New German Critique*, 6, 13-19.

Alcoff, L. (1988). Cultural feminism versus poststructuralism: The identity crisis in feminist theory. *Signs, 13*(3), 405-36.

Arac, T. (ed.) (1986). *Postmodernism and politics*. Minneapolis: University of Minnesota Press.

Aronowitz, S. (1981). *The crisis in historical materialism: Class, politics, and culture in Marxist theory*. New York: Praeger.

———— (1983). Mass culture and the eclipse of reason: The implications for pedagogy. In D. Lazere (ed.), *American media and mass culture* (pp. 465-71). Berkeley and Los Angeles: University of California Press.

Attali, J. (1987). *Noise: The political economy of music*. Minneapolis: University of Minnesota Press.

Barker, F. (1984). *The tremulous pivate body*. London: Methuen.

Baudrillard, J. (1983). *Simulations*. (P. Foss, P. Patton, & J. Johnston, Trans.). New York: Semiotext(e).

Benjamin, W. (1968). The work of art in the age of mechanical reproduction. In Hannah Arendt, ed., *Illuminations*. New York: Schocken Books, p. 244.

Bernstein, R. J. (1988). Metaphysics, critique, and utopia. *The Review of Metaphysics, 62*(2), 255-273.

Bloch, E. (1987). *The principle of hope* (3 vols.). Cambridge, Massachuettes: The MIT Press.

Brenkman, J. (1985). *Culture and domination*. Ithaca: Cornell University Press.

Brodkey, L. (1987). *Academic writing as social practice*. Philadelphia: Temple University Press.

Cherryholmes, C. (1988). *Power and criterion.* New York: Teachers' College Press.

Christian, B. (1987, Spring). The race for theory. *Cultural Critique, 6,* 51-63.

de Certeau, M. (1984). *The Practice of everyday life.* Berkeley: University of California Press.

de Lauretis, T. (1987). *Technologies of gender.* Bloomington: Indiana University Press.

Deleuze, G. and F. Guattari, (1983). *Anti-Oedipus: Capitalism and schizophrenia.* Minneapolis: University of Minnesota Press.

Eagleton, T. (1986). *William Shakespeare.* Oxford: Basil Blackwell.

———— (1985/86, Winter). The subject of literature. *Cultural Critique, 2,* 95-104.

Ellsworth, E. (1988). Why doesn't this feel empowering? Working through the repressive myths of critical pedagogy. Paper presented at the Tenth Conference on Curriculum Theory and Classroom Practice, Dayton, Ohio, October 26-29.

Fay, B. (1987). *Critical social science.* Ithaca: Cornell University Press.

Feher, M. (1987). Of bodies and technologies. In Hal Foster (ed.) Discussions in Contemporary Culture (number one) Seattle, Bay Press, 159-165.

Fine, M. (1988). Sexuality, schooling, and adolescent females: The missing discourse of desire. *Harvard Educational Review, 51*(1), 29-53.

Fiske, J. (1986). MTV: Post-structural, post-modern. *Journal of Communication Inquiry, 10,* 74-9.

———— (1989). *Understanding Popular Culture.* Sydney, Australia: Unwin Hyman, Inc.

Foster, H. (1983). Postmodernism: a preface. In *The anti-aesthetic: essays in postmodern culture,* Hal Foster, ed. Port Townsend: Washington: Bay Press, ix-xvi.

Gardner, H. (1985). *Frames of mind.* New York: Basic Books.

Geoghegan, V. (1987). *Utopianism and Marxism.* London: Methuen.

Giroux, H. (1983). *Theory and resistance in education: A pedagogy for the opposition.* South Hadley, Massachuettes: Bergin and Garvey Publishers.

———— (1988). *Schooling and the struggle for public life*. Minneapolis: University of Minnesota Press.

Giroux, H., and P. McLaren, (1989). Schooling, cultural politics, and the struggle for democracy: Introduction. In H. A. Giroux & P. McLaren (eds.), *Critical pedagogy, the state, and cultural, struggle*. New York: State University of New York Press, xi-xxxv.

———— (in press b). Teacher education and the politics of democratic life: Beyond the Reagan agenda in the era of "good times." In C. C. Yeakey & Gladys Styles Johnston (eds), *Schools as conduits: Educational policymaking during the Reagan years*. Praeger Press.

Giroux, H., and R. Simon, (1988a). Critical pedagogy and the politics of popular culture. *Cultural Studies*, 2(3), 294-320.

Grossberg, L. (1986b). Teaching the popular. In C. Nelson (ed.), *Theory in the classroom*. Urbana: University of Illinois Press.

———— (1986a, Summer). History, politics, and postmodernism: Stuart Hall and cultural studies. *Journal of Communication Inquiry*, 10(2), 71-77.

———— (1988). Rockin' with Reagan, or the mainstreaming of postmodernity. *Cultural Critique*, 10, 123-149.

Levin, C. (1987). Carnal knowledge of aesthetic states. In A. Kroker & M. Kroker (eds.), *Body invaders* (99-119). New York: St. Martin's Press.

Litchman, R, (1982). *The production of desire*. New York: The Free Press.

McCabe, C. (1981). On discourse. In C. McCabe (ed.), *The talking cure: Essays in psychoanalysis and language* (188-217). New York. St. Martin's Press.

McLaren, P. (1989a). On ideology and education: Critical pedagogy and the politics of resistance. In H. Giroux & P. McLaren (eds.), *Critical pedagogy, the state, and cultural struggle*. Albany, New York: State University of New York Press, 174-202.

———— (1989b). *Life in schools*. White Plains, New York: Longman, Inc.

———— (1988). Culture or canon? Critical pedagogy and the politics of literacy. *Harvard Educational Review*, 58(2), 213-34.

———— (1988). On ideology and education: Critical pedagogy and the politics of education. *Social Text*, 19/20, 153-85.

———— (1986). *Schooling as a ritual performance*. London: Routledge and Kegan Paul.

McLaren, P. and M. Dantley, (in press). Leadership and a critical pedagogy of race: Cornel West, Stuart Hall, and the prophetic tradition. *Journal of Negro Education.*

McLaren, P. and R. Smith, (in press). Televangelism as pedagogy and cultural politics. In H. A. Giroux & R. Simon (eds.), *Popular Culture — and Critical Pedagogy.* South Hadley, Massachuettes: Bergin and Garvey.

Megill, A. (1985). *Prophets of extremity.* Berkeley: University of California Press.

Merod, J. (1987). *The political responsibility of the critic.* Ithaca and London: Cornell University Press.

Pfeil, F. (1988). Postmodernism as a "structure of felling." In C. Nelson & L. Grossberg (eds.), *Marxism and the interpretation of culture.* Chicago: University of Illinois Press, 381-403.

Porter, C. (1988). Are we being historical yet? *South Atlantic Quarterly,* *87,* 744-86.

Ross, A. (1988). Introduction. In A. Ross (ed.), *Universal abandon?* (vii-xviii). Minneapolis: University of Minnesota Press.

Scherpe, K. R. (1986/87, Winter). Dramatization and de-dramatization of the end: The apocalyptic consciousness of modernity and post-modernity. *Cultural Critique, 5,* 124.

Scholes, R. (1988, Winter). Deconstruction and communication. *Critical Inquiry, 14,* 278-295.

Scholle, D. J. (1988). Critical studies: From the theory of ideology to power/knowledge. *Critical studies in mass communication, 5,* 16-35.

Schulte-Sasse, J. (1986/87). Imagination and modernity: Or the taming of the human mind. *Cultural Critique, 5,* 23-48.

——— (1987/1988). Electronic media and cultural politics in the Reagan Era: The attack on Libya and hands across America as postmodern events. *Cultural Critique, 8,* 123-152.

Shumway, D. (in press). Reading rock 'n roll in the classroom: A critical pedagogy. In H. A. Giroux & P. McLaren (eds.), *Critical Pedagogy, the state, and cultural struggle.* Albany, New York: State University of New York Press.

Silverman, K. (1988). *The acoustic mirror: The female voice in psychoanalysis and cinema.* Bloomington: Indiana University.

Stephanson, A. (1988). Interview with Cornel West. In A. Ross (ed.), *Universal abandon?* (pp. 269-286). Minneapolis: University of Minnesota Press.

Turner, B. (1984). *The body and society.* Oxford: Basil Blackwell.

Turner, C., and Carter, E. (1986). Political somatics: Notes on Klaus Theweleit's *male fantasies.* In V. Burgin, J. Donald, & C. Kaplan (ed.), *Formations of fantasy* (pp. 200-213). London and New York: Methuen.

Turner, D. (1983). *Marxism and Christianity.* Oxford: Basil Blackwell.

Walzer, M. (1987). *Interpretation and Criticism.* Cambridge: Harvard University Press.

West, C. (1989). *The American evasion of Philosophy.* Madison: The University of Wisconsin Press.

Yudice, G, (1988). Marginality and the ethics of survival. In A. Ross (ed.), *Universal abandon?* (214-236). Minneapolis: University of Minnesota Press.

CHAPTER 6

Notes

1. I use the terms "going out dancing" or "popular dancing" to refer to forms of contemporary social dancing that take place in clubs, dances, and parties, usually involving leaderless, improvised movements.

2. Jenny Taylor and Dave Laing, reviewing the Frith and McRobbie article, criticize the notion that rock music is inherently more sexual than other popular cultural commodities (1979, 43). However, given rock's role in social regulation through its construction of masculinity and femininity in often polar extremes and its presence in the clubs, a link between rock music, dancing and the learning of sexuality seems probable.

3. Queen Street West has a similarity to rue St. Denis or rue St. Laurent in Montreal, or Soho in New York, districts where a certain portion of the contemporary art scene, soft punk culture, style-driven consumerism, and the market's co-optation of desirable commodities intersect to produce a "scene" clearly defined by physical boundaries, taste, and a look—In this case a recognizable Queen Street style.

4. Fashion is one crucial sphere that intersects with dancing. Careful consideration for what is worn on the dance floor is one way to maximize

the pleasure of the experience. One woman told me, "Getting dressed up is like doing a painting for me. I am painting my body. It is a creative gesture. It's an inner expression as well as just an outer thing." Clothes as an outer expression are a form of signification to which others attach meaning, and are related to the colonization of women's (in particular) bodies (Sawchuk 1987).

5. Although Hebdige is referring to particular British youth subcultures in his fascinating *Subculture: The Meaning of Style*, his description of the ground of contestation is relevant here. "Tensions between dominant and subordinate groups can be reflected in the surfaces of subculture.... The meaning of subculture is, then, always in dispute, and style is the area in which opposing definitions clash with dramatic force.... But it ends in the construction of a style, in a gesture of defiance or contempt, in a smile or a sneer. It signals a Refusal" (1979, 2-3).

6. This contradicts the common sense notion that meanings are obviously and entirely encoded within a text or practice, to be "read" by the individual, resulting in the unmediated consumption of dominant meanings. This is the issue at the root of the debates concerning the apparent sexism and violence in much of rock and roll music (and television). We need to consider how the messages that *are* encoded within the music intersect with rock's articulation with wider social structures and individual subjectivities, producing a multiplicity of possible readings, within certain limitations (Grossberg 1986).

7. Ellen Dubois and Linda Gordon argue that feminists (among others) have been guilty of exaggerating the coerciveness involved in prostitution and stripping, denying the women roles other than passive victim (1984, 33).

8. I disagree with Lourde's notion of an essential femaleness, although there is a shared relationship to our bodies and sexuality that is born out of no women escaping the dominant social, political, historical construction of their sexuality.

9. Both Kerry and I experienced unknown men deliberately brushing parts of our bodies as they moved by. Those are not innocent gestures but intrusive, violent, and degrading ones. It was partly my fear of violence that stopped me from doing no more than swearing at the offender and partly how the scene itself seemed tolerant of and even conducive to violations that would be unacceptable elsewhere. It is a site of curious contradiction for me to appear to be accepting of a stranger's unwanted intrusion.

10. Another kind of pervasive example is romance fiction, a form of literature especially popular with women. It is encoded with the dominant myths and practices of Western culture, reinforcing patriarchal social

288 Notes and References

relations. The female readers experience resistance of a particular kind, related to escaping the reality of their lives, of spending family funds for their own pleasure, and of imagining themselves in a different reality, for example. The vicarious pleasures of the text, however, subvert any real attempts to change their situation of domination within patriarchy. Thus popular culture in general, and language in particular, become a source of subjective regulation for these women (Radway 1986).

References

Alonso, A. M. (1988, March). The effects of truth: Re-presentations of the past and the imagining of community. *Journal of Historical Sociology*, 1(1), 33-57.

Apple, M. W. (1982). *Education and power* (Ark edition 1985 ed.). Boston: Ark Paperbacks.

Aronowitz, S. (1981). *The crisis in historical materialism: Class, politics and culture in marxist theory*. South Hadley, Massachuettes: J. F. Bergin.

Bennett, T. (1986). Popular culture: Defining our terms. In T. Bennett et al. (Eds.), *Popular culture and social relations* (75-87). London: Open University Press.

Carter, E. (1984). Alice in the consumerland: West German case studies in gender and consumer culture. In A. McRobbie & M. Nava (Eds.), *Gender and generation* (185-214). London: MacMillan.

Chambers, I. (1986). *Studies in Communication. Popular culture*: The metropolitan experience. New York: Methuen & Co.

Corrigan, P. (1987). *Playing...contradictions, empowerment and embodiment: Punk, pedagogy and popular cultural forms*. Draft manuscript. (Toronto: Ontario Institute for Studies in Education).

Coward, R. (1984). Female desire. London: Granada.

Dimien, M. (1984). Politically correct? Politically incorrect? In C. Vance (Ed.), *Pleasure and danger: Exploring female sexuality* (138-148). Boston: Routledge & Kegan Paul.

Dobkin, A. (1985). Sexism and racism and rock and roll: A lecture by Alix Dobkin. *One, Two, Three, Four, A Rock 'n' Roll Quarterly*.(Toronto: Ontario Institute for Studies in Education).

DuBos, E. C. and L. Gordon. (1984). Seeking ecstasy on the battlefield: Danger and pleasure in nineteenth-century feminist sexual thought. In C. Vance (Ed.), *Pleasure and danger: Exploring female sexuality* (31-49). Boston: Routledge & Kegan Paul.

Foucault, M. (1983). Afterword: The subject and power. In H.L. Dreyfus and P. Rabinow (Eds.), *Michel Foucault: Beyond structuralism and hermeneutics* (second ed.) (208-226). Chicago: University of Chicago Press, 1982.

Frith, S. and A. McRobbie. (1978/79, Winter). Rock and sexuality. *Screen Education*, (29), 3-19.

Giroux, H. A. and R. I. Simon (1988, January). Critical pedagogy and the politics of popular culture. *Cultural Studies*, 294-320.

Grossberg, L. (1986). Teaching the popular. In C. Nelson (Ed.), *Theory in the classroom* (177-200). Urbana: University of Illinois Press.

Hanna, J. L. (1988). *Dance, sex, and gender*. Chicago: University of Chicago Press.

Haug, F. (1987). *Female sexualization*. London: Verso.

Hebdige, D. (1979). *Subculture: The meaning of style*. New York: Methuen & Co.

Hebdige, Dick (1988, April 11). *What is Soul*: Post-Modernism and Pop Video. Presentation, University of Toronto.

Kuhn, A. (1985). *The power of the image: Essays on representation and sexuality*. London: Routledge & Kegan Paul.

Lourde, A. (1984). *Sister outsider*. New York: Crossing Press.

Martin, R. (1988). *Performance as a political act: The embodied self* Unpublished manuscript.

McDonough, D. (1987, Winter). Dance as a feminist project. *Kick It Over*, (20).

McRobbie, A. (1984). Dance and social fantasy. In A. McRobbie and M. Nava (Eds.), *Gender and Generation* (130-161). London: MacMillan.

Radway, J. (1984). *Reading the romance: Women, patriarchy and popular literature*. Chapel Hill: University of North Carolina Press.

Roman, L. G. (1988). Intimacy, labor and class: Ideologies of feminine sexuality in the punk slam dance. In L. G. Roman, L. K. Christian-Smith W. E. Ellsworth (Eds.), *Becoming feminine: The politics of popular culture* (143-184). Philadelphia: Falmer Press.

Rossiter, A. (1988). *From private to public: A feminist exploration of early mothering*. Toronto: Women's Press.

Rowbotham, S. (1972). *Women, resistance, and revolution*. Middlesex: Penguin.

Saunders, L. (Ed.). (1987). *Glancing fires: An investigation into women's creativity.* London: Women's Press.

Sawchuk, K. (1987). A tale of inscription: Fashion statements. In A. & M. Kroker (Eds.), *Body invaders: panic sex in America* (61-77). Montreal: New World Perspectives.

Stall, S. (1897). *Self and Sex Series. What a young man ought to know.* Philadelphia, Pennsylvania: Virginia Publishing.

Swanson, G. (1986, Sept-Oct). Rethinking representation. *Screen,* 27(5), 16-28.

Taylor, J. and D. Laing. (1979, Summer). Disco-pleasure-discourse: On rock and sexuality. *Screen Education,* (31), 43-48.

Vance, C. (Ed.). (1984). *Pleasure and danger: Exploring female sexuality.* Boston: Routledge & Kegan Paul.

Wexler, P. (1982). *Structure, text, and subject: A critical sociology of school knowledge.* In M.W. Apple (Ed.), *Cultural and economic reproduction in education: Essays on class, ideology and the state* (275-303). Boston: Routledge and Kegan Paul.

Williamson, J. (1986). *Consuming passions: The dynamics of popular culture.* London: Marion Boyars.

CHAPTER 7

Notes

These citations are complementary to two other writings: "My(?)Body, My Self(?): Trying to see (with) My Masculine Eyes", *Resources for Feminist Research,* 1983/84; "The Body of Intellectuals/The Intellectuals' Body", *Sociological Review,* 1988.

1. E. H. Goddard, *Reminiscences of a Headmaster: Aske's School,* 1932-1961 (London: Hutchinson Benham, privately published, 1972, p. 193). I am most grateful to my Mother, Norah Rebecca Frances Corrigan, for obtaining a copy of this now out of print book.

2. A. Wilden, *The Rules Are No Game* (London, Boston: Routledge & Kegan Paul, 1987); *War and Peace, Man and Woman* (London, Boston: Routledge & Kegan Paul, 1987).

3. E. H. Goddard, *op. cit.,* n 1 above; I have also been helped by (a) my journal 1956 to 1960; (b) letters 1958 to 1962 from George, Philip, Arthur; (c) memories of Antony Harding, who "saved" me for the school

when I walked out in 1959 and introduced me to the writings of Ezra Pound, T.S. Eliot, and above all Gertrude Stein.

4. "Clocking-in", does that mean *anything* to readers in the 1980's? In England (as also elsewhere) workers, including clerical workers like many, had to *register* their arrival at/for work, by inserting a card into a clock that punched in the time of arrival. This determined pay, security of employment, reliability, and so forth. School registers (regulated by law) are like this too!

5. W. E. Marsden, *Unequal Educational Provision in England and Wales: The Nineteenth Century Roots* (London: Woburn Press, 1987).

6. A. Wilden, *The Rules Are No Game*, op. cit., n. 2 above, pp. 3-63 has some contextualized memories of Christ's Hospital, as a scholarship boy.

7. I've always been cynically cruel to George Orwell, calling him "A Ghost uncertain where he is supposed to haunt", but he did "write very well" (to quote from a letter *about my own writing* from E. H. Goddard to me a few years after I had left school). Why or even how I was "in touch" I cannot recall, but the fact displays precisely the ambivalence that pervades this writing now. This year, 1988, I read *Orwell Remembered* (edited by A. Coppard and B. Crick; London, BBC/Ariel Books, 1984) which changed my understanding of Orwell via a kind a shock of self-recognition—his "curious" placement in rural Southwold and his late years on Jura, his capricious obstinacy / latent violence, his constant writing, writing, writing; the repertoire of "eccentric" Englishness/Masculinity. But also this:

> "Probably the greatest cruelty one can inflict on a child", wrote Orwell in *Keep the Aspidustra Flying* "is to send it to school among children richer than itself". (Christopher Hollis, 1956, *Orwell Remembered* on Blair at Eton, p. 47).

But also, finally in an essay on the Boy/the Body, there is much to reference about Orwell's Body and the structuration of his thought, life, writing around the deep logics: Purity/Danger, Sacred/Profane *and* Englishness Aliens. Koester (169ff.). The persistent theme of "sordidity" (101) as fascination and fear, versus bathing, keeping oneself clean is the key to his politics, and old-fashioned English gentleman, decent, straightforward, homophobic, and patriarchal! Before I knew this "context" I'd teased some of it from his 1984: P. R. D. Corrigan, "Soft messages, Hard machines" in *Nineteen-Eighty-Four* in 1984 (P. Aubrey & D. Morley, eds., London: Comedia, 1984). Recall how the working classes "smell" and "stink".

8. Bert did well, emigrating in 1926 to Tasmania, Australia, where he became Electoral Officer, to return in 1965 (was it?) to obtain has CBE

gong from Her Majesty. Sadly, he died on the ship trip back home. His wife, Mabel, from Ireland, whom I do not recall, was a painter.

9. Goddard, *op. cit.*, n. 1 p. 5; Length of name means a lot, but inversely. There are codes of ruling class masculinity that need no words, or no words that can be found even in the full Oxford English Dictionary, like "Pop" (for Eton), so mostly single words (or sometimes, with these aboriginals, grunts and sighs, smirks, and itching of the crotch!) will signify "I was there" (with you, with you) a homosociality which (most) would deny as horrific if developed into the loving of the other's body that the private-public-masculine school promotes and denies. Importantly the Aske's conglomerate involved at least four schools, two private, one for boys, one for girls, and two state or semi-state, one for boys (mine, huh!) and one for girls (down Telegraph Hill, where my cousin, Brenda, Charley's daughter, freshly returned from the Rhodesian reality, went). How we boys/men-fantasized the girls/women there!

10. See "My(?)Body, My Self(?)", *op. cit.*, noted above, but also "In/forming Schooling", chapter 2 in D. Livingstone (ed.), *Critical Pedagogy and Cultural Power*, (South Hadley, Massachusetts: Bergin & Garvey, 1986); P. Corrigan, B. Curtis, & B. Lanning, "The Political Space of Schooling", chapter 1 in T. Wotherspoon (ed.), *Political Economy of Canadian Schooling* (Toronto: Methuen, 1987).

11. P. Willis, *Learning to Labour* (Farnborough, Saxon House, 1977); P. Corrigan and P. Willis, "Cultural Forms", *Media, Culture and Society*, 2, 1980; P. Willis and P. Corrigan, "The Orders of Experience", *Social Text*, 8, 1983.

12. If this seems "extreme", have a look at any of the writing by Jeremy Sebrook; or Patrick Wright, *Living in an Old Country* (London: Verso, 1985), or P. Corrigan & D. Sayer, *The Great Arch: English State Formation as Cultural Revolution* (Oxford, New York: Blackwell, 1985).

13. The hisory I abbreviate here is given more fully in Goddard, *op. cit.*, n. 1, pp. 5ff. and subsequently, in more detail, for the years of his Headship.

14. I did not tell my parents, so I had to leave each day, in school uniform; I rode the trains all over southeast England with money I earned from my Saturday job, working in a male clothing store. Antony Harding came to visit my parents (and me), then, and in a subsequent conversation in his own house, he persuaded me to return.

15. One feature of elite masculine speech in England is to drop any article or descriptor before a noun, thus "Hall" means the school Hall (in Oxford and Cambridge it means where you can eat breakfast, lunch, and dinner).

16. One pleasing feature since 1946 was that a proportion of the governors had to be from the LCC and also from the locality, e.g. Deptford. This meant, for all the elocution exercises, I could occasionally hear a good South London accent *from the mouth of Authority*.

17. The contribution of boredom to regulation has been for too long neglected (Roland Barthes considered it a form of distress), but see I. Illich "The Ritual power of daily humdrum", *Utne Reader*, November-December 1987; I. Goodson and I. Dowbiggin, "Docile Bodies: Some Commonalities in the History of Psychology and Schooling" (unpublished paper, Graduate School of Education, University of Western Ontario, 1987); more generally see M. E. Mishkind and others, "The embodiment of masculinity", *American Behavioural Scientist*, 29(5) 1986; R. Connell, "Men's Bodies' (1979), chapter 2, in his *Which Way Is Up?* (Sidney: Allen & Unwin, 1983) but, most profound, for me, P. Leach, "The rigid child", *Anarchy*, 6(64), 1966.

18. As I signal in "Masculinity as Wrongs: Notes on the Difficulty", *Sociological Review*, 1990, forthcoming, we lack good studies of masculine-adolescence *like* some of the new material appearing within a feminist writing, but see P. Roth "My Life as a Boy", *New York Times Book Review*, October 18, 1987, and as two contrasting resources: Esquire, "The American Man, 1946–1986; Growing Up Male: The Way it Was", theme issue, June 1986 (I am most grateful to Ruth Pierson for the provision of this essential reference document), and "He's 50!" (Super—an....), cover story, *Time Magazine*, March 14, 1988.

19. Goddard, *op. cit.*, n. 1, links his attention to "the voice" to acting (Shakespeare especially). His rhetoric is quite classical, in fact, as might be found from reading H. S. Tremenheere, who was the second of Her Majesty's Inspectors of Education, 1839 onwards, studied by P. R. D. Corrigan, *State formation and moral regulation* (Durham, England, University, unpublished PhD thesis, 1977).

20. In this sense Lindsay Anderson's film *If* is a useful study which contains some real sense (for me) of "Yes, that *is* partly what it was like!" But equally important is Tom Courtenay's performance in the film version of Alan Sillitoe's story *The Loneliness of the Long Distance Runner* whilst other features are revealed in *The Class of Miss McMichael, Educating Rita* and, for the moment of the 1950's, John Osborne's *Look Back In Anger* and *The Entertainer*.

21. I did not know the term then, but had it explained to me by a very good friend who had the distinction of "winning" both the Military Medal (for "other" ranks) and the Military Cross (for officers) in the 1939–45 period (he won the first by being so drunk that he snatched up a Sten-gun and sprayed all around, thus killing some some Nazi comman-

dos that were a-creeping up; he won the second by being, on the last day, in the last hours, of "The War", advancing across a field and finding he had stepped on a mine, of the release sort; "Run like hell men", he yelled, later being the only officer to enter/capture a "German" village with a bleeding bum and no trousers/pants!). Anyway, when ordered by a brigadier to lead his platoon to a certain map reference, he did so: they were neck high in the sea!

22. Apart from the material cited in notes 17 and 18 above, cf. C. L. Moore, "Body metaphors", *Interchange*, 18(3) 1987; D. Kion and others, "What Is Beautiful Is Good", *Journal of Personality and Social Psychology*, 24(3), 1972 and link to N. Hellmich, 'our ideal bodies: Thin is Out, Muscles In", *USA Today*, June 21, 1988, pp. 1, 5; M. Douglas, "The Two Bodies", in her *Natural Symbols* (New York: Pantheon, revised edition, 1982); R. Barthes, "Encore le corps" (1978), Critique, 38(425), August-September 1982; G. Ostrander, "Foucault's Disappearing Body", *Canadian Journal-of Political and Social Theory*, 11(1-2), 1987; and see other references in Corrigan, "My(?)Body, My Self(?)", *op. cit.*

23. P. Corrigan: "Playing Contra/Diction" in H. Giroux and R. Simon (eds) *Popular culture, schooling, and everyday life* (South Hadley, MA; Bergin and Garvey, 1989); "Politics of feeling good" in R. Gruneau (ed) *Popular Cultures and Political Practices* (Toronto, Garamond, 1988); "Innocent Stupidities" in G. F. Fyfe and J. Law (eds) *Picturing Power* (Routledge, 1988); *Social Forms/Human Capacities: Essays in Authority and Difference* (Routledge, 1990). *Note also*: P. Connerton "Bodily Practices" ch. 3 in his book *How Societies Remember* (Cambridge U.P., 1989); J. Gallop *Thinking Through the Body* (Columbia U.P. 1989; of A. Snitnow "Textual Intercourse" *Women's Review of Books* 8(1) October 1989); P. Brown *The Body and Society* (Columbia U.P., 1988); and R. Porter "Body and History" *London Review of Books*, 31 August 1989.

CHAPTER 8

Notes

1. Editorial, "The Biggest Secret of Race Relations: The New White Minority," *Ebony Magazine* (April 1989), p. 84, John B. Kellog, "Forces of Change," *Phi Delta Kappan* (November, 1988), pp. 199–204.

2. Michelle Fine, *Framing Dropouts* (Albany, New York: State University of New York Press, forthcoming).

3. Kirk Johnson, "A New Generation of Racism is Seen," *The New York Times*, August 27, 1989, p. 20; Kathy Dobie, "The Boys of Bensonhurst," *The Village Voice*, 54:36 (September 5, 1989), pp. 34–39.

4. Chantal Mouffe, "Hegemony and New Political Subjects: Toward a New Concept of Democracy," in Cary Nelson and Larry Grossberg (eds), *Marxism and the Interpretation of Culture* (Urbana: University of Illinois Press, 1988), p. 102. It is important to note here that in talking about democracy, critical democracy, or democratic public culture, I am referring to democracy as a system of social relations based on forms of pluralism and popular power that encourage social forms that extend and encourage rather than deny the realization of a variety of human capacities. At issue here is a conception of public life inspired by a redistribution of power and material and ideological capital in ways that extend the relations of equality, liberty, and justice to all spheres of social and economic life and not merely to the sphere of political formalism. For an extensive discussion of critical democracy, see Henry A. Giroux, *Schooling and the Struggle for Public Life* (Minneapolis: University of Minnesota Press, 1988).

5. Jon Pareles, "There's a New Sound in Pop Music: Bigotry," *The New York Times*, Section 2, Sunday, September 10, 1989, pp. 10 & 32.

6. This theme is taken up in Stanley Aronowitz and Henry A. Giroux, *Education Under Siege* (Granby, Mass.: Bergin and Garvey Press, 1985).

7. This position was first made famous in Daniel Moynihan, "The Moynihan Report," [The Negro Family: The Case for National action. Washington, D. C. U.S. Department of Labor, 1965. For two critical responses to this report, see Marian Wright Edelman, *Families in Peril: An Agenda for Social Change* (Cambridge: Harvard University Press, 1987); Hortense J. Spillers, "Mama's Baby, Papa's Maybe: An American Grammar Book," *Diacritics* 17:2 (Summer 1987), pp. 65–81. See also a special issue of *The Nation*, (July24/31, 1989), entitled "Scapegoating the Black Family: Black Women Speak."

8. Ernesto Laclau, "Politics and the Limits of Modernity," in Andrew Ross (ed.), *Universal Abandon? The Politics of Postmodernism* (Minneapolis: University of Minnesota Press, 1988), pp. 63–82; Nelly Richard "Postmodernism and Periphery," *Third Text* 2 (1987/1988), pp. 5–12.

9. Gayatri C. Spivak, *In Other Worlds: Essays in Cultural Politics* (London: Metheun, 1987); See the two special issues of *Cultural Critique* on the nature and context of minority discourse, Numbers 6 & 7, Spring and Fall of 1987.

10. Cornell West, "Marxist Theory and the specificity of Afro-American Oppression," in Cary Nelson and Larry Grossberg (eds), *Marxism and the Interpretation of Culture* (Urbana: University of Illinois Press, 1988), pp 17–26; for an elaboration of West's perspective on racism,

see Peter McLaren and Michael Dantley, "Cornel West and Stuart: Towards an Afro-American Pedagogy, *Journal of Negro Education* (in press).

11. David Kolb, *The Critique of Pure Modernity: Hegel, Heidegger, and After* (Chicago: University of Chicago Press, 1986), especially the first and last chapters.

12. Stuart Hall, "Gramsci's Relevance for the Study of Race and Ethnicity," *Journal of Communication Inquiry* 10:2 (Summer 1986), pp. 5–27.

13. Stanley Aronwitz, "Postmodernism and Politics," *Social Text* 18 (1987/1988), p. 113.

14. Scott Lash and John Urry, *The End of Organized Capitalism* (Madison: University of Wisconsin Press, 1987).

15. Two important critiques of Marxist economism can be found in Stanley Aronowitz, *The Crisis in Historical Materialism* (Granby, Mass.: Bergin and Garvey Press, 1983); Ernesto Laclau and Chantal Mouffe, *Hegemony and Socialist Strategy* (London: Verso Books, 1985).

16. Two important references on these issue are Cornel West, *Prophesy Deliverance: An Afro-American Revolutionary Christianity* (New York: Westminister Press, 1982); Cornel West, *The American Evasion of Philosophy* (Madison: University of Wisconsin Press, 1989); Coco Fusco, "Fantasies of Oppositionality: Reflections on recent conferences in Boston and New York," *Screen* 29:4 (Autumn, 1988), pp. 80–93.

17. See Henry A. Giroux, *Theory and Resistance in Education* (Granby, Mass.: Bergin and Garvey Press, 1983).

18. For example, see the work developed in John Young, ed. *Breaking the Mosiac: Ethnic Indentities in Canadian Society* (Toronto: Garamond Press, 1987). Thomas Popkewitz, "Culture, Pedagogy, and Power: Issues in the Production of Values and Colonialization," *Journal of Education* 170:2 (1988), pp. 77–90.

19. Hazel Carby, "The Canon: Civil War and Reconstruction," *Michigan Quarterly Review* XXVIII: 1 (Winter, 1989), p. 39.

20. Richard Dyer, "White," *Screen* 29:4 (Autmn, 1988), pp. 44–64.

21. Toni Morrison, "Unspeakable Things Unspoken: The Afro-American Presence in American Literature," *Michigan Quarterly Review* XXVIII: I (Winter, 1989), pp. 1–34.

22. Ibid., P. 11.

23. Issac Julien and Kobena Mercer, "Introduction: De Margin and de Centre," *Screen* 8:2 (1987), p. 3.

24. Popkewitz, op. cit.; Hazel Carby, "Multi-Culture," *Screen Education* 34 (Spring 1980), pp. 62–70.

25. I make clear the distinction between critical and conservative forms of postmodernism in Henry A. Giroux, "Postmodernism and the Discourse of Educational Criticism," *Journal of Education* 170:3 (1988), pp. 5–30.

26. Robert Merrell, "Ethics/Aesthetics: A Post-Modern Position," in Robert Merrill (ed.), *Ethics/Aesthetics: Post-Modern Positions* (Washington, D.C.: Maisonneuve Press, 1988), pp. vii–xiii.

27. Hal Foster, Ed. *The Anti-Aesthetic: Essays on Postmodern Culture* (Towsend, Washington: Bay Press, 1983); Hal Foster, Ed., *Discussions in Contemporary Culture, Number one* (Seattle, Washington: Bay Press, 1987);

28. Jean-Francois Lyotard, *The Postmodern Condition: A Report on knowledge* (Minneapolis: University of Minnesota Press, 1984).

29. Sygmunt Bauman, "Strangers: The Social Construction of Universality and Particularity," *Telos* 78 (Winter 1988–1989), p. 12.

30. Dick Hebdige, "Postmodernism and 'the other side'", *Journal of Communication Inquiry* 10:2 (1986), p. 81.

31. Ibid., P. 91.

32. Frenc Feher, "The Status of Postmodernity," *Philosophy and Social Criticism*, 13:2 (1988), pp. 195–206.

33. Jim Collins, *Uncommon Cultures: Popular Culture and Post-Modernism* (New York: Routledge, 1989).

34. Foster, op. cit., 1983.

35. A characteristic example of this work can be found in the wide-ranging essays on culture, art, and socal criticism found in B. Wallis, (Ed.) *Blasted Allegories* (Cambridge: MIT Press, 1988).

36. Cora Kaplan, "Deterritorializations: The Rewriting of Home and exile in Western Feminist Discourse," *Cultural Critique* 6 (1987), pp. 187–198.

37. Larry Grossberg, "Putting the Pop Back into Postmodernism," in Andrew Ross, (ed.), *Universal Abandon? The Politics of Postmodernism* (Minneapolis: University of Minnesota Press, 1988), pp. 167–190.

38. Teresa DeLauretis, *Technologies of Gender* (Bloomington: Indiana University Press, 1987); Meighan Morris, *The Pirate's Fiancee: Feminism Reading, Postmodernism* (London: Verso Press, 1988).

39. These themes are taken up in Ernesto Laclau and Chantal Mouffe, *Hegemony and Socialist Strategy* (London: Verso Books, 1985); Stanley Aronowitz, *The Crisis in Historical Materialism* (South Hadley, Mass: Bergin and Garvey, 1981). On the changing economic, political, and cultural conditions that characterize the postmodern condition, see Scott Lash and John Urry, *The End of Organized Capitalism* (Madison: University of Wisconsin Press, 1987) and David Harvey, *The Condition of Postmodernity* (New York: Basil Blackwell, 1989); Jean Baudrillard, *Selected Writings*, edited and Introduced by Mark Poster (Stanford: Stanford University Press, 1988).

40. Bruce James Smith, *Politics and Remembrance* (Princeton: Princeton University Press, 1985). See also Richard Terdiman, "Deconstructing Memory: On Representing the Past and Theorizing Culture in France Since the revolution," *Diacritics* (Winter 1985), pp. 13–16.

41. Jim Collins, op. cit., p. 115

42. Ibid., p. 115.

43. Mouffe, op.cit, in Ross, ed. 1988.

44. For an analysis of this issue as educational criticism, see Linda Brodkey, *Academic Writing as a Social Practice* (Philadelphia: Temple University Press, 1987).

45. Sharon Welch, *A Feminist Ethic of Risk* (Fortress Press, forthcoming).

46. Mouffe, op. cit., in Ross, ed. 1988, p. 41.

47. Cornel West, "Black Culture and Postmodernism," in Barbara Kruger and Phil Mariani,(eds.), *Remaking History* (Seattle: Bay Press, 1989), p. 90.

48. Richard Bernstein, "Metaphysics, Critique, and Utopia," *The Review of Metaphysics* 42 (1988), p. 267.

49. Among the many anthologies on black women writers, one of the better ones is Mari Evans, ed., *Black Women Writers (1950–1980): A Critical Evaluation* (New York: Anchor Press, 1984). Important theoretical works discussing the writings of black women include: see Barbara Christian, *Black Feminist Criticism* (New York: Pergamon, 1985); Susan Willis, *Specifying: Black Women Writing—The American Experience* (Madison: University of Wisconsin Press, 1987); Hazel V. Carby, *Reconstructing Womanhood: The Emergence of the Afro-American*

Women Novelist (New York: Oxford University Press, 1987); Sharon D. Welch, *A Feminist Ethic of Risk* (Fortress Press, 1990).

50. Christian, op. cit. p. 159.

51. Cited in John McCluskey, Jr. "And Call Every Generation Blessed: Theme, Setting and Ritual in the Works of Paule Marshall," in Evans, op. cit., p. 316.

52. See for instance, Audre Lorde, *Sister Outsider* (Freedom, CA.: The Crossing Press, 1984); Bell Hooks, *Talking Back* (Boston: South End Press, 1989); June Gordon, *On Call* (Boston: South End Press, 1987); and Carby, op. cit., *Reconstructing Womanhood*.

53. Lorde, op. cit.

54. Carby, op. cit., "The Canon: Civil War and Reconstruction," p. 39.

55. Fusco, op. cit., p. 90.

56. Hooks, op. cit., "The Politics of Radical Black Subjectivity," *Talking Back*, 1989, p. 54.

57. Lorde, op. cit., p. 112

58. Ibid., p. 112.

59. Ibid., p. 118

60. Ibid., p. 112

61. Ibid., p. 45.

62. Barbara Christian, *Black Feminist Criticism*, op. cit.

63. Hooks, op. cit., *Talking Back*, pp. 11–12.

64. June Jordan, op. cit., *On Call*, pp. 30–31.

65. Barbara Christian, "The Race for Theory, *Cultural Critique* 6 (Spring 1987), p. 52.

66. Toni Cade Bambara, "Evaluation is the Issue," in Mari Evans, ed., *Black Women Writers (1950–1980): A Critical Evaluation* (New York: Anchor Press, 1984), p. 46.

67. For sustained and clear analysis of the works of these particular Afro-American women writers, see Susan Willis, *Specifying: Black Women Writing—The American Experience* (Madison: University of Wisconsin Press, 1987).

68. Michelle Gibbs Russell, "Black Eyed Blues Connections: From the Inside Out," in Charlotte Bunch and Sandra Pollack (eds.), *Learning Our way: Essays in Feminist Education* (Trumansburg: The Crossing Press, 1983), pp. 274, 275).

69. June Jordan, "Where is the Love?" in Barbara H. Andolsen, Christine Gurdorf and Mary Pellauer (eds.), *Women's Consciousness Women's Conscience* (New York: Harper and Row, 1985), p. 203.

70. Sharon Welch, "Feminism, Modernity, and Postmodernism," *A Feminist Ethic of Risk*, (forthcoming), p. 5

71. Henry A. Giroux, *Schooling and the Struggle for Public Life* (Minneapolis: Univeristy of Minnesota Press, 1988). Chantal Mouffe, "Hegemony and New Political Subjects: Toward a New Concept of Democracy," in Cary Nelson and Larry Grossberg (eds.), *Marxism and the Interpretation of Culture* (Urbana: University of Illinois Press, 1988), pp. 89–104.

72. Henry A. Giroux, "Border Pedagogy in the Age of Postmodernism," *Journal of Education* 170:3 (1988), pp. 162–181.

73. Chantal Mouffe, "Radical Democracy: Modern or Postmodern," in Andrew Ross, ed. op. cit., p. 42.

74. D. Emily Hicks, "Deterriorialization and Border Writing," in Robert Merrill (ed.), *Ethics/Aesthetics: Post-Modern Positions* (Washington, D.C.: Maisonneuve Press, 1988), pp. 47–58.

75. For excellent theoretical and practical examples of how this approach to anti-racist education works using particular films, see Roger I. Simon, John Brown, Enid Lee, and Jon Young, *Decoding Discrimination: A Student-Based Approach to Anti-Racist Education Using Film* (Ontario, Canada: Althouse Press, 1988).

76. Stuart Hall, "Teaching Race," in Alan Jones and Robert Jeffcoate (eds.), *The School in the Multicultural Society*, (London: Harper and Row Ltd., 1981), p. 61.

77. Some important books that develop a broad theoretical perspective for understanding racism in ideological, structural, and pedagogical terms are: Hazel Carby, et al., *The Empire Strikes Back* (London: Hutchinson, 1982); Lois Weiss, ed. , *Class, Race, and Gender in American Education* (Albany, SUNY Press, 1988); Barry Troyna and Jenny Williams, Racism, Education and the State (London: Croom Helm, 1986); W.W.B. Du Bois, *Against Racism: Unpublished Essays, Papers, Addresses, 1887-1961*, edited by Herbert Aptheker (Amherst: University of Massachusetts Press, 1985); John Brown Childs, *Leadership, Conflict, and Cooperation in Afro-American Social Thought* (Philadelphia: Temple University Press, 1989);

Authur Brittan and Mary Maynard, *Sexism, Racism and Oppression* (New York: Blackwell, 1985) ; Houston A. Baker, Jr. *Blues , Ideology, and Afro-American Literature* (Chicago: University of Chicago Press, 1984), and Cornel West, *Prophetic Fragments* (Trenton: Africa World Press, Inc., 1988).

78. Some important literature which explores this issue from a variety of pedagogical interventions include: Carter Godwin Woodson, *The Mis-Education of the Negro* (Washington, D.C.: The Associated Publishers, Inc., 1933); Gloria Ladson-Billings, "Like Lightning in a Bottle: Attempting to Capture the Pedagogical Excellence of Successful Teachers of Black Students," Paper presented at the Tenth Annual Ethnography in Education Research Forum, February 24-25, 1989, University of Pennsylvania, Philadelphia, Pennsylvania; Joyce Elain King and Gloria Ladson-Billings, "The Teacher Education Challenge in Elite University Settings: Developing Critical Perspectives for Teaching in a Democratic and Multicultural Society," *European Journal of Intercultural Education* (forthcoming); Joyce King, "Black Student Alienation and Black Teachers' Emancipatory Pedagogy," *The Journal of Black Reading and Language Education* 3:1 (May 1987), pp. 3–12; Cameron McCarthy, "Rethinking Liberal and Radical Perspectives on Racial Inequality in Schooling: Making the Case for Nonsynchrony," *Harvard Educational Review* 58:3 (1988), pp. 265–279.

79. Andrew Hannan, "Racism, Politics and the Curriculum," *British Journal of Sociology of Educaton,*" 8:2 (1987), p. 127.

80. Lisa Delpit, "The Silenced Dialogue: Power and Pedagogy in Educating Other People's Children," *Harvard Educational Review* 58:3 (1988), pp. 280–298.

81. Ibid.

82. Signithia Fordham, "Racelessness as a Factor in Black Students' School Success; Pragmatic Strategy or Pyrrhic Victory?" *Harvard Educational Review* 58:3 (1988), pp. 54–82.

83. Stuart Hall, "Teaching Race," in Alan Jones and Robert Jeffcoate (eds.), *The School in the Multicultural Society* (London: Harper and Row Ltd., (1981), pp. 58–69.

84. Roger I. Simon, "For a Pedagogy of Possibility," *Critical Pedagogy Networker,* 1:1 (February 1988), p. 2

85. Richard Johnson, "What is Cultural Studies Anyway?" *Social Text* 16 (Winter 1986/1987), pp. 38–80.

86. These issues are taken up in Catherine Belsey, *Critical Practice* (New York: Metheun, 1980); Tony Bennett, "Texts in History: The

302   Notes and References

Determinations of Readings and Their Texts," in Derek Atridge, Geoff Bennington, and Rogert Young, eds. *Post-Structuralism and the Question of History* (New York and London: Cambridge University Press, 1987); Henry A. Giroux, "Reading Formations, Texts, Voice, and the Role of English Teachers as Public Intellectuals," in Stanley Aronowitz and Henry A. Giroux, *Postmodern Education: Border Pedagogy, Politics, and Cultural Criticism* (University of Minnesota Press, 1991).

87. For specific ways in which voice and difference are treated in critical pedagogical terms, see Bell Hooks, *Talking Back* (Boston: South End Press, 1989); Henry A. Giroux and Roger I. Simon, "Popular Culture as a Pedagogy of Pleasure and Meaning," in Henry A. Giroux and Roger Simon, (eds.), *Popular Culture, Education and Everyday Life* (Granby, Massachusetts: Bergin and Garvey Press, 1989), pp. 1–30; Paul Smith, "Pedagogy and the Popular-Cultural-Commodity-Text," in Henry A. Giroux and Roger Simon, (eds.), *Popular Culture, Education and Everyday Life* (Granby, Massachusetts: Bergin and Garvey Press, 1989), pp. 31–46; Henry A. Giroux, "Schooling and the Politics of Student Voice," in *Schooling and the Struggle for Public Life* (Granby, Massachusetts: Bergin and Garvey Press, 1988).

Index